Jerry Hopkins has been chronicling popular music since his graduation from Washington and Lee University in 1957. He has written for dozens of publications as a freelance journalist and is the author of many major rock books including *No One Here Gets Out Alive* (on Jim Morrison of the Doors), *Elvis: A Biography*, and *Elvis: The Final Years*. He is also a contributing editor to *Rolling Stone* magazine.

Jerry Hopkins

Bowie

I was David Jones from Brixton who wanted to do something artistically worthwhile. But I hadn't the courage to face the audience as myself.

David Bowie, 13 Feb 1979

CORGI BOOKS

BOWIE
A CORGI BOOK 0 552 12709 4

Originally published in Great Britain by
Elm Tree Books/Hamish Hamilton Ltd.

PRINTING HISTORY
Elm Tree/Hamish Hamilton edition published 1985
Corgi edition published 1986

Corgi Books are published by Transworld Publishers
Ltd., 61–63 Uxbridge Road, Ealing, London W5 5SA, in
Australia by Transworld Publishers (Aust.) Pty. Ltd.,
26 Harley Crescent, Condell Park, NSW 2200, and in New
Zealand by Transworld Publishers (N.Z.) Ltd., Cnr. Moselle
and Waipareira Avenues, Henderson, Auckland.

Printed and bound in Great Britain by
Cox & Wyman Ltd., Reading, Berks.

This book is dedicated
to the ones I love the most,
Rebecca, Erin, Nicky and Kessel

CONTENTS

ACKNOWLEDGEMENTS

Thanks are due to more than those named. Many talked-off-the-record, some of them fearing that if they were identified, it would endanger their relationships with David. And, of course, others talked merely because David's protector and aide-de-camp, Coco Schwab, had told them *not* to.

This was not surprising, considering David's penchant for privacy and determination to stay in complete control of all aspects of his life and career. It was totally in character, for example, that when David allowed Chet Flippo "inside" the Serious Moonlight tour to produce a text for the official tour book published in 1984, it was only after Chet agreed in writing never to use anything he learned on the tour for any other purpose.

Most of those approached agreed to participate. Of these, special thanks go to Ken Pitt, Angela (Bowie) Jones, Herb Helman, Mary Finnigan, Charles Shaar Murray, Barry Miles, Mike Garson and Ava Cherry.

Others who contributed include, in alphabetical order, Pat Antoniou, Toni Basil, Rodney Bingenheimer, John Blake, Trevor Blythe, Victor Bokris, Chris Charlesworth, Colin Clark, Richard Crinkley, Cameron Crowe, Jules Fisher, Ken Fordham, Louise Frogley, David Geffen, Bill Hassell, Jim Haynes, David Hemmings, Jack Hofsiss, Roy Hollingworth, Dennis Katz, Andy Kent, Brian Lane, Martin Last, Jean Louis, Nick Massey, Harry Maslin, Paul Mayersberg, Tony McGrogan, Patty Mitsui, Richard Neilson, P. G. Nunn, Ron Oberman, Nagisa Oshima, D. A. Pennebaker, Mark Pritchett, Roger (Wooten) Raven, Mark Ravitz, Nicolas Roeg, Ronnie Ross, Ken and Pat Scott, Michael Thomas, John Tobler, Roger Tomlinson, Dr Jerome Tucker, George Underwood, Don Wardell, Sandy

Watson, Michael Watts, Chris Welch, Geoff Weston, Robin Whitecross and Olav Wyper.

Interviews with Barrie Bethel, Dek Fearnley, Louis Marks, Tony Visconti, Rick Wakeman and Alan Yentob were provided by John Tobler.

A rare and revealing interview with David's mother, Peggy Jones, came from Charles Shaar Murray.

More help came from several avid Bowie fans, the keepers of the unofficial archives. These are the young men and women who have saved or acquired virtually everything one can possess that concerns David Bowie's life and career — clippings and magazines, photographs, bootleg records, tapes of radio interviews, memorabilia (one has a shirt encased in glass in his bedroom), films and videos. The three who helped the most were Carmen Jacobson, Kevin Cann (an editor of a Bowie fan magazine *Starzone*, P.O. Box 225, Watford, Herts WD1 7OG) and Madeline Bocchiaro.

Previously published books which contributed much understanding and chronological detail include *Bowie: An Illustrated Record* by Roy Carr and Charles Shaar Murray; *David Bowie: A Chronology* by Kevin Cann; *David Bowie: The Pitt Report* by Ken Pitt; *David Bowie Black Book* by Barry Miles; and *Free Spirit* by Angie Bowie.

Thanks also to the staff and files and libraries of the British Film Institute, Music Sales Ltd, *New Musical Express*, *Melody Maker*, the *Sun* and *Daily Express* in England; the Margaret Kerrick Library of the Academy of Motion Picture Arts & Sciences, the Performing Arts Research Center at Lincoln Center, RCA and the *Los Angeles Times*, the *New York Times*, *Creem* and *Rolling Stone* in America.

Finally, for spiritual, emotional and psychological support, Frank and Linda Lieberman, Rona Elliot and Roger Brossey, Corb and Melantha Donohue, Denne and Wanda Petitclerc, my agent Esther Newberg and my editor Barry Lippman.

THE CHILD, THE BOY,
AND THE STUDENT

Britain emerged from the Second World War with a well-developed sense of pride, but she also came out of it exhausted. The British people had grown accustomed to restrictions which before the war they would never have endured. Recovery was slow.

Entire residential blocks lay in rubble; even the standing homes and buildings bore the scars of battle, pock marks from shrapnel in the brick and stone. Food prices remained high and many items were available only on the black market. Petrol was exceedingly scarce. People still stood in long queues for nearly all products and services. The currency was shaky. Telephone service was minimal. If there were any toys, they were left over from pre-war days. Many children were being raised by single mothers and aunts because so many men were still in the services, occupying Europe, or were dead. Nearly all the teachers in the schools were women, whereas before the war they had been primarily men.

It was into this austere but hopeful environment that at nine o'clock in the morning on Wednesday, 8 January 1947, David Robert Jones was born in a small terraced house at 40 Stansfield Road, Brixton.

The father was Hayward Stenton Jones, called John. He was short and slight with thin, sandy hair and protruding ears. His blue eyes projected sincerity, honesty and intensity and according to everyone who knew him, he was 'very quietly spoken'.

Mr Jones was a Yorkshireman, from Doncaster. Born in 1912, he was the son of a prosperous shoe and boot manufacturer. His parents had died when he was young and after having grown up in the care of relatives, at the age of twenty-one he was given his inheritance of £4000.

It was a large sum for 1933 and he sank much of it into a small nightclub near London's Euston and King's Cross rail stations. It was a small, but cosy place and most of the regulars came to hear a singer named Hilda Louise Sullivan, who said she was French. She won the hearts of all men, including John who married her.

In time, the club failed and John went into partnership with a man who had leased a bar near Piccadilly Circus, close by the fleshpots of Soho and the theatres of the West End. It was during this period that John began to drink heavily. It all came crashing down, as John put it later, when his partner 'did a midnight flit and left me holdin' the can'.

That was the end of John's nightclubbing days and soon afterwards, in 1939, he began six years of service with the Eighth Army in Montgomery's drive to push the Italians and Germans out of Africa.

Like so many other marriages of the time, John's was a wartime casualty and at the war's end, in 1945, John and Hilda were permanently separated.

John went to work for Dr Barnardo's Homes, and in his travels around the city as the organization's publicity director, he visited the Ritz Cinema Restaurant, where within a year he met a sometime waitress, sometime usherette named Margaret Mary Burns. Her friends called her Peggy.

Peggy had been born in 1913. One of six children, she was sternly brought up by her father who frequently used a broad leather army belt he had continued to wear after a career as an army bandsman. She was a quick, pretty girl who rebelled against her father's strictness, leaving school at fourteen to seek a job as a nanny. In 1937, when she was twenty-four, Peggy was working as a nanny to people who owned a small hotel. There, Peggy met the son of a wealthy furrier, who disappeared as soon as she announced her pregnancy. Terrance Guy Adair Burns was born on 5 November 1937, taking his mother's surname, although he was not at first raised by her. Peggy gave him to her parents, who looked after him full-time for the first nine months, part-time after that when Peggy moved home again, but continued to work.

When the war came, Peggy worked in a factory that made military uniforms and parachutes. It was there that she met the father of her second child, a daughter born in 1943. The girl was given the name Myra Ann and at the age of ten months, was given up for adoption. Peggy never saw her again.

In 1945, Peggy was still living at home with her mother and father and her son, Terry, who was now seven. Peggy's hopes seemed slight. She had had two children by two men and still had no family of her own. While her mother looked after Terry, she worked as a waitress and usherette.

In 1946, life brought her John Jones. He was thirty-four and she was thirty-three.

Although he was still married to Hilda, John and Peggy shared a flat, at first in North London, then after Peggy got pregnant, in the cheaper Brixton district. John's wife filed for divorce, charging adultery. The divorce dragged on and on and David was eight months old before his parents could marry.

There was nothing unusual about illegitimate births in Brixton, but John and Peggy were not proud of the fact that both the boys had been born out of wedlock. Both had been raised in strict, conservative surroundings and the word 'bastard' rang of sinfulness and brought with it a lot of guilt.

David was the favoured child, so much so that Terry felt almost scorned. John admitted years later that he virtually ignored the boy, while David was the one he and Peggy fawned over, and bragged about. They never talked baby talk with David, regarding him as a small adult. In part, this was because David seemed so bright. Even before he could talk he was feeding paper into his father's typewriter, and at three he could use the telephone.

The poverty of Brixton was a grinding presence. David remembers seeing some of his schoolmates coming to class without shoes. John's employment was regular, but working for a charity offered him rewards which were more spiritual than material, so there rarely was money for anything extra. None the less, John and Peggy vowed to leave the tough, gritty neighbourhood as soon as possible.

3

They did so in the late summer of 1957, when David was ten (Terry enlisted in the Royal Air Force at the same time), moving their modest belongings into another four-room, two-storey house, at 4 Plaistow Grove, Sundridge Park, Bromley.

The house was tiny – like the Brixton home, two rooms upstairs and two down – and it was one of about twelve terraced houses. David had the small bedroom on the second floor in the back, overlooking a little garden surrounded by a wooden fence. A small shed stood at one corner of the garden and beyond that, across a narrow driveway, was the back of the neighbourhood pub, the Crown.

If the two houses were about equal in size, the move from Brixton to Bromley was nevertheless significant. Brixton was a working-class neighbourhood when the Jones family left it, and Bromley was decidedly middle class. (It was also well-known as the birthplace of H. G. Wells.)

*

Like much of Europe, postwar England looked to the United States for support. In the 1950s, Uncle Sam was the source of staggering largesse. Along with money and material to rebuild came millions of tons of goods. And as might be expected, American clothes, American films, American slang, American music – all were hungrily consumed by a country looking for a way out of the drabness that had been with them for so long.

In a few years' time, much of England became 'Americanized', as Things American became expressions of the new affluence, as well as cultural liberty. In no area was this more evident than in something brand new – and American – called rock and roll.

It arrived in November 1955 when David was eight. The movie, *Blackboard Jungle*, gave Britain the first look at American juvenile delinquency, and a soundtrack that included the first rock anthem, 'Rock Around the Clock'. English youth, 'digging' the loud, raw invitation to 'rock and roll till dawn's daylight', tore up the cinema seats to celebrate.

Within a year, Elvis Presley had had three number one hits in England – 'Heartbreak Hotel', 'Hound Dog' and 'All

Shook Up' – and others who reached the No. 1 or No. 2 position on the same British charts included the Crickets, the Teenagers featuring Frankie Lyman, the Everly Brothers and Johnny Otis.

England was never the same again.

David later said, 'I saw a cousin of mine dance when I was very young. She was dancing to Elvis's "Hound Dog" and I had never seen her get up and be moved so much by anything. It really impressed me, the power of the music. I started getting records immediately after that. My mother bought me Fats Domino's "Blueberry Hill" the next day. And then I fell in love with the Little Richard band. I never heard anything that lived in such bright colours in the air. It really just painted the whole room for me.'

The town where he lived changed his horizons, too. Although his own situation hadn't changed much, he was now for the first time getting to see really nice houses. Only a short distance from his home, on the way to school, was a golf course, another symbol of middle class gentility. And *he* still lived in a tiny terraced house, a home so small it could be shoved inside a servant's cottage. In Bromley, David Jones became aware of class difference first hand. The Jones family had changed towns, but their lifestyle, and their class were the same: not exactly poor, but only a little better, and David wanted out.

In September 1957, David Jones was accompanied by his father to his first day of classes at Bromley Technical High School (now called Ravenswood School for Boys). Classmates and teachers agree that David was not a remarkable scholar. 'He was a run-of-the-mill student,' says classmate Colin Clark today. 'There were a few who were extremely good, but he, like me, wasn't one of them. He was more interested in things outside of school.' Adds Trevor Blythe, 'He was a very bright guy, but he never applied himself. He was fairly good at art, but overall he tended to wander through. He was a bit of a butterfly. I was old-fashioned and could knuckle down and do the job. He was the opposite to that. There was a creative spirit, but no one could've guessed where it was headed.'

Initially David seemed to be aiming at a career in art. In his third year, after studying English, history, maths,

5

geography and other basic courses, David entered the 'art stream'; now he focused his energies on what the school was known for, the tactile and visual arts.

At home, David's major influence was his brother, Terry. Terry completed his three-year tour of duty with the RAF in 1959, when he was twenty-two and David was twelve, and moved in with his Aunt, Pat Antoniou, who lived in North London, an hour's train ride from Bromley. According to Pat, Terry wasn't made to feel welcome at the Jones home, so his visits to Bromley were limited. None the less, David glued himself to his older half-brother. David hero-worshipped Terry. When Terry shared stories about his military service in Malta and North Africa, David said that when he grew up he'd travel to the same places. Terry had learned to box while in the RAF and taught David some of the rudiments of shadow boxing.

Terry also introduced his younger brother to some of the American 'beat generation' writers of the late 1950s who would, in turn, exert their own strong influence. The young David was especially struck by Jack Kerouac's second novel, *On the Road*, and the characters in it, the 'mad ones, the ones who are mad to live, mad to talk, mad to be saved, desirous of everything at the same time, the ones who never yawn or say a commonplace thing, but burn, burn, burn like fabulous yellow Roman candles exploding like spiders across the stars.' It all seemed hopelessly romantic to him.

On special occasions, Terry took David to London, to glamorous and 'sinful' Soho, a neighbourhood rich in bohemian tradition, and in the 1950s, the location of London's best jazz clubs, the centre of the country's film and fashion industries, as well as the home of burlesque.

David walked with his big brother as if they were attached at the hip, his eyes looking left and right, unable to take it all in fast enough. David was small and blond, his brother taller and much darker, and the relationship in ways was that of a student and his teacher.

By now, David was enthralled by American rock 'n' roll and when he discovered the saxophone – first in a recording of Little Richard's and then in the backing tracks of several other late 1950s recording stars – it was a simple matter for Terry to introduce his brother to jazz. Jazz was Terry's

6

favourite music and at the time it was closely identified with many of the 'beat' writers.

'Who's the best saxophone player here?' David asked one day. 'Here, in England . . .'

Terry didn't give it a second thought.

'Ronnie Ross,' he said. So saying, Terry walked David past one of the clubs where Ross was currently playing.

The year before, in 1958, Ross had represented the United Kingdom at the Newport (Rhode Island) Jazz Festival and was voted 'new star' in America's esteemed *Down Beat* magazine poll. In 1959, between dates in the Soho clubs, he toured England with the Modern Jazz Quartet and Woody Herman's band. Ross was not just England's best reed player (clarinet and flute as well as sax), he was what the noted American musician Gerry Mulligan called 'the first important challenge' on what was Ross's and Mulligan's primary instrument, the baritone sax.

So it must have taken some courage, and a touch of innocence or arrogance, for David to look up Ross in the telephone directory and call him to ask him to teach him how to play that instrument.

'I had only two or three students at the time,' Ross says today. 'I didn't mind teaching if the pupil was really interested, and David seemed interested.'

David studied with Ross once a week, taking the train to Orpington, where Ross lived, about twenty minutes away. Ross charged about £2 a lesson.

'I taught him the basics,' Ross says. 'You had to have a solid grounding before you specialized. I was teaching him about music in general – how scales were formed, about harmony, how to blow and breathe and a little about how to read music. I don't think we entered into anything syncopated. The basics only.

'I told him that playing the sax was like trying to get sounds you hear in your head out through a horn and into a room,' Ross says. 'It wasn't just reproducing notes you saw on paper. It was creating a new language. Communicating your visions without speaking them.'

David studied with Ross for six months, finding a refuge in music that he hadn't known was there. Neither his mother nor his father were demonstrative. It was not easy for them

7

to touch David, to hug him, to kiss him, and so he had grown up somewhat distanced from normal parental love. When he discovered that music could give him a sort of substitute warmth, he immersed himself in it, determinedly and gratefully.

One of his closest companions of the time was George Underwood, a handsome, dark-haired boy he'd met when they were both ten. They were in the arts stream together at Bromley Tech, and when David began to study the saxophone, George told him that he played the guitar and wanted to be a singer. Typically, the two began to play together, at first after school and later for school functions, or just for fun on the school steps between classes.

On Saturdays, David began working in a record store on Bromley High Street, where as he entered his final years at Bromley Tech, he began to listen to recordings in the import bins by James Brown, Ray Charles, Lloyd Price, the Drifters, Dinah Washington, Jackie Wilson and other black American artists.

Eventually David and George formed small groups and joined existing bands to play at neighbourhood dances. The first of these was the Kon-rads, a five-piece combo that required its members to wear more or less matching dark suits, white shirts and striped ties. In the early publicity pictures, David looked almost exactly as he would twenty years later – rail-thin with intense, brooding eyes, his hair platinum blond. At the time, his hair was copied from the Teddy Boys. David wore his in what was called an 'elephant's trunk', the hair on the sides slicked back into the 'duck-tail' popularized by Elvis Presley, and combed forward from the top to form a 'horn' or 'trunk' of hair that projected out and down from the forehead. It was held together with spray and it was quite uncommon in Bromley. No one else in the band styled his hair in any way similar.

They played for dances in local dance halls and country clubs. David sang three or four numbers in a flawed but energetic voice and played an uninspired but happy saxophone as George sang all the other vocals.

For a hometown band whose oldest member was eighteen, the Kon-rads fared well, playing at dances at the nearby Ravensbourne School of Art and at Justin Hall in West

Wickham. But the pay was minuscule. Even the local country clubs paid the band a mere £10, which, when split five ways, hardly covered more than the cost of petrol and the price of cleaning their suits. Soon David and George dropped out, becoming a duo and calling themselves the Hooker Brothers after the American blues guitarist John Lee Hooker.

By now, David and George were school celebrities and according to his classmates, David was the centre of his group. 'He set the trends,' says Trevor Blythe, 'and the rest of us followed. He was the one to cut off the point of his school tie and unravel the end, which became a fad. And when we were all wearing winkle-pickers, he was wearing chisel-points. And he kept changing his hair styles. It sounds twee, but at the time, small things like that were significant.'

David was an individualist, studiedly. He listened to American football scores on the BBC's World Service and the following day mystified his classmates with a rambling monologue about the Green Bay Packers and the Baltimore Colts. One class assignment was for each student to create an activity for the entire class; David suggested everyone wear kilts and carry handbags. Another time, he showed up with a bright streak of orange in his hair.

At the same time, he was forging his sexual identity. One girl who dated him at the time recalls that when it came to kissing, he was a bit 'zero-rated', was a little on the 'girly' side. David himself said later, 'When I was fourteen, sex suddenly became all important to me. It didn't really matter who or what it was with, as long as it was a sexual experience. So it was some pretty boy in class in some school or other that I took home and neatly fucked on my bed upstairs.'

There were two serious incidents when David was sixteen that gave his fellow students much to talk about. David had let his hair grow long and periodically added more vegetable dye. At a party the day before school pictures were taken some of his classmates took exception to his defiant style, held him down and gave him a haircut, taking great chunks of hair away with a sharp pair of scissors. The next day he went to the barber shop on Bromley High Street (wearing a hat) to have his hair cut into an American style crew-cut.

The second incident was more serious, and involved a fight between David and George Underwood. George says today it was over a girl, but others say it was over a boy. David will not talk about the fight. If precisely what happened is not clear, the results are. David was badly beaten, and with both of his eyes punched shut, he was rushed to a London hospital for emergency surgery.

For a time there was a danger of his losing his sight. Recovery was slow and for four months his mother and father visited him in the hospital every evening. First, the sight returned to the right eye, and then to the left. But the eyes seemed a different colour now – one blue, the other green – and the pupil of the left eye was locked in an open position, giving him an off-balance, almost other-worldly look.

The medical term for this injury is traumatic mydriasis and it is caused when there is a blow to the eye forceful enough to damage the tiny sphincter muscles in the pupil that allow it to open and close according to available light. Once the pupil is dilated permanently, all such control is lost. Although most who suffer the injury are not bothered excessively by moving from a dark environment into a lighter, or even bright one, others may experience reduced vision or later develop secondary cataracts.

When David resumed classes at Bromley Tech, he and George were not speaking. Thus, when George put another band together for the end-of-term concert, David was not a part of it. He performed in the show nonetheless, at the last minute rejoining the Kon-rads, who still were limping from weekend to weekend.

There were two shows, one in the afternoon (a dress rehearsal for the students), the other in the evening for the parents. The school choir sang selections from *Oklahoma* and then one of the office staff sang 'There's a Hole in My Bucket', after which a youngster named Peter Frampton, the son of David's art teacher, who was later to make a name for himself with the Herd and as a solo singer, came on with his first band, the Little Ravens. The Kon-rads ended both shows and David was given the only standing ovation of the evening.

Two months later, in June 1963, David reported to his

vocational counsellor, who asked him what he wanted to do in a month when he left school.

'I'd like to be a saxophonist in a jazz band,' David said.

The counsellor said he thought that was quite a fancy dream. He smiled and told David he'd make some calls and let him know.

A few days later the counsellor called David into his office.

'Mr Jones,' he said with a wide grin. 'I have some first-rate news. There's a firm nearby that makes harps and I think that a bloke with musical talent like yours would fit right in. What do you say? Shall I put you up for an interview?'

THE MOD

David ignored his counsellor's advice and went, instead, to his art master, Owen Frampton, who had offered to help find jobs for pupils who were leaving – jobs which might be appropriate for those who had studied art. It was in this way that David left school a week early, in May, to join the London office of an American advertising agency, J. Walter Thompson, as a 'junior visualizer', someone who helped ink in the illustrations and story boards. He didn't like it much, but at least it was in 'art', more or less, and it took him to his beloved London.

By mid-summer, David's friendship with George Underwood was revived, when George called with an apology and an invitation to join another weekend band. David missed playing in a group and accepted immediately. He couldn't have picked a better time to do so, because in 1963 the English pop music scene was exploding. For seventeen years, American music had dominated the British record charts and then in January, 1963, an obscure band from Liverpool began touring Scotland to promote its first single, 'Love Me Do'. The Beatles released a second single, 'Please Please Me', that month and a month after that it was No. 2 on the British charts. In April, they released another single, 'From Me to You' and as it was climbing to the No. 1 spot, another band from Liverpool, Gerry and the Pacemakers, had its first No. 1 hit, 'How Do You Do It?'. By June, Billy J. Kramer was at No. 2 with 'Do You Want to Know a Secret?', which was written by John Lennon and Paul McCartney. In August – when David was completing his first month of work in London – yet another group from Liverpool, the Searchers, went into first place with 'Sweets for My Sweet'. And so it went for much of the remainder of the year until in December, *Variety*, the entertainment business weekly, announced that the 'Liverpool beat' had boosted total British record sales by an astonishing 40 per cent.

One by one, the bands from the north came to London, first to record and then to live.

At the time, London was the world's most populous city, but it was rather sedate. It changed, or seemed to, with the arrival of the Beatles and the horde of bands that bobbed up in their irridescent wake – from Newcastle a gritty bunch of millworkers' sons who called themselves the Animals; from Manchester the Hollies and a peculiarly fey milkman with an ill-fitting wig (Freddie and the Dreamers); and from London, the Dave Clark Five, the Who (then calling themselves the Detours) and the Rolling Stones. All burst on to the record charts in 1963 and from that year on, it was not just London, it was 'Swinging' London, the centre of everything pop.

Throughout the city, dozens of pubs and small working men's clubs switched to a live entertainment policy and in Soho, several new clubs opened and some of the older ones began headlining the young rhythm and blues bands which previously had been presented only during the intervals. Georgie Fame and His Blue Flames opened the new Flamingo that summer and Alexis Korner's legendary Blues Incorporated moved into the Marquee, which until then had featured jazz almost exclusively.

All this activity only made David Jones itch, and when George Underwood offered him the opportunity to join a band he immediately said, 'Let's do it then.'

Three other musicians – a drummer named Robert Allen, bassist Frank Howard and lead guitarist, Roger Bluck – were, according to David, found in a barbershop. Sometimes David said the barbershop was in Bromley, other times in Brixton. The truth is that with all the fuss being made about long-haired rock and roll musicians, David loved the irony of saying he had found *his* musicians getting their hair *cut*.

David and George decided to call their band the King Bees, after the blues lyric, 'I'm a king bee, baby, buzzing 'round your vine' and as might be expected, much of the slapped-together repertoire was comprised of rhythm and blues hits from America.

Says George Underwood: 'It was me and David, forcin' our tastes on the other three.'

For four or five months the King Bees worked the South London circuit, picking up jobs wherever they could, never finding a place to call home. In part this was because of increased competition. The sudden and enormous success of the Beatles and other English bands had inspired thousands of others to form bands in far greater number than even the expanded number of venues could accommodate. David grew somewhat depressed, which was unusual for him; normally his confidence bordered on arrogance.

During the week, of course, he continued to work at the advertising agency, but the pay there was minimal, too, and after train fares and lunch – which he often skipped – there was precious little left for records, clothing and entertainment.

David was nearing his seventeenth birthday when he went to his father for advice about his music. Mr Jones wasn't an especially imaginative man, but he wasn't simple either. He read several of the national newspapers and when David started bringing home copies of the London music paper, *Melody Maker*, he read that, too. So he knew the story of how a businessman named Brian Epstein had 'discovered' and backed the Beatles in Liverpool, becoming their manager.

'Ay, David,' he said one night, 'this Brian Epstein, what do you know of 'im?'

David answered as best he could, sharing some of the gossip he'd heard in Soho.

'David,' his father said, 'it looks to me you need a man like that. A manager. A gentleman with a few bob to 'is name.'

David thought it over and a few days later he suggested John Bloom, a London entrepreneur who had made millions selling washing machines. In 1963 he was one of the most gossiped-about London party-givers. Fast new money was a passport to the pop scene and with all the latest pop stars reported in attendance at the Bloom parties, David thought he was a likely prospect. He and his father composed a letter, asking for his support.

'If you can sell my pop group like you sell your washing machines,' David wrote, 'you're on a winner.'

Bloom was impressed, or at least intrigued, but not wishing to get involved, he sent a telegram to David to that effect. However, he suggested that David write to a friend of his, Leslie Conn, and he called Conn to tell him what he'd done.

'I've had a letter from a cheeky sod,' Bloom said, 'but I like his style. Give him an audition and tell me what you think.'

Conn was a young hustler with a reputation for running with the London avant garde. Among his friends he counted the soon-to-be-famous hair stylist Vidal Sassoon and the playwright Harold Pinter, and at the time of Bloom's call, he was working as a talent scout in the office of Dick James, the Beatles' music publisher. It seemed a terrific break for David.

Conn listened to David's band and told Bloom he liked what he heard. Bloom then offered to pay £20 to have the group perform at a wedding anniversary he was hosting for friends at a Soho club. Conn said he thought the boys would be interested and managed to increase the price to £100.

David later described the evening – a posh event at the Jack of Clubs – as 'a bit embarrassing'. The truth was, it was a disaster. The guests were dressed formally, and the band showed up in T-shirts and jeans. To make matters worse, most of the guests reacted to the band's first song, 'Got My Mojo Working', with shocked or pained expressions. Some even held their hands to their ears. At the end of the second song, 'Hoochie Coochie Man', Bloom was on his feet shouting. 'Get 'em off! They're ruining my party!'

Conn seemed unaffected by the Bloom incident when David called the following day.

'Put it aside, mate,' Conn said. 'I've got good news. Decca wants an audition.'

'Decca?'

David was stunned. Decca was one of the strongest record companies in England, with a long line of hit-making acts that included the big bands of Mantovani and David Whitfield, middle-of-the-road vocalists like Vera Lynn and Anthony Newley, and pop newcomers Tommy Steele, Jet Harris, the Bachelors and the Tornados, all of whom had had No. 1 hits in recent years. Decca also had the Rolling

Stones, while Buddy Holly and Bill Haley and the Comets were on two of the company's subsidiary labels.

It was one of Decca's subsidiary labels, Vocalion, which was principally devoted to jazz and R&B, that wanted the King Bees. Of course, David wanted to leave his London job immediately. But his father's will prevailed.

'It's only an audition, David. Let's take it a step at a time.'

The King Bees were nervous and they sounded like a watered-down version of the Rolling Stones with a little of the Animals thrown in, but that was considered acceptable, because that sound seemed to be The Next Big Thing. Decca offered to release a 45 rpm single, withholding an album offer for when and if the single was a hit.

While selecting material and waiting for the May recording date, Leslie Conn took David to meet Dick James. James had been bitten by the Beatles bug, and bitten badly. As the Beatles churned out hit after original hit, his tiny Soho music publishing company was under a state of siege as more and more artists showed interest in recording Lennon-McCartney songs. Other callers wanted James to publish *their* songs, believing James had a magic touch. In fact, the Beatles had fallen into the publisher's lap only a year after he had started his business, and then only because years before, when he was a crooner himself, some of his recordings had been produced by the Beatles' producer, George Martin. In 1964 – as the Beatles began to conquer America – James was determined to become another Brian Epstein, discovering and developing his own stable of talent. When Conn took David to meet him, James was so unimpressed, he almost barked at his talent scout: 'Get that long-haired git out of the office and find me another Beatles!'

None the less, James published the song that was selected for the feature side of the King Bees' first record, 'Liza Jane', which Conn took credit for writing. It was actually an old Negro spiritual that they had played around with, and turned into what was then called in London a 'rave-up' tune, the sort of song used in the middle of a set to get the customers off their bums and on to the dance floor. The lyrics were simple and repetitious, with a typical call-and-response between David and his backup musicians; David sang a verse and the band chorused, 'Little Liza, little Liza Jane!' and then David sang another verse. The emphasis was on the pounding, monotonous bass line and David's energetic but somewhat undisciplined vocal. He also got to play saxophone, but that, mercifully, was buried in the record's mix.

The B-side of the record was a 'cover' of a song by a then-obscure American group, Paul Revere and the Raiders, called 'Louie Louie Go Home'. Again the lyric was simple to the point of starkness and while the little vocal 'woo-woos' sounded rather like the Beatles (doing their impression of Little Richard who was still one of David's favourites), the rest was reminiscent of the Animals and the Rolling Stones.

The record was released 5 June 1964, and the following day David appeared on the BBC television programme *Juke Box Jury*, a show built upon the premise of having a panel of 'experts' (usually well-known entertainers, some of whom may have had nothing to do with music) listen to and evaluate new records. Judges that day included sex symbol Diana Dors and comedian Charlie Drake, both of whom thought the record had potential.

Decca pressed 3,500 copies of the record and sent them out the same day it shipped a similar 45 rpm single by a group called David John and the Mood (a band from Preston). Decca really didn't care which David hit, merely hoping that one of them would.

Both flopped.

Before that happened, however, David left the advertising agency. 'I had me flirt with capitalism,' he said later. 'I decided it was time to get on with being a musician.'

The King Bees continued to work weekends – sometimes making as much as £100 at one of the universities – but the expenses climbed as well. When 'Liza Jane' failed, Decca showed no interest in recording any more material.

In an attempt to breathe some life into things, Les Conn urged his boss Dick James to throw himself personally behind David, give him the star push. James declined, so Conn took David to Mickie Most, a young record producer who had been instrumental in getting the Animals their recording contract (and who later guided in one way or another the careers of Herman's Hermits, Donovan, Jeff

Beck and, in the 1970s, the Sex Pistols). Most also said no.

Meanwhile, the King Bees were falling apart. 'We didn't quite jell,' George Underwood says. 'And we weren't going great guns, so David found another band he could front. He felt he was the only one taking it seriously, because the rest of us were in school and he was devoting his everything to music. So he split.'

The new band David drifted into was called the Manish Boys, six instrumentalists from Maidstone, Kent. Like the Rolling Stones, they took their name from a Muddy Waters song, a song of sexual braggadocio about a boy who was nearly a man – a 'manish' boy.

By now, David had left Leslie Conn, who later said, 'David had total belief in his own talent and was totally dedicated to what he did. He believed with a passion that he was going to be a big star. I believed in him as much as he believed in himself. My biggest problem was I hadn't the resources to back my judgement. David was too ambitious to hold under the existing conditions. And to my regret, I let him go.'

As David began to rehearse with his new backing group, he indulged himself: he began to do what he had wanted to do for years and that was to 'hang about' in the London music scene. In 1964, it was quite something.

The Beatles were the darlings of all America by now and the British 'invasion' force was in full and rewarding attack. American performers continued to make themselves known to American record buyers in 1964, but it was the English contingent that sold out the biggest American arenas and stadiums, earned the biggest dollars on *The Ed Sullivan Show*, and grabbed nearly all of the media. In 1964 the Beatles toured the US twice, dominated record bestseller charts, were on the covers of twenty-six national magazines, and released their first movie, *A Hard Day's Night*. And in the wake of all this came the Rolling Stones (who also toured the US in 1964), the Yardbirds, the Animals, the Kinks, the Searchers, the Dave Clark Five, and Gerry and the Pacemakers. Even the big, new network television show debuted by ABC in August, *Shindig*, was produced by an Englishman, Jack Good.

In London in 1964, the focus on British pop musicians

was even sharper than it was in America. In March, for the first time in British recording history, all Top 10 singles in England were by English acts. In the same month, Britain also got its first pirate radio ship, anchored outside the three-mile limit to escape national regulation; this effectively broke the forty-year broadcast monopoly of the BBC, which had shunned rock music, and by the end of the year there were seventeen such ships. In May, Princess Margaret and Lord Snowdon were in attendance at the premiere of *A Hard Day's Night*. In Soho, the owner of the Marquee shifted his club's music policy from slick jazz to hard R&B, booking the Rolling Stones and the Who, and from America, Rufus Thomas and Wilson Pickett. And just four blocks away was Carnaby Street, now erupting with new clothing shops.

The excitement around him, coupled with his own sort of meandering success, made David all the more determined. He was going to be a star, he told friends in Bromley. And towards that end, he decided to change his image.

Until now, David's image had been ill-defined visually – a thrown-together mix of student bohemianism and the conventional suit and tie, with a bit of the Mod and Ted tossed in.

When David was still at Bromley Tech and playing with the Kon-rads, his carefully coiffed ducktail and elephant trunk was a Teddy Boy hair style. The 'Teds' were a peculiar group, a proud, defiant bunch of swaggering Cockney street toughs who wore long, Edwardian drape jackets and stove-pipe trousers, with black bow-string ties and crepe-soled shoes. Elvis was god in this band of misfits and rockabilly was the religion.

The Mods were cooler. Like the Teddy Boys, membership of the subculture was rooted in the working class, but here the wardrobe was more conventional and while the Teds were absolutely stuck in one fashion, Mod styles were changing nearly every week. The Mods were consumers – in fact *massive* consumers, buying and discarding clothes and other goods in a manner that was quite alarming in a country whose older generation had still not recovered from the deprivations of war. Thus the Mods were the first subculture to represent postwar affluence.

The Mods also had an elitist approach to music, ignoring

the early white rock and roll of the Teds and Rockers, ignoring all the new copycat English performers with made-up names like Billy Fury and Dickie Pride and Marty Wilde, ignoring the folky sounds of the 'skiffle' craze which was reminiscent of America's jug-band sound, ignoring even the Beatles, preferring, instead, black musicians from America, especially the early sounds of Tamla-Motown from Detroit.

Make-up was another part of the Mod look: lipstick, blusher, eyeshadow and pancake powder (not Clearasil).

Pills were integral, too, but only amphetamines. Speed was the essence of Mod.

For David the choice between Ted and Mod was an easy one. He became a Mod. Without a job to help him dress the part, however, David often had to improvise with whatever he could find in the Carnaby Street dustbins, where haberdashers and trendy designers discarded the outfits with flaws. Consequently, David was always a tiny bit off, slightly mismatched or behind the constantly changing times.

David's hair was quite long by now, worn well below the collar and with a fringe, much like Brian Jones of the Rolling Stones. In November 1964, ever alert for publicity for himself and his group, the Manish Boys, David arranged an interview in the *London Evening News* to announce the formation of what David called the International League for the Preservation of Animal Filament (hair).

'It's really for the protection of pop musicians and those who wear their hair long,' David explained. 'Anyone who has the courage to wear hair down to his shoulder has to go through hell. It's time we united and stood up for our curls. Everybody makes jokes about you on a bus, and if you go past navvies digging in the road, it's murder!'

It was a clever publicity gimmick, and in the same week, David and his band signed with the esteemed Arthur Howes Agency. Almost immediately they were added as the opening band on a six-concert tour then being planned for the American singer Gene Pitney and Liverpool's Gerry and the Pacemakers. The shows were uneventful and although they did serve to give David and his mates a few pointers on life on the road, as is so often the case with opening acts, the Manish Boys generally went unnoticed.

Another group signed to the Howes Agency at the time was the Kinks, a quartet of working-class boys from North London whose hit records ('You Really Got Me', 'All Day and All of the Night') were being produced by an American exile in Britain, Shel Talmy. Talmy became the *second* person to 'discover' David Jones. (Les Conn being the 'first'.)

Talmy came to London from Los Angeles, where he had been an apprentice to Nik Venet, the Beach Boys' record producer. The way the story goes, when Shel decided to go to England, Nik gave him several tapes of Lou Rawls and the Beach Boys, telling him to say that he (rather than Nik) was the producer. In this way, Talmy was hired as a house producer for Decca. He met Ray Davies, started producing the Kinks and began looking for other acts.

Eventually, David and the Manish Boys recorded two songs with Talmy, which appeared in the shops on the Parlophone label in March 1965. The A-side was a song called 'I Pity the Fool', a No. 1 song on the American rhythm and blues charts in 1961 by Bobby 'Blue' Bland. David's version was a fairly close and sympathetic copy of the original, with added guitar by Jimmy Page, a young musician on nearly all of Talmy's sessions (and who later would go on to great fame as lead guitarist for the Yardbirds and Led Zeppelin).

The B-side was David's first recorded original, 'Take My Tip'. Like other groups of the period, David had realized that to be really successful you needed to write your own songs and avoid relying on other people for material. This song was more in the jazz tradition, with an emphasis on the keyboard style of the American pianist and singer Mose Allison (who was a great influence on many British musicians, including Zoot Money, Georgie Fame and Graham Bond). It also was remarkable for its tongue-twisting lyric, which showed David's love of language, a characteristic of his music for the rest of his life.

David did everything he could to promote the record. With his father's, and Talmy's, support, he resumed the crusade for the liberation of long-haired males when the producer of the BBC's pop music show, *Gadzooks! It's All Happening!*, reportedly threatened to ban David's group from appearing on the show unless David cut his hair.

Said the producer, Barry Langford, 'Kids today just don't want this long-hair business any more.'

David said in reply: 'I would rather die than get my hair cut. I wouldn't have my hair cut for the Prime Minister, let alone the BBC. It took nearly three years to grow and it's part of my stock-in-trade.'

As pickets organized by David's old friend Les Conn marched around the BBC studio carrying signs proclaiming, 'Be fair to long hair!', Langford proposed a compromise: David could appear on the show with only a trim, but if the viewers complained, David's fee would go to a deserving charity.

It was all a bit contrived, but London's daily newspapers seldom understood rock and roll and, consequently, stories about long hair generally evoked alarming headlines or cute ones. When the Rolling Stones first appeared on the scene, for instance, newspapers asked in blazing type: 'Would You Want Your Daughter to Marry a Rolling Stone?' In David's case, it went in the other direction. On the day before his appearance on the television show, David's picture appeared in several papers, a hair net being placed over his head for a 'trimming of his long blond locks.'

When the new record was released, David was unhappy with the way the record was packaged. A few months earlier he had told friends he didn't want to be known apart from his band, said he didn't want to be billed as David Jones and Whomever. Instead, he said, he wanted to be an equal part of the band, as Mick Jagger was just another Rolling Stone.

However, with the release of the new single, his tune changed. Paul Rodriguez, the tenor saxophonist in the Manish Boys, says there was a 'furious row' over billing once the record came out. Now David was livid about not getting billing above the group.

As the Manish Boys began to fall apart, David moved quickly to join another band. For a while he worked in both groups simultaneously.

The new band was called the Lower Third, originally a five-piece group from Margate. Three of the musicians – lead guitarist named Dennis Taylor, bassist Graham Rivens, and drummer Les Mighall – had come to London in search of fame and fortune. As a trio they found temporary employment at La Discotheque, another club in Soho. Their vocals were weak, however, and so they began auditioning singers. David was one of them. Another was Steve Marriott, who would go on to fame as a singer and guitarist for the Small Faces and Humble Pie. David seemed more confident and he got the job, quickly taking over the band.

David went to his father's tired old typewriter and created a flashy and hyperbolic letter, which he sent to a long list of agents, nightclub bookers and television producers:

This is to inform you of the existence of

DAVIE JONES and THE LOWER THIRD

Reputation-wise, Davie has a spotless chart. Having picked up the gauntlet in the now legendary 'Banned Hair' tale, he stormed the BBC 2's *Gadzooks*, leaving such an impression that he has been contracted for another impression this month.

THE LOWER THIRD

THE group to watch this year. Gaze on, as their record, BORN OF THE NIGHT (released shortly), rushes up the charts. Stand astounded at their brilliant backings for Davie.

TEA-CUP on lead
DEATH on bass
LES on drums

How does a three piece sound like a twelve piece? All this, plus Davie's earthy vocals, Tenor/Alto Sax and Hard pork, adds up to the most exciting evening of R&B that you've ever experienced.

A VERY FAIR SHOW FOR A VERY FAIR PRICE.

There was a remarkable single-mindedness about David and a surprising confidence for a young man of his age. When he appeared on television, in both his musical performances and news interviews, he appeared to be extraordinarily composed. Even in the mannered and somewhat stiff publicity photographs, in which the band members all gave the camera their best surly glare, David's was the most convincing. It was as if he *knew*, somehow, exactly who he was, or, like some cosmic card player, knew he had the ability to bluff better than anyone else in the game.

David was still living at home and hating it. By now, he rarely saw his older brother, Terry. Initially, they had parted musically, as Terry failed to understand David's fascination for rock and roll. But then Terry withdrew completely. There were long crying jags and then, as David said years later, 'he got to where he almost vegetated, wouldn't talk, read, wouldn't do anything.' For a while Terry saw a psychiatrist and later, during the period when David was raiding the Carnaby Street dustbins, Terry vanished.

David was fearful and shocked, but it was not a subject that was discussed at home. His mother was an emotional woman and got upset if Terry was mentioned. She also fretted over David's choice of a career. It was bad enough, she said, that one son had disappeared after behaving so poorly, but to have the remaining one wearing outlandish clothing and hair clear to the shoulders – well, that was even worse. Mrs Jones did not wish to discuss either Terry *or* rock and roll and her husband and son humoured her.

Initially, the Lower Third fared poorly. David's letter brought only a few jobs and the record he mentioned, 'Born of the Night', was nothing more than hope and hype; it was never released. And then the drummer Les Mighall quit, to be replaced by Phil Lancaster, a session musician who had recorded with the Dave Clark Five.

Talmy persisted, persuading Parlophone in August 1965 to release another single, two of David's original compositions, 'You've Got a Habit of Leaving', a lyric lament with an adenoidal vocal, and 'Baby Loves That Way', in which David sings more comfortably, against a choral backing similar to most other English groups of the period. In fact, both sides sounded very much like Talmy's other two groups, the Who and the Kinks, with some Herman's Hermits thrown in. This record also failed and Parlophone said it would *not* be interested in trying again.

David began carrying copies of his earlier records and

'dubs' of what he hoped would be his next release, from door to door along Soho's Denmark Street, centre of London's music business. In this way, he found himself one day in the office of an agent named Terry King, who then represented such acts as Screamin' Lord Sutch and the Savages, the Fortunes, the Rockin' Berries and the Zephyrs. King introduced David to a young agent who had recently left the Moody Blues after serving as their road manager. This was Ralph Horton, who auditioned the Lower Third in a pub near Soho.

Horton liked what he heard and began to get them work – first as the opening band for the Moody Blues at the Bromel Club in Bromley, where David's parents proudly sat in reserved seats, and then in a series of weekend end-of-summer engagements in resort clubs in Bournemouth and on the Isle of Wight.

'We were known as the second-loudest group in London,' Dennis Taylor said years later. 'The Who were the first. A publisher who was present at the recording session remarked that we sounded like a Lancaster bomber flying through the studio.'

David's recollection of the group was even less flattering: 'We were too loud on stage. We used feedback and sounds and didn't play any melodies. We just pulverized the sound, which was loosely based on Tamla-Motown. We had an ardent following of about a hundred Mods, but when we played out of London, we were booed right off the stage. We weren't very good.'

Good or not, David and the Lower Third went into the esteemed Marquee Club in September and October 1965 for a series of six Sunday afternoon shows which were being recorded and sponsored by Radio London, one of the pirate radio stations. It was their first showcase in Soho and they were playing second bill to the High Numbers – who soon would become the Who. It gave David and his band their first important Mod audience.

The shows also gave Ralph Horton the opportunity he needed to get several others in the business to come and see the act. When he was with the Moody Blues he'd met Tony Hatch, the record producer, and when Hatch heard David at the Marquee, he signed him to Pye Records for a period of six months, during which time Hatch promised to release one single.

Before the songs were recorded, Horton called yet another friend in the business, Kenneth Pitt.

Pitt was a reserved, erudite London-born sophisticate who entered show business as an artist designing movie posters for the J. Arthur Rank Organization. He then became a publicist for Rank, accompanying Jean Simmons and other starlets from interview to interview. In time, he left the film company and opened a management office, representing a number of English bandleaders and singers, including Ted Heath and Allan Dean. He also worked for many American performers when they appeared at the London Palladium – Jack Benny, Frankie Laine, Johnny Ray, Louis Armstrong, Duke Ellington, Stan Kenton, Billy Eckstine, Mel Torme, Vic Damone, Billy Daniels and, most recently, Bob Dylan, as manager of Dylan's English tours. At the time, Pitt was also managing from his offices in Mayfair a singer named Crispian St Peters (who would have a number of hit records in Britain the following year), and Manfred Mann, consistent hit-makers since 'Do Wah Diddy' topped both the British and American record charts in 1964.

Pitt didn't have time to get involved with David at that time, but he did have some advice.

Horton looked at Pitt. 'Wot's that, mate?'

'David should consider changing his name.'

'Why?'

'There are many young men named Jones,' Pitt replied, 'and there is one called Davy Jones, who has already been on the London stage, in Lionel Bart's production of *Oliver*. He's in America now and he has a record out. He's also just been cast in an American television show called *The Monkees*, a send-up on the Beatles. I don't think the world needs *two* singers with the same name and this other one has a leg up.'

Two days later, Pitt received a letter from Horton. He said David Jones was now David Bowie. Whenever anyone asked, David said he picked the name from Jim Bowie, inventor of the Bowie knife, a familiar weapon in American films.

In the months that followed there seemed to be some hope. First, Ralph Horton found an 'angel', a businessman who provided £4,000 in exchange for 10 per cent of David's earnings for the next three years. Then David got a luke-warm but encouraging review for his new single – two original songs, 'Can't Help Thinkin' About Myself' and 'I Say to Myself', both somewhat autobiographical – his first 'official' review (in *Record Retailer*) and the record went into the charts, rising to No. 34. This was followed by an interview in another of the music weeklies and an early March booking on *Ready, Steady, Go!* with the Yardbirds and the Small Faces, along with personal appearances in several London record shops.

None the less, the Lower Third broke up – again the reason being lack of money: the £4,000 was quickly spent, largely to cover longstanding debts – and with still another band (this one called the Buzz and comprised of guitarist John 'Hutch' Hutchinson, Derek 'Dek' Fearnley and organ-ist Derek Boyes), David was starting over. The band was living in Ralph Horton's flat, where creditors came calling daily. When the electricity was cut off, Ralph went into a manhole in the street and reconnected it. Finally, there was no food to eat.

Horton called Ken Pitt again, saying he wanted to bring him up to date. Horton was selling and selling hard when they met, on 5 April, counting off all David's accomplish-ments since he had changed his name at Pitt's advice. Pitt agreed to take a look on 17 April, when David and his band were appearing at the Marquee in the second of a series of Sunday 'Bowie Showboat' shows.

At the concert opening, David lit one of his pungent European cigarettes and using it almost as a baton, he signalled the band to begin, crashing into one of his orig-inals. Pitt was startled. Before him was a performer of surprising polish and confidence. Musically the band sounded raw, practically unrehearsed – not far off, consider-ing their brief time together – and rather like dozens, perhaps hundreds of other groups, but the singer was riveting. Never, Pitt said afterwards, had he ever seen anyone so completely in control, so intense.

Pitt was especially impressed by David's closing song,

which seemed totally misplaced in the Marquee: the stirring inspirational number from the American musical *Carousel* which had been such a hit for Judy Garland, 'You'll Never Walk Alone'. David belted it out as if he were on a West End stage.

Ralph Horton went up to Ken Pitt as the band was putting its instruments away. He suggested they go to a nearby pub for a pint. Pitt looked at Horton and suggested they go to his home instead.

Pitt lived the refined gentleman's life, in a Georgian townhouse built in 1780 not far from Regent's Park. He had a maisonette on the top two floors and in it one of London's most impressive collections of Victoriana. David was drawn immediately to the glass case full of rare books by Aubrey Beardsley and Oscar Wilde.

'Oh!' he cried. 'You've got this one!' He pulled one of the volumes from the shelf and turned the pages, then put it back and ran his finger along the row of old books. 'And this one, too!'

David turned to face the two men, who were seated nearby. He touched his hair, still damp from his Marquee performance and extricated a cigarette from his jacket pocket. Lighting it dramatically, he finally said, 'Ralph, let's do a deal with Ken.'

It was then that Pitt laid out his plan. He said he was impressed by David's potential to become more than just another rock star. Another English pop singer, Tommy Steele, had gone on to the stage and films, Pitt said, and that was what he wanted for David as well: 'to juggle, dance and act as well as sing and play guitar.'

'Super!' David said. 'That's what we'll do, then.'

Pitt agreed to handle all of the duties of a manager for a five-year period, freeing Horton to go back to what he knew best, working with the band on the road. Pitt's duties were to handle the paperwork, search for work, and keep the accounts. He also agreed to book David as a support act for two other bands in his stable, Crispian St Peters (who had just had his first English hit, 'You Were On My Mind') and Dave Antony's Moods.

The 'Bowie Showboat' continued at the Marquee on Sunday afternoons and in August Pye released another single. Again there were two Bowie originals, 'I Dig Every-thing' and 'I'm Not Losing Sleep'. When provided with an advance 'dub' of the record, *Ready, Steady, Go!* said no. The music trade papers ignored it. And so did the record buyers.

*

If success continued to elude David and his band, at least life was exciting. Even poverty could not make life in Swinging London dull.

Of course, insiders said that London was no longer swing-ing by 1966 – that it had become institutionalized by the time the media 'discovered' it. However true that appraisal may be, when *Time* magazine and *Life* and *The Saturday Evening Post* devoted their covers to the mini-skirted, long-haired, rock and roll phenomenon, the city was suddenly awash with American visitors looking for action. And London began to swing again.

No one enjoyed this more than David Bowie, the English-man with the American name. Although he worked at the Marquee only once a week, he was there virtually every night, listening to John Mayall's Blues Breakers and Cream (both featuring the guitarist Eric Clapton), the Spencer Davis Group, Alexis Korner's Blues Incorporated, and the Graham Bond Organization.

In the final months of 1966, the Mod's 'official' band, the Who, rode the top of the record charts with 'The Kids Are Alright' and 'I'm a Boy', songs of exultation. The Beatles sang about a 'Paperback Writer' and a 'Yellow Submarine'. Love songs were scattered all over the landscape, from the Troggs' 'Wild Thing' to Dusty Springfield's 'You Don't Have to Say You Love Me' to the Rolling Stones' 'Let's Spend the Night Together'. First Carnaby Street, and then the King's Road, blossomed into trendy focal points, where boutiques and hairdressers seemed to proclaim the youth revolution won.

And David was in the thick of it, with a choice of London flats to stay in when it was too late to catch the last train home to Bromley.

When he was using more than the usual number of Purple Hearts, the popular name for the heart-shaped tablets of methadrine, or smoking the occasional hashish, or had a 'bird' in a mini-skirt in tow, he headed for Ralph Horton's place, where a party raged until early every morning. When he was sober and alone, he went to Ken Pitt's home on Mansfield Street, climbing the twisting staircase to the large bedroom on the upper level.

On Sundays, David continued to perform at the Marquee and one day soon after Ken Pitt became his manager, Radio London came by to broadcast the show.

Radio London: And now a young British Boy whose career will surely develop him into one of the bigger names in the show-biz field. He's a great attraction here at the Marquee and his name is David Bowie. David, you're working with a backing group, the Buzz. Have you always been with them?

David: As David Bowie, yes. I've always been with them, for about six months.

Radio London: Why do you say 'as David Bowie'?

David: I was someone else before that.

THE MIME

And someone else he'd be again.

By the time David and the Buzz recorded an original song about the Mod movement, 'The London Boys', the Mod movement had peaked and David's interest in it was fading rapidly.

'London Boys' is a song that David sang as if he were giving advice to a would-be-Mod from the provinces who was trying to keep up with the London 'faces'. It wasn't worth it, David said, because eventually you came 'down' from the amphetamine rush of Swinging London life.

The song was recorded for Pye but never released, and by late summer of 1966, Pye and David were ready to call it quits, so Pye released the song to him. Ken Pitt then took the song to Deram, another subsidiary of the Decca label. 'London Boys' was a timely tune and Deram thought they'd find some success with it. However, by the time it was released in early December, David and the Buzz had split up – for the same reason the others had: no money – and David's career was moving in two new directions at once.

One was towards being a cabaret star – a slick, conservative lounge act with an appeal so broad that even the grandmothers could worship him.

The other direction was towards being an 'arts lab' hippy.

David's first moves towards the London underground seemed tentative. He did not, for example, join or express any sympathy for anti-Vietnam protesters marching in front of the American embassy. At the same time, however, he *did* attend a concert of Bob Dylan's at the Royal Albert Hall (a show that was promoted by his own manager, Ken Pitt) and talked of little else for weeks afterwards. He also started reading London's underground newspaper, *International Times*. None the less, when Pitt began negotiating with a small film company to use David in a short musical, David followed Pitt's advice and quickly wrote nine tunes of a sort aimed squarely at a broad pop audience. Some of these songs also were taken to Deram, in an attempt by Pitt to get an album contract.

At the time, an album was an unlikely prospect for David. In 1966, most artists generally had a hit single before an album was offered. But Pitt found a receptive audience in Decca's head of promotion, Tony Hall, and the label's album manager, Hugh Mendl. Mendl was especially taken by the songs and David's mainstream pop delivery. He said he was reminded of another artist whose records he supervised, the composer, vocalist, actor, and comic Anthony Newley.

The songs were a strange lot, only a little like anything David had done before. Years later a critic would refer to one of the songs on the album as 'West End musical fodder', and they almost certainly did come as a result of David's fascination at the time with Lionel Bart type musicals. In fact, nearly all fourteen songs which eventually appeared on the record fit that description.

The eternal child/reluctant adult motif was one of the recurrent themes, evident in 'Uncle Arthur', a whimsical story of an aging mama's boy; more regretfully apparent in 'This Is a Happy Land', where, David said, only children live; in 'Come And Buy My Toys', a simple song about 'monkeys made of ginger bread and sugar horses painted red'; and in 'Little Bombardier', a strange tale of a war veteran who liked to play with children and got run out of town by the police for doing so.

Other songs hinted at themes which David would explore years later. The apocalyptic 'We Are the Hungry Men' delivered a simplistic message about overpopulation and utilized a spoken 'Nazi' voice. And 'She's Got My Medals' tentatively looked at sex-role change, telling the story of a young woman who impersonated a man to be a soldier and then deserted just before disaster, returning to London as a woman again.

The only two songs that seemed to fit David's immediate past were those he wrote about the London he first examined in 'London Boys'. 'Join the Gang' was about Johnny the sitar-playing existentialist, Moddy the model who loved LSD, and Arthur the staggering rock band drunk. It was all a big illusion, but if you join the gang, you're 'in'. The other song, 'Maid of Bond Street', was a lesser work, a bittersweet lament about the trendy dolly-girls.

The album ended with probably the oddest song of them all, 'Please Mr Gravedigger', a sick joke about a man who mourned the death of a ten-year-old girl he had killed, as he was preparing to kill the gravedigger.

What made these songs even more unusual was the fact that David and his band rarely performed them, sticking instead to their R&B repertoire (no doubt because the club audiences wouldn't have stood for them). It was as if David had two separate careers in progress simultaneously, one aimed at the mums and dads, the other programmed for the kids at the Marquee.

The group was not faring well at the time. By now, some of the musicians were living in an old ambulance that they used to travel from job to job. David, of course, had an album scheduled for release, but those peculiar songs had little to do with the group, so it was not surprising when in the last month of 1966, David told his mates it was over. They had earned more than two thousand pounds during the year and had been advanced another four thousand by Ken Pitt and their businessman-angel, but they closed the year in grinding debt as the money didn't go far when divided up between them and, anyway, David had a tendency to spend money when he had it and starve later.

There was also a growing rift between Ken Pitt and Ralph Horton. When Ken Pitt was in the United States negotiating a publishing contract for David which would have netted him $30,000, Horton signed David to a London publisher for £500. Pitt was furious. It was, he says today, 'a blow from which we never recovered'.

Pitt never told David about the $30,000 offer. After meeting with David's father, they agreed it would only depress him. They also agreed that Horton should be eased out – contract or no contract – and that Pitt would be the new manager.

David's father supported his son unfailingly. On more than one occasion, before the band broke up and the ambulance had broken down out of town, Mr Jones got out of bed, drove forty or fifty miles and brought the stranded boys back home to London. He answered David's business correspondence and whenever there was a noteworthy event in his son's life he notified the local Bromley papers and called the music weeklies with the news. Most important, when David's mother began questioning her son's career, Mr Jones was inevitably quick to come to David's defence, saying, 'It's okay, mum, if we don't let David give it a bash, he'll be frustrated the rest of his life.'

Although there were no performances in the first three months of 1967, David stayed occupied, accompanying his manager to the theatres in the West End, meeting with Deram about an idea he had for a single, and then recording it.

The A-side was called 'The Laughing Gnome', in which David sang to a gnome whose speeded-up voice was exactly like those of the Chipmunks in America. David added to the gimmick some characteristic word-play, using the word 'gnome' as often as he could in the lyric, 'Gnome-man's land . . . metrognome . . . gnomads . . . London School of Ecognomics . . . like a rolling gnome.'

The single, released in April, failed to attract any following, and by May, Pitt was worrying about album sales. He pulled out all the stops, sending personally typed letters to some twenty producers at the BBC, sending demonstration tapes elsewhere, handling many of the promotional chores usually executed by the record company. He even paid for a half-page ad in *Record Retailer*, one of the music trade papers.

The first reviews were positive!

Said the *New Musical Express*: 'Here's a Cockney singer who reminds me of Anthony Newley and Tommy Steele, which can't be bad. Yes, we have another Tony Newley here all right. A very promising talent.' While the *Disc and Music Echo* called the LP 'a remarkable creative debut'.

The album – released in June – failed on the marketplace anyway. David's loyal fans from his Mod and R&B days stayed away from the album in droves. And no one else seemed ready for another Tony Newley.

After all, that was the summer of 1967, a very special time. In America they were calling it the 'Summer of Love'.

The week David's album had gone into London shops, Brian Jones was introducing Jimi Hendrix at the Monterey Pop Festival in California (where in a spectacular display, Hendrix set fire to his guitar, upstaging the Who, who had merely destroyed their instruments with their fists and feet). June was also when the Beatles released their masterwork, *Sgt Pepper's Lonely Heart's Club Band* and when Rolling Stone Keith Richard was found guilty of allowing his home to be used for the smoking of cannabis. In the US the top song was Aretha Franklin's first major hit, 'Respect', and in the United Kingdom the No. 1 record was Procol Harum's surrealistic and somewhat stately 'A Whiter Shade of Pale'.

And David was spending more and more time in London. His nocturnal habits were interrupting his parents' sleep. He liked playing his records late at night and sometimes, high on amphetamines and anxious to play his guitar, he didn't want to go to bed at all. Ken Pitt has a note in his diary that it was on 11 June that Mr Jones drove David and the last of his belongings up from Bromley, moving them into Pitt's larger bedroom with the idea that David probably would not come back.

As he left, Mr Jones gave his son his best smile and said he liked Pitt's flat.

'It's very masculine,' Mr Jones said.

David burst out laughing.

Friends say David took full advantage of his manager, who seemed to worship his young charge, even clearing up David's room for him. David was a messy flat-mate, Pitt says today, and after a while he had to ignore the cascade of paper all over the floor and kick the abandoned underwear under the nearest chair. 'Finally, I just closed the door,' he says. 'I figured if I couldn't see it, it wouldn't bother me.'

David also exasperated his manager by getting raging drunk at record parties and bringing girls home for the night, or by walking around the flat nude, so the neighbours could see.

And yet, David respected Ken Pitt. Once, after making a fool of himself and dragging some teenager home with him, David appeared sheepishly at Pitt's office the following day with a box of chocolates and an apology. At the same time, he did continue to do whatever Pitt wished him to do to advance his drooping career, even to the point of agreeing to appear in a film in which two nude men kissed. He also told Ken to have Deram release as his next single the Tony Newley soundalike song, 'Love You Till Tuesday'.

Deram released the record in July and again the reviews were good. The writer in the *Record Mirror* used words like different, amusing, stand-out. *Record Retailer* said it was a 'mature and stylish performance which could easily make it'. Chris Welch wrote in *Melody Maker*, 'Dave Bowie is one of the few really original solo singers operating in the theatre of British pop. He writes very unusual material, he's good-looking, and while his voice has Anthony Newley connotations, it matters little while he makes fine songs of this ilk. And if you don't know what ilk means, it's like having a hit . . .'

Chris Welch was wrong and Penny Vallentine was right when she said in *Disc*, that David was somewhat wonderful, but the record appealed to a 'connoisseur's market'.

Which means the record was less than a success.

The following month, the album and single were released on the US-Deram label in America.

Again, the records sank without a ripple.

Finally, David said the hell with it. He had long suspected that anything 'artistic' was almost by definition non-commercial and his own lack of financial success in music only confirmed that opinion. David fancied himself an artist and it was for this reason that he began to drift away from Ken Pitt's more conventional direction and towards that of the London underground.

More and more, he found himself occupied by an interest in Tibetan Buddhism, enrolling in a mime troupe, and becoming involved with an 'arts lab', where young designers, actors, dancers, film-makers, singers, musicians, artists, poets and crafts people came together in a commune-like environment.

David has claimed through the years that his interest in Buddhism went back to his high school days. More likely, a casual interest evident in early interviews was fanned to flame in 1967, when he visited the basement office of the Tibet Society in London's Eccleston Square, a combined welfare and educational organization formed by refugee monks who had fled Tibet when the Chinese invaded some years before. It was there that he met Chogyam Trungpa, a young monk who was, according to others on the scene, often witnessed running around the King's Road in a robe, with a thousand-year-old dagger stuck in his belt. It was a time when such people were given guru status by pop musicians; the Beatles recently had stumbled into and then away from the camp of India's Maharishi Mahesh Yogi and many others were proclaiming themselves followers of this and that yogi. When the young monk opened a monastery in Scotland, David even went for a visit, saying he might become a monk himself.

He changed his mind when he met one of the truly outrageous characters on the London scene, a mime called Lindsay Kemp. Kemp had studied briefly with Marcel Marceau in Paris and after directing a small avant garde theatre in Edinburgh, he moved into a basement studio that was part of an experimental arts laboratory run by an American expatriate in London's Covent Garden.

'Lindsay was twenty years older than I was,' David said later, 'and had spent much of his early life living the whole Left Bank existence in Paris. He was very militant about being gay, unusual in those days. He introduced me to the way he lived – life started at seven in the evening and one went to bed at seven or eight o'clock the next morning. The walls of his apartment were painted black and the shades were drawn always; daytime didn't exist any more. It was the perfect bohemian existence.

'Lindsay was sort of a leftover from the beatnik period. And as far as I was concerned, his mime company was the most wonderful and definitely the most experimental mime company in Europe at that time. His thing wasn't about putting on masks, miming walking against the wind, and all that stuff. He was far more interested in putting the ideas of Genet or Baudelaire or Cocteau on the stage. And in England, in the mid-sixties, that was incredibly brave. He asked me to do some music for his backgrounds, and I asked him to teach me about mime. I stayed with him for three years, off and on, and we did a lot of tours together. I was learning about how to combine music with theatre, and the guy who played the piano for the company introduced me to

John Cage, to Stockhausen, to the early German electronic music, and the newer, improvisational electronic music from America. I'd never heard stuff like that before.

'At the same time, I was learning about the history of the avant-garde in Europe – surrealism, and before that, of course, dada. And throughout my career, I've held on to the central idea of dada, the idea that an idea becomes obsolete when it works.'

David also attended classes about once a week, at eleven o'clock in the morning. There were about twenty students, all of whom worked in facing rows at first, and then David was paired with Robin Whitecross, a slender young woman from Portsmouth.

'We worked together as a couple,' she says today. 'Our sizes weren't too different and Lindsay would give us an idea and we'd improvize.'

The students lined up and Kemp called out the assignments.

'David and Robin! Two birds!'

David and Robin would flutter and flap and coo.

'David and Robin! Wind!'

David and Robin moved their arms and bodies in an approximation of wind.

'David and Robin! Birth!'

And they would improvize, using their bodies and learning not to be afraid of them.

However much of his day was consumed by his interest in Buddhism and mime – and listening to the endless talk about free sex and anarchy in the arts lab coffee shop – David never entirely abandoned his manager, who continued to work towards moving David into cabaret, the theatre and film. David wasn't really all that interested in that world these days, but he needed money as well as acceptance of any kind, so he figured what the hell: let old Ken Pitt do his thing and he'd go along, taking whatever might come.

It was in October, a month after Pitt obtained an Actors Equity membership for David, that David met Michael Armstrong, a young director who immediately cast David in a short silent film, *The Image*.

Originally, the film was to last thirty minutes and there were only two characters in the film, an Artist played by

Michael Byrne, and the Boy, played with a sort of wooden determination by David. The film opened on a dark, rainy night with Byrne contemplating a portrait on his easel which looked very much like the Boy, who suddenly appears outside the window, his nose pressed against the pane.

The Boy's entrance into the studio follows and there is a fight in which the Boy is killed with a bronze bust. As Byrne goes back to contemplating his painting, the Boy returns to life. Now Byrne stabs him repeatedly with a knife, wrestling him down a flight of stairs and finishing him off with the knife. Byrne is so filled with remorse he rips his portrait to shreds and falls weeping on it. At which point he and the film come – thankfully – to rest.

There were a number of other film auditions as well, including ones for the anti-war vehicle *Oh, What a Lovely War* (David was turned away), another for a feature film about the military, *Virgin Soldiers* (this time, David was given a non-speaking role), and for a period musical on the BBC, where David was cast to dance a minuet while wearing a powdered wig. Both roles took only a few days and so with little else to do, David continued working with Lindsay Kemp, becoming a favourite and finding himself in the third role in an original production called *Pierrot in Turquoise*. His first appearances came only a month after he began taking classes, at the Oxford Theatre, on 29 December, and then in Cumberland in the first week of January 1968.

The reviews were good and because David's role was more musical than mime, that dictated the direction of the criticism.

Said the critic for the *Oxford Mail*: 'David Bowie has composed some haunting songs, which he sings in a superb, dreamlike voice.' David's contribution was called 'inventive' by *The Stage* and even when the reviewer for the *Financial Times* said David's songs 'tend to follow ambition beyond the boundaries of his talent,' he added that 'I am on his side, though, because (among other reasons) he sings without a microphone.'

However much David enjoyed the bohemian artist's concept that artistic success demands commercial rejection, the poverty began to tell on him. He was growing tired of scrapping for a living. When he travelled with the Lindsay

Kemp troupe, often it was with six others and all the props and costumes and personal effects squeezed into a single Volkswagen van. Ken Pitt discovered the same month that Decca was withholding royalties from the sale of David's singles to cover a meagre £100 advance he had been given for the album. Pitt felt that this was a violation of the recording contract and whether or not he was right is irrelevant. Five years and four record companies into his career, David was still at square one, and his manager was waging battle with his record company over a paltry £100!

In mid-March David went back into the studio to cut another two songs. These were sent to Decca for consideration and Decca rejected them. This was followed by another blow to his artistic pride. Selfridges was promoting a special 'Decca Week' and Pitt went to see what part David played in it, taking David with him.

They entered the record section, where a large booth had been constructed to display Decca product. Two sales persons in special uniforms were in attendance. Not seeing David's name or photograph, or being able to find any copies of his album, Pitt went up to one of them. David stood nearby, listening.

'Pardon me,' Pitt said, 'I'm seeking a gramophone record by an artist named David Bowie. Can you assist me?'

The young woman searched through the piles of albums nearby, then looked at some of the promotional leaflets provided by the company.

Finally, she said, 'I'm sorry, he's not with Decca.

Hugh Mendl said he was embarrassed when Pitt called half an hour later, adding, 'I cannot blame you if you wish to leave.'

David obtained his official release from the label on 22 April and the next day Pitt was in the office of the Beatles' Apple Music Limited, and there followed, according to Pitt, a three-month experience of 'deplorable disorganization, sheer amateurism and downright rudeness.'

During the spring and summer months, David continued to drift, finally putting together a trio called Feathers. His two partners in this venture were Hermione Farthingale, a freckled, red-haired nineteen-year-old daughter of a suburban lawyer he'd met while dancing the minuet for the

BBC and who, by now, was his first steady girlfriend; and 'Hutch' Hutchinson, the bassist from David's old band, the Buzz. They read poems, played tapes, performed pantomime skits about the Chinese massacre of Tibetan Buddhist monks in Tibet, and in the first six months earned less than £60.

At the same time David's manager was pleading with him to prepare an act for the cabaret circuit. This was a development of the English music hall, small theatres where middle-of-the-road performers sang and told jokes to conservative, middle-of-the-road audiences, the sort that loved David's hero, Anthony Newley, and Tom Jones and Tommy Steele.

Pitt repeatedly told David: 'You tell me you're tired of being skint. In cabaret you can earn £100 a week!'

For several weeks, David toyed with the idea, then accepted it, and finally plunged into the project with what Pitt describes as 'great energy and the usual Bowie determination and confidence'.

Songs were taken out of the act and put back, or replaced. The between-songs patter was created. New songs were written and then discarded. Nearly forgotten songs were given new life. David rehearsed almost daily, at first in his manager's flat and then in his office, where, in August, he auditioned for several booking agents.

One agent asked him to audition on a nightclub stage and afterwards gave the act the traditional kiss of death.

'Ken, the boy's tremendous,' he said. 'It's a marvellous act, but where can I book it? It's too good!'

The frustrations of doing cabaret began to tell on David and his manager and they began to separate under the strain. Pitt continued to work for David, sent him on auditions for a number of films, including John Schlesinger's *Sunday, Bloody Sunday*, and booked him on to some German television shows, but David seemed increasingly disinterested. Pitt had no interest in Dylan, mime, the growing arts lab movement, Buddhism, or any of the other odd things to which David wanted to give his time.

David still had a key to his manager's flat, but he seldom used it and in the late summer of 1967, he had rented a small room in a two-storey terraced house at 22 Clareville

Grove in South Kensington, where he and Hermione lived together for about six months. It was a happy time for David. He loved Hermione as he'd loved no one before her. For a long time, Ken Pitt didn't even know they were living together. And he was irked when David failed to check in regularly.

As was his custom, David went home to Bromley for Christmas to be with his parents. It was not a joyful holiday. Tragedy had come to the Jones family in 1968 and no matter how apart David felt from his family and home, it was an event he could not dismiss.

It was, in fact, something that would grow to monstrous proportions for David, haunting him for much of his young adult life.

THE 'AQUARIAN'

David's brother Terry had been found.

That was the good news. The bad news was that he was found in a psychiatric hospital in Cane Hill about ten miles from Bromley, where he had been diagnosed an 'incurable schizophrenic'.

Cane Hill Hospital was an old Victorian building surrounded by some of England's greenest countryside, but it was not a pleasant place to visit. Most of the 800 to 900 patients slept in wards and were totally alone – either without families and friends or abandoned by them. Visitors could not escape the cries of the seriously disturbed, or avoid their desperate, frightened eyes.

Sometimes when David and his parents went to visit Terry, he seemed 'normal'. He chatted freely, acknowledged their visits graciously. Other times he wouldn't speak, seemed not to know them, and in the end, David said, 'I've never been able to get through to him about how he really feels. I guess nobody has.'

Initially, David and his parents visited every two weeks, taking a hamper of sandwiches and apples, new shirts and clean clothing that they had taken home dirty and laundered after their previous visit. Terry was happy to see them, David said, but even though Terry had talked at first, he soon became mute again, lying on the hospital lawn all day, looking at the sky. David told interviewers for years afterwards that he wondered if he would ever find himself on his own back looking at the same grey English sky.

It was ironic that just as David reached this emotional low, he was to write a song that would take him to the first pinnacle of success. The song was 'Space Oddity'. Before he wrote the song though, David made his first television commercial for a new ice cream product:

'Luv, Luv, Luv,' David sang. 'Let me give it all to you. Let me know that some day you'll do the same for me. Luv, Luv, Luv!'

David spoke the next line: 'Now from Lyons Maid. Everybody needs it.'

David sang again: 'Luv, Luv, Luv!'

And finally, a closing spoken line: 'The pop ice cream. Nine pence.'

Ken Pitt had decided in January 1969, to put up nearly £3000 of his own money to make a half-hour film of David singing the songs from his last Deram album. Pitt figured that the film would then be made available to television stations all over Europe, which would recover part of the cost, the rest being regained as the Deram album began to sell on the basis of the broad and unique exposure.

David and Ken Pitt met, agreeing that there was a need for a final song – something 'special, something with enormous power for the times'.

During the final days before filming was to begin, David and Hermoine saw one of the most popular films of 1968, the science fiction fantasy of Arthur C. Clarke, *2001: A Space Odyssey*.

This was a crucial film of the time. Of course, some critics dismissed it as the opposite of what 'good' science fiction should be. To others, especially to the young, it represented the ultimate audio-visual 'trip', the perfect cinematic experience for a psychedelic, computerized society on the threshold of space exploration.

David was inspired and went home to write a song about an astronaut who left his 'tin can' a hundred thousand miles above the earth, refusing to come back.

David was carrying his guitar by its neck when he entered his manager's office.

'I have a song,' he said.

'What's it called?'

'"Space Oddity",' David grinned.

He sank cross-legged on to the carpet and began to strum. 'Ground control to Major Tom . . .'

The filming went well. Everyone was pleased. David had even memorized – phonetically – German translations to the songs, so that a second version of the film could be broadcast by his friends in Hamburg and Munich. The photography was excellent and Ken Pitt was excited about having a professional showcase to use in finding his 'talent' work.

None the less, when the filming was finished, in February 1969, so were David and Hermione.

They had fought frequently during the filming. Hermoine never liked the economic insecurity that was so much a part of David's life, and she didn't like not knowing where he was on the frequent nights he failed to come home to their little room in South Kensington. Ken Pitt says Hermione helped David with the film as a 'parting gesture' to David and because she was 'a professional'.

In February, David performed an acoustical act in support of Marc Bolan and Tyrannosaurus Rex, playing in Birmingham, Croydon, Manchester, Bristol, Liverpool and Brighton. He auditioned – and was turned down – for a role in *Hair*. And he wrote two of the most personal and candid songs of his career, both of them to Hermione.

The songs, 'An Occasional Dream' and 'Letter to Hermoine', were sad laments revealing much pain. David rarely talked about the breakup at the time and in the years following, he *never* spoke of it, but in 'Letter' he told the cause: there was another man, who made Hermoine laugh.

'Did you ever call my name –' David cried, 'just by mistake?'

'I care for no one else but you,' he sang. 'I tear my soul to cease the pain . . .'

Not wishing to return to his manager's flat and not having anywhere else to go, he returned home to Bromley.

Very little was happening in David's life. Ken Pitt's pet project, the film he was calling *Love Me Till Tuesday*, was in the final post-production stages, but because Hermoine had been in some of the scenes, David was losing interest in it. There were no jobs – none at all. And still no interest from a record company. Even the auditions were drying up. David was left to play his acoustic guitar and pass a hat in Soho folk clubs.

One day in March, David visited some old friends, Barrie and Christine Jackson in Beckenham, only a mile or so from

Bromley. Sitting on the window ledge of their upstairs flat, he began to play and sing.

A voice cried out from below: 'Hi, you up there! Anybody fancy a cuppa?'

This was Mary Finnigan, a friendly, twenty-eight-year-old former Fleet Street journalist and single mother of two who would become the next major influence on David's life.

David and the Jacksons came down for coffee and two days later David returned to Mary's flat, to play and sing at a small party she was hosting. She admits today that she was absolutely entranced by him.

'He had a runny nose and watery eyes and lots and lots of jokes,' she says, 'and all this glorious music kept pouring and pouring and pouring out, song after song after song.'

David told her he was penniless, had just broken up with his girlfriend and was living at home and hating it. He said he wanted to get rid of his manager because he didn't understand him and wanted him to become some sort of cabaret star like Tommy Steele. Mary felt sorry for David and offered him her spare bedroom. He moved in the next day, bringing with him several car-loads of guitars and recording equipment.

Within a few days, David and Mary were talking about starting a folk club, to give David a place to work. The following day, they walked into the Three Tuns pub in Beckenham High Street where, in exchange for the added business the owner thought the musicians and singers would bring him, they were given the use of a back room on Sunday nights rent-free to stage their little shows.

Fifty people attended the first Sunday to hear David and some other folksingers and to watch a light show projected on a sheet hung on a wall behind the stage. The second Sunday there were a hundred paid admissions and on the third or fourth week, David asked if those in attendance wanted to turn the place into an 'arts lab'. The audience roared loudly, 'Yes!' A tie-dye class was organized. A small newspaper was started. Musicians began to jam together.

David was smoking hashish heavily, and drinking beer and barley wine. Although his flatmate Mary Finnigan was taking LSD regularly David steadfastly refused to join her on her 'trips'. He was frightened of the effects of the mind-altering drug. He told her, and others, that his strange, mismatched eyes showed he was a potential schizophrenic. He was known to say, 'I'm mad! Stark raving banaaaaaaaaaaaanas!'

'However,' Mary Finnigan says, 'he was never out of control. I don't think I ever saw him lose control. I don't think there are many people around who are honest with themselves who would not admit there's a lot of confusion going on inside, and I think he was being quite Buddhist about the way he approached this. He wasn't trying to pretend to the outside world that he was sane and ordinary, because if you meditate for any period of time, you stir up the shit, you get down to the psychic sludge and that illusion of 'normality' is quickly dispelled. And he'd been through that process of self-examination. I don't think he was kidding himself at all. And I think that Terry was probably the yardstick he used to judge himself by.'

*

David had not been ignoring his recording career entirely. For a couple of months he had been frequenting the offices of Mercury Records, where he had an affair going with a tall, thin, aristocratic Chinese-American, Calvin Mark Lee. He arranged a meeting between Ken Pitt and some of the people at Mercury and that resulted in a modest but encouraging recording contract, which was accepted. 'Doctor' Lee, who had a PhD in chemistry and wore his hair to his waist, also introduced David to a girl he was dating at the time . . . and David quickly went for her. 'When I met Angie,' David said later, 'we were both fucking the same bloke.'

Angie was Angela Barnett, a slender, vivacious American whose father was a mining engineer living in Greece, and who had grown up in Europe, becoming multi-lingual and poly-cultural. She was an outrageous creature given to dramatic explosions and coarse language. She also had a very large heart, she seemed to love everyone and everything, and she was also bisexual.

She met David at a press party for a band called King Crimson. 'Do you jive?' David asked her.

'Jive?' she said. 'Certainly . . .'

Angie had no idea what David was talking about, but followed the young, intense singer on to the dance floor.

David took her out the following evening and spent the night with her. When he rose to leave the next morning, Angie protested. She wanted him to stay. He said he had to leave and descended the stairs to the street. Angie, still in her nightclothing, threw herself down the stairs to stop him.

David didn't stop. But he called again the following day and a few days later moved Angie into his room at Mary Finnigan's flat.

David and Angie were totally honest with each other. She told him that she had been kicked out of a boarding school for having a lesbian affair with another student . . . and it quickly became very clear to her that (in her words) 'he was fucking everything in sight'. Within a week, Angie was sleeping with Mary, who had been sleeping with David since he moved in.

Somehow it seemed to work. Mary and Angela enjoyed each other, liked babbling on in French to confuse the others in the room . . . and Angie was happy to help with the housework and spend time with Mary's two children when Mary was away. The party continued.

It was decided that the first single release on his new record label would include the song he recorded last for his film for Ken Pitt. Mercury thought 'Space Oddity' should be re-recorded, so David went into a studio on 20 June 1969, and twenty minutes later left. The record was released in England, and in America the following month.

During the summer of 1969 the scene in America was having its dawn, with the Woodstock Festival, and almost simultaneously its dusk. Jimi Hendrix and the Jefferson Airplane's bassist, Jack Casady, had been arrested for drugs in May, and John Lennon had been declared an 'inadmissible immigrant to the US' for a drug conviction the year before.

Outdoor rock festivals were attracting crowds of 100,000 and more while the bands were paid as much as $100,000 for each performance, the 'vibes' were anything but good, as small, violent groups of malcontents crazed on 'reds' (downers) rushed the festival gates, causing injury, arrests and headlines.

In Berkeley, California, National Guardsmen shot and killed a young man protesting at the city's refusal to let 'the people' use a vacant lot as a park.

In England, Mick Jagger and Marianne Faithfull were arrested for marijuana possession, and what one journalist called 'the latest mutation in far-out youth, the Skinheads, [came] down from the trees and [began] to give English police some cause for concern.' The Skinheads wore their hair cropped short and wore steel-toed army boots for fights.

And then the Rolling Stones' guitarist Brian Jones was dead. In July, the Stones gave a free concert for 250,000 fans in London's Hyde Park, a tribute to Brian.

In the meantime, David and Mary Finnigan were focusing most of their attention on planning a 'free festival' which was to be sponsored by their arts lab and held in a Beckenham park.

And then came a dramatic event. On 20 July, Mary and her children and half a dozen others gathered round the television to watch Neil Armstrong take man's first steps on the moon. As the ship landed, the BBC played David's song. Angela became hysterical – a common state, according to those around her – laughing and crying and screaming and rolling around on the carpet. The others reacted in a similar manner. In a way, it didn't make any sense. 'Space Oddity' was about a loser who drifted off into space rather than complete his mission. It was as if the BBC hadn't listened to the words. On the other hand, the song's prominent use on the BBC convinced everyone in the room that David had a hit.

The only one missing was David, and no one in the room knew where he was.

He was at Ken Pitt's and two days later he left town with Ken to compete in song contests in Malta and Italy. His hair was quite long by now and he had to pull it back into a tight pony-tail to appear more middle-of-the-road than he was. He also wore a suit and sang 'When I Live My Dream', one of the Anthony Newley type ballads from his album of the year before.

It seemed an odd move for David, but it was a commitment he had made, so he kept it. He also used the contest in Italy as an excuse for a vacation and when it was over, Angela joined him. Together they returned to London on 3 August, just in time to go on stage at the Three Tuns pub.

At the end of the evening, Mary casually mentioned a telephone call she had had earlier from David's father.

'He said he was sick,' she said.

'Why didn't you tell me before?' David cried.

'I dunno. He sounded all right to me.'

David was furious. He rushed to the telephone and called home, then tore away from the pub without a word.

John Jones was gravely ill. Smaller and even thinner than David, his constitution had never been good and the stomach operations from years before had taken their toll. Lingering lung problems from a bout with pneumonia the previous winter only made things worse.

David entered his father's bedroom in Plaistow Grove. He was shocked by what he saw. His father seemed so lifeless, so pale. David held a small trophy, awarded him in Italy for his contribution to the festival.

'Look, pa,' David said, 'look what they gave me.'

His father looked up and smiled, but said nothing.

He died the next day.

David was devastated by his father's death and furious with his mother, accusing her of failing to care for his father properly. Why, he shouted, didn't she take him to the hospital? He stormed out of the house and returned to Mary Finnigan's, where he stayed mostly by himself and could be heard crying in an adjacent room.

After David had calmed down he moved back into the Bromley house to assist his mother with the funeral arrangements. His father was buried on the 11th, and David then returned once again to Mary Finnigan's to join in the final preparations for the arts lab festival, scheduled for that Saturday, 16 August.

The mood of the day was typical of the event and time; the three-day Woodstock Music and Art Fair had opened in New York the previous day. In a city park in Beckenham, too, the vibes were exceptional; even the mayor and the police chief attended the event.

Angela had stayed up the entire night before, preparing

hamburgers for a stall she ran out of a wheelbarrow. Others organized stalls for the sale of exotic tea, ceramics, jewellry, homemade clothing, Tibetan curios and books. There were puppet shows and on a small gazebo, more than thirty musicians and singers performed, including the Strawbs, Keith Christmas, John Peel and Junior's Eyes.

Only David had a miserable time. When he performed, he performed cheerfully, but the rest of the day he was in a deep, angry funk. He still hadn't forgiven his mother and he was upset that Mary hadn't called him when she first heard his father was sick. Most of all, he was upset that his father had died before David had become the success he predicted; John Jones had had such incredible faith in David, that David felt as if he'd somehow let his father down by not achieving that success sooner. David took his feelings out on everyone all day and that night in Mary's flat, as Angela and the others counted the money they'd received – realizing a profit of £150 – David stalked into the room and said, 'Ah, you bunch of mercenary shits!' And stalked out again.

*

Ken Pitt did everything within his power to make 'Space Oddity' a hit. When someone appeared in his office and asked for £100 in exchange for getting the song on to the British charts, Pitt gave the stranger the money he asked. Even when he returned a few days later and requested an additional £40 – to boost sales in the Midlands – Pitt agreed. He says now that he felt it was worth the risk.

It's unlikely that the money had anything to do with the success that followed. After two months of sporadic radio exposure and only a handful of personal appearances – all of them outside London – 'Space Oddity' finally appeared on the *New Musical Express* bestseller chart on 6 September, at No. 48.

Pitt immediately called the producer of *Top of the Pops* (the leading TV pop programme since the demise of *Ready, Steady, Go!*). The producer said he wanted to see what the record did the following week.

The following week there was no sign of 'Space Oddity' on the chart.

But the next week, on 20 September, it reappeared at No. 39 and in subsequent weeks, it went up again. All the way to No. 5.

Now, *everybody* wanted David.

An advertisement appeared in all the music trade papers, showing David endorsing the Stylophone, a pocket-sized keyboard instrument he used to create some of the 'other-worldly' effects on 'Space Oddity'. *Top of the Pops* booked him, as did club owners throughout London. And disc jockey Anne Nightingale, one of the leading voices of London's pop scene, wrote a story for one of the big circulation national dailies that started, 'Hooray, leap about, applaud, cheer, wave flags – we have something to celebrate. The finest single disc made this year, "Space Oddity", has finally lifted off the charts.'

It was a strange album, showcasing several of David's musical influences and styles and although the songs were well-written and produced, they seemed a carelessly thrown-together hotchpotch.

Besides 'Space Oddity', David included his two songs to Hermoine – Angela was less than thrilled – along with a romantic tribute to the arts lab, 'Memory to a Free Festival', which astonished Mary Finnigan, because what she remembered of the festival was David's rotten mood. In still another direction, David sang 'Unwashed and Somewhat Slightly Dazed', a Dylanesque song of black lyricism ('phallus in pigtails ... blood on my nose/my tissue is rotting where the rats chew my bones') performed to a Bo Diddley rock and roll beat.

The most interesting, and important, song on the album was generally overlooked. If 'Space Oddity' was the show-piece that revealed where David had been – in terms of story-telling in the acoustical, folkie style of music he once preferred – 'Cygnet Committee' showed the way to David's grander theatrical future.

This dramatic scenario was nearly ten minutes long, and in it David again revealed his ability and willingness to offer incisive comment about his closest peers and to tell a story while doing so. In a way, it was similar to songs such as 'London Boys' and other early material commenting on the Mod Scene. Now it was the British arts lab/hippy scene that came under the Bowie knife, and this time in greater detail.

However much reward he got from the Sunday scene in the Three Tuns, David was growing tired of it. Mary Finnigan says, 'The pseudo hippies and hangers-on who came to hear David sing and made no contribution eventually turned David off, and he stopped coming.'

David wasn't alone. By now, the bloom was definitely off the hippy rose. In America, many of the good 'vibes' so praised at the Woodstock Music and Arts Festival in August were gone only two months later when the Hell's Angels beat a spectator to death at a free festival given by the Rolling Stones at Altamont, California. By late 1969, much of the so-called 'underground' around the world seemed to have been taken over by opportunists and 'phonies' and David was disillusioned.

David was establishing himself as a commentator, a songwriter who had something to say, reflecting a clear and incisive point of view. In the years to come, this stance would reap great reward, once David learned how to marshal his thoughts and then choreograph them.

As the album went out to lacklustre public response – never going on the bestseller charts and attracting little critical attention – David and Angie were skint and shifted back and forth between Mary's flat in Beckenham and his mother's terrace house in Bromley. By mid-September, it was getting tense at both places. David never enjoyed his mother's company very much and when she, in turn, made it clear that she couldn't stand Angela, the loud arguments began. Then when Mrs Jones walked into David's room and found them making love in the middle of the afternoon, she told them to get out.

Things were no better at Mary's house.

From the day that he moved in, David partied, noisily and late into the night. There was a convent directly across the street and Mary's children attended the school there. It became clear to Mary that her flatmates were not appreciated. Mary once walked down the road to see how far away from the house she had to get before she couldn't hear the noise. She walked half a mile.

'The sexual shenanigans weren't having a terrific effect

on my kids, either,' Mary says today. 'The nuns totally hated me. Irresponsible as I was in those days, I did have some sense. I was profoundly relieved when they left.'

Their next home was not far away. Also in Beckenham, at 24 Southend Road, it was the ground floor flat in Haddon Hall, a decaying mansion left over from the Victorian era of grotesque architectural excess.

*

The jobs were coming more frequently now. In late October, David performed a solo acoustic act in support of Humble Pie, a new band that included his art teacher's son from Bromley Tech, Peter Frampton. He then opened for Herman's Hermits and the Troggs. This was followed in early November by a nine-day tour of Scotland, part of the off-and-on album promotion.

It was disastrous. David later said he was naive. He thought he'd just go out and sing his songs, like a medieval troubadour, and that would be that. He hadn't counted on there being another pop subculture in his audience. These were the Skinheads, young working-class toughs who shaved their heads and regarded fighting as a recreational sport. David was greeted with taunts, and had burning cigarettes flicked at him.

Still another subculture was called in at Ken Pitt's invitation. Ken had a theory on which he hoped to base a new campaign for David. Having worked with Judy Garland, Ken had seen crowds of gay men in her audience and at the stage door. They often sent flowers to her dressing room. He had watched the same men carry Marlene Dietrich aloft to her car, running alongside until its gathering speed took her away. Ken Pitt thought the time was right for a male personality who attracted the same gay audience. He began to call editors of gay magazines, setting up interviews.

Whatever the sexual preference of David's audience, it was clear that it was growing rapidly now, thanks to 'Space Oddity', of course, but also due to two major London performances. The first, at the Purcell Rooms on the South Bank on 20 November, attracted the attention and ebullient praise of Tony Palmer, one of the brightest and most respected critics. In his review in the *Observer*, he described

David as 'devastatingly beautiful ... every schoolgirl's wonder movie star,' and said David could 'dazzle you with niceness. Then, suddenly, he tears into you with a violent, passionate, angry, stamping song about fear and despair.' David's observations on the absurdities of technological society were 'razor-sharp' Palmer said, and his off-beat approach to the space race' on 'Space Oddity' made the song 'spectacularly good'.

The album reviews, over all, were not favourable, but it didn't seem to matter. David was given the Ivor Novello award by the Songwriters' Guild of Great Britain for the most original song of the year ('Space Oddity') and with Tony Palmer's stamp of approval, and a performance on 30 November at the London Palladium in the presence of Princess Margaret – to whom he was presented – his audience expanded to include many older fans.

In other ways, too, it seemed that success was imminent; 'Space Oddity' was named Best Commercial Single in *Disc* magazine and David was named the Best Newcomer in *Music Now!* When Ken Pitt added up his income for 1969, he discovered that David had made almost £4000, twice his income for the year before and a figure well above the national average.

None the less, David was in a state of drift again, uncertain of what he wanted. After the first flush of activity following the album's release, the jobs fell off and after six years in the business, he still had no booking agent.

Fortunately, he had Angela, who took some of the 'Space Oddity' royalties and, adding some of her own money, began to decorate their Haddon Hall flat as if it were the home of an established star. Angela believed that if you were going to be a star you had to live like one. So in the bathroom she put art nouveau fabric on the walls (spraying it with Scotch Guard to waterproof it) and in the bedroom, a huge bed with a carved Chinese headboard.

A problem arose with Angela in December, when her visitor's visa expired. She and David talked about her going to work for Ken Pitt so that she could acquire a work permit, but they decided it was a bad idea. So Angela left England for the required month before another visa could be issued, flying to Cyprus to be with her parents.

The week after Christmas, David proposed marriage on a card: 'Please come back. We will marry. I promise, this year.'

David followed the card with a telephone call and played a tape of a song he had written for her. She flew back to London the following morning.

By now, David had surrounded himself with a sort of musical commune, many of whose members were sharing the Haddon Hall flat. First of all there was an American Hustler named Tony Visconti, an accomplished bassist who had been working with David off and on for about a year and who moved into the second bedroom in the flat with his girlfriend Liz.

Tony introduced Mick Ronson, a guitarist in the Jeff Beck tradition who came from Hull. 'Ronno' was loud, bright and energetic, in his playing and as a person, and he had an understanding of musical theory and a flair for arranging. He spent his nights in a sleeping-bag on the loft that ran along one side of the vaulted living room.

Together David, Tony and Mick recorded another two songs for Philips, using John Cambridge on drums and Marc Bolan on second guitar. Marc and David were very close and David, ever the musical chameleon, for a while adopted some of Bolan's warbling vocal style. This was clear on the two new songs – 'Prettiest Star', the song David wrote for Angela and had played to her on the telephone while proposing, and 'Conversation Piece', an absurd dialogue that was more or less a throwaway.

In February 1970, David announced the existence of another new band – Ronno on guitar, Cambridge on drums, and Tony Visconti on bass. He called it Hype.

Hype also may be what he had in mind when, after a few break-in shows outside London, he put the band into super-hero costumes for a performance as warm-up band for Country Joe and the Fish, a California band appearing late the same month in London's prestigious Round House. David, as 'Rainbowman', wore a silver lamé jump suit with a blue and silver cloak. Even his hair was dyed silver and blue. While Tony was dressed up as 'Hypeman', John as 'Cowboyman' and Ronno as 'Gangsterman'.

The audience in the big, former railroad roundhouse

seemed utterly confused. 'We died a death,' David said of that performance. 'And of course the boys said, "Look, we told you so. Let's get back to being a band again."'

'I just about stopped after that performance,' David recounted later, 'because I knew it was right. I knew it was what I wanted to do and I knew it was what people would want, eventually.'

On 6 March, Philips released 'The Prettiest Star' and the week after that, Decca put its revamped version of David's first album on the market as a part of their low-budget 'World of . . .' series, calling it *The World of David Bowie*. The week after that, David and Angela were married almost secretly, and almost weren't married at all.

On Thursday 19 March, they went to the Kensington antique market, where Angela bought a pink and purple bridal gown and where David found tight black satin trousers and a cream-coloured satin shirt with flared sleeves for the wedding, which was planned for the following day at the Beckenham registry office. They then drove to visit a girlfriend who asked them to stay for dinner. They stayed the night. Angela says it was the first time she had slept with a man and a woman at the same time, and although she regarded it as 'rebellious' and 'outrageous', she admitted quite freely that she enjoyed it – and apparently so did everyone else, so much so, in fact, that they slept until 10.50 the next morning, only ten minutes before they were due at the registry office.

'Sorry, everyone,' David said as he got out of the car half an hour late, 'the traffic was dreadful out of London. We got caught in a jam.'

There were only a handful of people present, including David's mother, who says she learned of her son's wedding plans on her own. The others were their friend from the night before, who had agreed to be their witness; Tony Visconti's girlfriend Liz; drummer John Cambridge; and Roger Fry, who served as David's roadie when he went on tour and who had moved into Haddon Hall with all the rest. Visconti was at a recording session and Ken Pitt remained at home, refusing to go because David hadn't invited him (although he had heard of David's plans from Mrs Jones).

Back at Haddon Hall, David toasted his new bride and his guests, but disappeared into the bedroom in mid-afternoon, telling Angela, 'I don't think I've ever made love so much since meeting you.'

By now, David's new single, 'The Prettiest Star', was clearly a commercial flop, selling fewer than 800 copies throughout England. At the same time, sales of his first album in America, released by Mercury as *Man of Words/ Man of Music*, crept past the 5,000 mark in sales, a figure that was regarded at the time as only barely encouraging. None the less, a new album was commissioned. Tony Visconti and the others were anxious to get going, but there was a new problem.

'This man would just not get out of bed and write a song,' Tony said. 'We'd go into the basement and make a lot of noise and David would just sort of drift down and say, "Hey, what's going on?" We'd get him away from Angie for about fifteen minutes.

'Later, we just laid down the chords, the arrangement, the guitar solos, the synthesizers, and David would be out in the lobby of Advision (the recording studio) holding hands with Angie and going coochie-coochie-coo. It was as sickening as that.

'Then . . . we had about three days left and I said, "David, you're going to have to throw some lyrics on these songs, and vocals – how about that?"

'And he went in, and I was totally infuriated with him that I had to work so close to the deadline and of course we had hardly any time left to mix that album. David wasn't around for most of the mixes, either. He came up with a lot of clever bits, like the little talking section in the middle of "All the Madmen", but, really, the album was me and Mick Ronson. David just wasn't there.'

However Visconti felt about David's contribution during the recording process, it was clear when the album was completed that his presence was very evident – so evident, in fact, it seemed ominous. Never before had David written such dark material. David was not alone. It was a dark time. The previous year had given the world Woodstock, and the hope that that gathering implied, but it had ended with Altamont and bloody riots during the Democratic presidential nominating convention in Chicago. Jim Morrison had taken his Nietzschean outlook to London in 1968 and David was in the audience, just as he had been in Dylan's audience a few years before; both were significant influences on David.

The opening song on the album, 'Width of a Circle', was another of his long, Dylanesque compositions, more than eight minutes of unrelieved surrender and spiritual rape, played against a rough and raunchy R&B backdrop.

'After All', which seemed at first hearing to take a children's party as its theme, really conveyed a message of extreme despair: 'Man is an obstacle sad as the clown (oh by jingo)/So believe in nothing and he won't let you down (oh by jingo).'

A somewhat similar message was in 'All the Madmen', which David said was inspired by his brother Terry, who was still in Cane Hill Hospital. In the song, David asked his listeners to challenge everything they believed, suggesting that the only sane people left were already in the asylums.

In 'Running Gun Blues', David told the story of a fragmented Vietnam veteran who became a sniper, picking off innocent civilians from a tower somewhere.

In 'Saviour Machine', a computer begged the humans who used it to rebel against the 'system', else the computer would kill them in a show of its utter contempt.

Years later, David was asked why the album was so dark. He said it was because of the amount of hashish he was consuming at the time – in pipes, or cooked by Angie in his meals, or crumbled into the hand-rolled cigarettes that he smoked, often lighting one from the other.

Angie talks of the poverty they experienced during this period – the constant, desperate need for cash. In the late winter and early spring of 1970, David was supporting a small commune of people and he was always broke.

Just as the pocketbook was empty, so too were some of the old relationships. With the completion of the album, David and Tony Visconti separated for a period of four years, not speaking, because of the difficulties they had experienced working together. At the same time, David finally left Ken Pitt.

David went to see Olav Wyper, the merchandizing manager for Philips Records in London, who told him that the record company had to take a neutral stand. Wyper consequently sent David to a young solicitor's clerk, a pugnacious cigar-smoker from East London named Tony DeFries.

DeFries was only a few years older than David, and considerably less well educated. But he had a scintillating photographic memory; he liked to have visitors to his office pull law books randomly from the bookshelf and read off the title, whereupon DeFries would begin to recite the book's first page, word-for-word. DeFries was a rag and bone man's son from the East End who had worked hard to escape his lower-class background, even learning to speak with a proper Oxford accent.

DeFries examined David's contracts and said he could get him away from Ken Pitt – who still had more than a year to go on his contract – and from Mercury/Philips. He said he would sign David to a big American company like CBS or RCA. David was a big star, Tony said, and he deserved a big record company, though it would be some time before DeFries' words were actually proved true.

David was enthralled. Later, he said, 'I just sat there and openly wept. I was so relieved that somebody was so strong about things. I was always stronger than everybody else around me, more determined and wanting to do more things and everybody else was mousy and didn't want to take any risks. It was like going up a hill, trying to drag kids with you. "Oh, come on, will you!" And nobody would go with you. And there was this pillar of strength. It was like everything was going to be different.'

How different David didn't know. Nor did he have a clue about the problems that would come with the promises when they were delivered. But at the time, in the summer of 1970, Tony DeFries sounded like the answer to his prayers.

THE TRANSVESTITE

It was not an overnight change. David's leaving Ken Pitt and Mercury/Philips dragged on for several months, forcing David to fend for himself and to accept whatever his record company delivered. Fortunately, there were those at Mercury in Chicago who cared.

'Space Oddity' had gone Top 10 in several American cities but only to No. 124 nationally, and the album, *The Man Who Sold the World*, had flopped completely, but one of Mercury's publicists, Ron Oberman, had visited David in London and believed in him. He also believed that David could become a media 'darling' as had some earlier intellectual songwriters, including Van Dyke Parks and Randy Newman. With that in mind, he managed to convince his bosses that they should bring David to the US not for a concert tour, but for a blitz of interviews in four or five cities. Once accepted by the media, Oberman argued, David could make the leap to essential radio airplay and from that to rewarding record sales.

David had a plan as well.

By now, David was 'dressing up' quite frequently – wearing some of Angie's dresses at first, and then having a garment especially designed and made for him, a long-sleeved, full-length dress cut down the front to well below the sternum. Sometimes he wore it when he went shopping and he even wore it in the photograph he had taken for the cover of *The Man Who Sold the World*. Why the open cross-dressing? Years later, David would say it was for the shock value, a common tactic for the late sixties and early seventies.

For the American release of the same album, an innocuous drawing was substituted for the picture of David in a dress, reclining on a chaise longue. David was amused by America's puritanism and so when he packed his bags for his first visit, in January 1971, he did what any self-respecting transvestite would have done: he packed his nice dress along with his jeans.

America would remember David Bowie after this trip, of that David was confident.

*

The tour began badly.

By 1971, airline employees were used to seeing outrageously dressed, long-haired Britons travelling from London to America. But David seemed somewhat odder than most, and he was travelling alone, unusual for a pop musician.

Mostly the problem was his looks. His hair was particularly long, hanging well below his shoulders. His lankiness and high, angular cheekbones accentuated it. With a full-length, purple greatcoat and effeminate hand movements, he appeared more female than male. Some said – and photographs largely confirmed – he was a dead ringer for Lauren Bacall. And yet, his passport said he was named David.

Upon landing David was held aboard the flight for an hour after everyone else had deplaned while he was searched and his bags were pulled aside and examined.

Outside, his American record company publicist, Ron Oberman paced the airport terminal floor.

'What happened?' Ron said when David finally appeared. They had met twice before, when the young publicist had gone to England. He liked David and was embarrassed and concerned. 'What'd they do to you? Are you all right?'

Whatever anger David felt, it passed quickly. For years America and things American had held him entranced, and now, finally, he was actually on American soil. As Ron drove David to his hotel from the airport, and David took in the sights, his annoyance was replaced by excitement. He began to ask questions, questions about America.

In the three weeks that followed, David crossed America in much the same way – he said years later – as Jack Kerouac and his friends must have travelled in *On the Road*. From Washington, he went to New York, from there to Chicago – headquarters of Mercury Records – and thence on to Los Angeles, travelling the 3000 miles entirely by bus.

Rodney Bingenheimer, who worked for Mercury, took him to a party in a big house high above the Sunset Strip (where David sat cross-legged on a bed and sang for most of the evening); introduced him to Gene Vincent and the Andy Warhol movie star Ultra Violet; and walked him past Hollywood High School, where his dress attracted loud whistles and hoots.

For what it was set up to do, the tour was an unqualified success. Radio stations gave him interview air time and played his records. The tour also provided David with his first important American interview, with John Mendelsohn of *Rolling Stone*. John liked David's album, *The Man Who Sold the World*, and when his story was published in April – with a picture of David wearing his floral print dress and holding a wilted flower – it contained a sentence that would be quoted widely for a long time: 'Tell them,' David said, referring to *Rolling Stone's* readers, 'they can make up their minds about me when I begin getting adverse publicity – when I'm found in bed with Raquel Welch's husband.'

Even with this publicity, neither the album nor the single, 'All the Madmen', sold very well. He may have been on his way to becoming a 'media darling' like Randy Newman and Van Dyke Parks. But what Mercury may have overlooked was the fact that *they* didn't sell many records, either.

Back home, Angela was showing her pregnancy – now nearly six months along – and loathing it. Often, she visited friends and cried, sitting in a chair or on a bed, her shoulders heaving as she wailed, 'I've got to have this baby! I've got to do it, get it over with.'

David was unaware of most of this. Angela took most of her complaints, and fears, elsewhere, as David busied himself with resuming his English career. First, Mickie Most called to say that Peter Noone of Herman's Hermits was going to record a song that David had written for his own next album, 'Oh You Pretty Things', an upbeat song about the youth revolution. The song was picked to be the former Hermit's first single as a solo artist and in May, it entered the British pop music charts, where it went to No. 12.

As Noone's version of David's song moved up the charts, *The Man Who Sold the World* was finally released in England, six months after its release in America. David made himself available for interviews and everyone zeroed in on the outrageous album cover.

The press coverage was predictably cute.

'Dressed up for the Bowie Life' was the way the *Daily Mirror* headlined its story. 'When you're a fella and you wear a frock . . .' The accompanying picture showed David in his calf-length purple greatcoat, boots and hair so long he still looked like Lauren Bacall, while the story barely mentioned the album at all.

'I get all sorts of abuse showered on me,' David said. 'It doesn't worry me any more what people say. I get called a queer and all sorts of things. But my sexual life is normal.'

Angela was present during the interview and she agreed. 'That should be obvious to anyone,' she said, patting her stomach. She was at the time two weeks from delivery.

Duncan Zowie Haywood Jones was born in Bromley Hospital on 28 May. David was at home listening to a Neil Young record when he got the news by phone. Later that day, he wrote a song called 'Kooks' to commemorate the event: 'We'll tell you what to say when people pick on you/ Because if you stay with us, you're going to be pretty kooky, too.'

Meanwhile, the meetings between Ken Pitt and Tony DeFries continued and finally, in the late spring of 1971, the contract with Pitt was dissolved and David signed another with DeFries, agreeing to giving him 50 per cent of all his earnings for a period of ten years.

It was a staggering sum and a long time. Most managers took only 15 per cent and usually asked for five to seven years. David also agreed to pay all of his new manager's business expenses.

Tony Visconti was furious. He hated DeFries and told David that he was being ripped off. Standing on the sidewalk outside DeFries' Regent Street offices, Visconti said, 'I just don't think that by changing managers it's going to solve all your problems. This last album was so goddamned difficult, and you have to take responsibility.' David looked at Visconti with tears in his eyes and then walked upstairs to sign the final agreements.

David was desperate. Eight years in the business and what did he have to show for it? He hadn't worked at all in

1971 – not once. And after a dozen singles, four albums and six different record companies, he was still without a record contract. (After the failure of *The Man Who Sold the World*, Mercury in America and Philips in England both turned their backs on David.) What was worse was that David didn't even have a band, as John Cambridge and Mick Ronson soon followed Tony Visconti, to seek whatever work they could.

Under such circumstances, 50 per cent may not have seemed too much to give away. As the saying goes, 50 per cent of nothing is nothing.

Besides, the more David learned about Tony, the more he found he liked him. While he wasn't someone he wanted to spend his spare time with, he was enchanted when he heard that Tony had once tried to organize all the models in London into a union. David also enjoyed the fact that Tony had a photographic memory even more impressive than his own.

Such mental dexterity served DeFries well in his quest for a new recording contract and soon he told David he had both Columbia and RCA interested in America. Columbia was Bob Dylan's label and RCA had Elvis Presley. David was impressed.

However, DeFries said, before he could make any deal, he needed half a dozen new songs to show the companies what they were bidding for. So, with DeFries agreeing to pay the cost of recording, David went back into the Trident Studios, calling Ronno to play guitar, Woody Woodmansey (who had played on *The Man Who Sold the World*) to fill in for John Cambridge on drums, and Rick Wakeman (who had played mellotron on 'Space Oddity') to handle the piano parts. In Tony Visconti's absence, Ken Scott, who had engineered David's last two albums, agreed to take over as producer.

First, David recorded his own version of 'Oh You Pretty Things' and an upbeat rendition of 'Kooks'. The third song was the strongest. This was 'Changes', which he used to open the demo tape and which later would become his first American hit. In it, and in 'Oh, You Pretty Things', David spoke of the unrest he had witnessed in America, particularly over Vietnam, and he championed the cause of youth.

The tracks were good, containing echoes of very successful groups. The stuttering 'Ch-ch-ch-ch-ch–CHANGES!' was reminiscent of the Who's anthem, 'My Generation' and Rick Wakeman's piano in 'Oh You Pretty Things' sounded a little like Paul McCartney's in the Beatles' 'Martha, My Dear'. And yet the mix was original. David's strong lyric gift was amply evident – at one point, in a song called 'Quicksand', he effectively rhymed 'Garbo's eyes' with 'Churchill's lies' – and in almost every verse of every tune there was something of substance to think about.

Eventually, Clive Davis, the president of Columbia, bowed out, telling colleagues that DeFries was asking too much money for someone who wasn't even sure what sex he was. That left RCA.

At the time, RCA was not America's flashiest rock and roll label. It was true that the company roster included Elvis Presley and Jefferson Airplane, but that was about it, until a young A&R man named Katz mounted a campaign to change the company's image. By the time David signed his contract in Katz's office, Katz had signed the Kinks and Lou Reed.

David's agreement was fairly standard for the time. RCA got David Bowie's services as a recording artist for a period of five years, during which time David was to provide sufficient material for two albums a year. In exchange, David received a $100,000 cash advance against future record royalties and the promise of a low-interest loan to be used to underwrite the cost of his first tour of America – which was to coincide with the release of his first RCA album and single.

It wasn't a fabulous deal, but a liveable one, and even if DeFries immediately put half the advance into his own pocket, the remaining $50,000 – minus some expenses claimed by DeFries – was much more than David had ever received before. At the time, it seemed a small fortune.

Tony DeFries returned to England after verbally making the deal, to visit RCA's offices in London. Heads turned swiftly as Tony made his way past the receptionist. He was wearing a full-length fur coat, he was carrying a handbag, he had a cigar clenched between his teeth, and his hair, moustache and sideburns were long and frizzed.

Ken Glancey, the chairman, swallowed noticeably and began explaining the details of the David Bowie campaign.

'This is what we're going to do for David,' he said. 'We're going to put all our efforts behind him straightaway and we're . . .'

Glancey talked for about ten minutes, finally sitting back to get Tony's reaction. Tony took the cigar from his mouth and spoke the only words he was to utter at the meeting: 'You're not going to do anything. I'm going to send *my* team over here and we'll tell *you* what to do. You don't tell *us*. We tell *you*.'

'And so saying, he got up and left.

The next day a bunch of unusually dressed people arrived. One of them said, 'Hiiiiiiii. Myyyyyyy naaaaaaame is Z.'

'Hullo, Z,' said Barry Bethel, the director of artist development. 'Did you cut yourself or is that lipstick?'

'It's lipstick, silly. And I want to talk to you about David's artwork.'

'Artwork?' Barry said, surprised. 'We don't even have an album yet.'

In a few days, the contract was ready and RCA flew David and Angela to New York for a formal signing ceremony.

All the top executives gathered in their dark suits in the office of the president.

The executives looked at the two strangers in the room. Herb Helman was RCA's director of publicity and he figured it was his job to step forward, introduce himself to David and then introduce everyone else in the room. But both of the strangers looked so much alike, it was eerie. Herb assumed that the one with the shortest hair was David and he marched confidently across the room and stuck out his hand.

'Hello, David. My name is Herb Helman and . . .'

The person holding his hand said, 'I'm Angela.'

David laughed and within a few minutes, much of the initial awkwardness had passed and David had been introduced to a young writer-producer named Richard Robinson, who with his wife Lisa was at the centre of New York's pop elite. With RCA's approval, Richard quickly organized a party, introducing David to a group of individuals who would empower David's artistic direction, confirming some of his own ideas, proving he wasn't alone, and providing a comradeship that artistic risk seldom offered. This was the Andy Warhol crowd, a band of freewheeling social anarchists, artists, film-makers and scene-stealers who in 1971 ruled New York's decadent 'in' crowd.

Andy Warhol had made a name for himself in what was called pop art, with his meticulous paintings of Campbell's soup cans, and from that base, he consructed New York's most avant garde creative 'commune' of the period – spinning off incomprehensible films (where the camera was fixed and very little happened for several hours) and creating an overall aura of sexual kinkiness.

Two months earlier, David had attended a performance in London of a play called *Pork*, one of the travelling productions emanating from the Warhol 'Factory' on New York's Lower East Side. This was a play loosely based on Warhold's life. The posters warned: 'This play has explicit sexual content and "offensive" language. If you are likely to be disturbed, please do not attend. MATURE ADULTS ONLY!'

Afterwards, David went backstage to meet the Warholians – Tony Zanetta, who actually looked like Warhol, but unlike him actually talked; director Tony Ingrassia; Cherry Vanilla; and several others. David was happy to see the group again at the party in New York. This was the first time, however, that he met the shy, albino-esque and quirky Andy Warhol, who demonstrated his awkwardness by taking polaroid pictures of David and refusing to speak. David also met Lou Reed, a veteran of the heroin and homosexual underground then writing and singing songs for Warhol's Velvet Underground, a rock band known largely for its 'hip' sexual ambivalence.

It was a brief visit to America, but a thrilling one. Besides meeting the Warhol crowd, they stayed at the Plaza Hotel and the night after signing his contract, RCA arranged for David and his party – including RCA's president – to see Elvis Presley, who was performing at Madison Square Garden.

David returned to London in a fever, calling Ken Scott (his producer on *The Man Who Sold the World*), Ronno and Woody and Trevor, and plunged into the recording of not one, but *two* albums, almost back-to-back.

When they started, in late September, Ken and the boys in the band only knew about the first album, which came to be called *Hunky Dory*.

Several of the tracks already had been recorded – 'Oh, You Pretty Things', 'Changes' and so on – the songs which had persuaded RCA to offer him a contract. Now it was just a matter of recording a second side. The impact of his recent trip to America was instantly revealed. In a song called 'Andy Warhol', David provided an acoustical guitar arrangement which, he said, was his answer to the Velvet Underground's electric guitar arrangements. 'Song for Bob Dylan' was somewhere between sour tribute and affectionate parody. And 'Queen Bitch' clearly was inspired by Lou Reed and sung, again, in the manner of Bob Dylan.

The rest of the side contained a song by the American pianist Biff Rose – a flower power-ish sort of message called 'Fill Your Heart' – and an obscure song-poem called 'The Bewley Brothers' that David said was written with an American audience in mind, for them 'to read whatever in hell they want to read into it.'

However, it wasn't hard to see David's brother in the song. 'The Bewley Brothers' was a title he would later use for a music publishing company. In it, David referred to the Bewleys as 'the moon boys' and said, 'My brother lay upon the rocks, he could be dead, he could be not, he could be you/He's chameleon, comedian, Corinthian and caricature . . .'

'The Devil may be here,' David sang, somewhat ominously.

Overall, the album was more positive than *The Man Who Sold the World*, despite the long, Dylanesque overtones and the moods of madness and kinkiness in selected songs. And it contained several good rockers, notably 'Oh, You Pretty Things' and 'Changes'. The album was finished in early November and rushed to America for release in mid-December with an album cover photograph that now made David resemble Greta Garbo. As soon as the tapes were shipped, David went to Ken Scott.

'I don't think you're going to like this next album,' he said.

'Why not?'

David looked at his producer, his strange, mismatched eyes intent, one pupil seeming enormous next to the other. David puffed on his unfiltered European cigarette.

'Well,' he said, 'it's very different to anything I've done before. It's going to be much, much heavier, and much stranger. It's called *The Rise and Fall of Ziggy Stardust and the Spiders from Mars.*'

'Ziggy really set the pattern for my future work,' David later said. 'Ziggy was my Martian messiah who twanged a guitar. He was a simplistic character. I saw him as very simple . . . fairly like the character Newton I was to do in the film [*The Man Who Fell to Earth*] later on. Someone who dropped down here, got brought down to our way of thinking and ended up destroying his ownself. Which is a pretty archetype story line.'

And so it was. The loss of innocence was a common dramatic theme, in fiction as well as in life. Youthful self-destruction was another popular theme; the live-fast-die-young-and-make-a-good-looking-corpse mentality was a romantic tradition that spanned centuries . . . and was perfectly suited for rock and roll.

It opened with 'Five Years', an apocalyptic song that took its cue from the Beatles' 'Day In the Life'. In this instance, the news was even grimmer: only five years remained before Armageddon. There was a spare, dramatic piano punctuating David's angry lament, for much of the song's duration, and then came a full studio orchestra, with everyone in the band crying over and over again: 'Five years! Five years! Five years!'

The track ended with a Sgt Pepperish cacophony of sound effects wrapped in echo . . . then, finally, a lonely drumbeat . . . which segued neatly into the second song, introduced by another, softer drumbeat. This was 'Soul Love', a romantic interlude full of innocence and slurpy saxophone parts, which gave the listener a chance to collect himself psychologically following the end-of-the-world beginning.

In the third song, 'Moonage Day Dream', the character of Ziggy Stardust began to emerge. 'I'm an alligator . . .' David sang, 'I'm a space invader/I'll be a rock and roll bitch for you.'

The next two songs that David included in the original

version of the album really didn't fit, perhaps in part because they were written by other composers – Ray Davies' much-recorded 'It Ain't Easy' (a contemporary, white blues about the difficulty of growing up) and Jacques Brel's 'Port of Amsterdam'.

It was on the second side of the album that Ziggy appeared in every song and it was here that David created his first truly cohesive song cycle. Ziggy emerged in full-blown androgynous confusion in the first cut, 'Lady Stardust': 'Lady Stardust wore make-up but he was all right!' The audience may have laughed, he sang, but it was clear that Ziggy would more than muddle through.

The plot thickened a bit in the following songs, 'Star', where David took the long hair and make-up of 'Lady Stardust', a bit further and said, 'I could play the wild mutation as a rock and roll star!' and saw stardom as a means of finding personal salvation: 'I could fall asleep at night as a rock and roll star/I could fall in love all right as a rock and roll star . . .' And then he closed the song, saying 'Watch me now!'

'Hang On To Yourself' opened with a windmilling, buzzsaw Ronson guitar reminiscent of 'Summertime Blues' (a three-time hit, for its composer Eddie Cochran in 1958, for San Francisco's power trio Blue Cheer in 1968 and for the Who in 1970) and a positive lyric that urged the listener/audience: 'Come on, come on, we really got a good thing going/If you think we're gonna make it, you better hang on!'

'Ziggy Stardust', the title song, was next and the second of three hard rockers in a row. In this song David summarized the entire album's plot and captured the essence of the rock and roll experience in a single line: 'He took it all too far, but, boy could he play guitar!' In the studio, he reminded his musicians and Ken Scott of Jimi Hendrix, who had died in London a few months earlier of an overdose.

From that, David and his band crashed into one of his own personal favourites, 'Suffragette City'. (Eventually he recorded it several times, re-releasing it on three other albums.) This was a song that roared and screamed, propelled by Ronno's relentless piano chords and infernal buzzing guitar, with an arrogant lyric that thundered to a closing

71

line appropriated from T. S. Eliot's classic poem, 'The Wasteland', 'Wham, bam, thank you, ma'am!'

What could follow other than a song called 'Rock 'n' Roll Suicide'? This was the album's haunting, almost religious epitaph. 'You're not alone,' he cried to his audience, *give me your hands!*

The preacher-ish laying-on-of-hands at the story's end was not accidental, but planned. In fact, Angela claims she had something to do with it, urging David to write something 'where you can go to the front of the stage and he wrote "give me your hands", because I watched and I know it looked good when he did that whole sort of messiah thing.'

It was more than a concept album. *Ziggy Stardust* was conceived as performance, too. Leafing through a copy of *Vogue* magazine, David spotted a picture of a model wearing a short, spikey red hairdo and said he wanted Ziggy to have a similar haircut. At the same time, he was creating the costumes for Ziggy and his band, sending Angela all over London to find fabric, giving his friend, the outrageously fey Freddie Buretti, design ideas, which he then quickly stitched into jackets and pants.

Rock theatre was well beyond infancy in 1972, but not yet fully developed. For a short while, of course, Andy Warhol's Exploding Plastic Inevitable had led the movement, preaching the gospel of whips and chains. Then in the late 1960s, Jim Morrison had crumpled on stage when 'shot' in a mock military execution, Lou Reed, Marc Bolan, Gary Glitter and others had all added feminine make-up to their acts, and Alice Cooper had appeared in torn women's tights and a garter, carrying a boa constrictor. While Arthur Brown had worn a flaming headdress, Screamin' Lord Sutch had sung from a coffin, Frank Zappa had impaled dolls on bayonets, the Who had detonated smoke bombs and destroyed their amplifiers, and Jimi Hendrix had set fire to a long line of Stratocaster guitars.

Then, in mid-January 1972, something occurred which moved the concept of rock theatre in a direction never imagined before, Ziggy Stardust stepped off the record and on to the concert stage.

ZIGGY STARDUST

Once *Hunky Dory* was in the shops – and while Ziggy was still in the studio – the young, long-haired journalists from London's flashy pop music press began ringing David's management, requesting interviews. This was the custom for almost every established artist with a new record and the writers were by now especially fond of David, because he was articulate and intelligent, characteristics not always attached to pop stardom.

In recent months, interview requests had been turned away. With the new album to sell and an English tour to promote, Tony DeFries reversed his policy and now said yes to everyone.

One after another, the writers took the train to Beckenham to visit David at home, or interviewed him in a London rehearsal hall, where he was preparing his new stage show. Generally, the same ground was covered for each, as David boasted of selling 100,000 copies of *The Man Who Sold the World* in the US (half that figure was closer to the truth), answered questions about *Hunky Dory*, or talked excitedly about his upcoming concert tour, which he said would be 'quite outrageous . . . very theatrical . . . costumed and choreographed . . . quite different to anything anyone else has tried to do before.'

When Mick Watts arrived from *Melody Maker*, the conversation took a different turn. By now, London's pop journalists had stopped asking David about his effeminate ways. In fact, some had ignored the subject even when David talked about his dresses without being asked. 'I covered it up,' says Chris Welch, who then wrote for the *New Musical Express*. 'I said, "Oh, dear, I don't want people to think David is bent." So I skated right over it.' Not Mick Watts. He went into the interview with the question that the respectful British writers had not until then had the nerve to ask. 'Are you gay?' he asked.

'Yes, of course,' David said. 'I'm gay and always have been, even when I was David Jones.'

Mick's editors had expected him to return from the interview with a predictable bit of pop music fluff, to fill out one of the back pages. Once they read what Mick wrote, they filled up the front page instead with a picture of David and a bold headline that shouted, 'OH, YOU PRETTY THING!'

'Even though he wasn't wearing silken gowns right out of Liberty's, and his long blond hair no longer fell wavily past his shoulders,' Mick wrote, 'David Bowie was looking yummy. He'd slipped into an elegant patterned type of combat suit, very tight around the legs, with the shirt unbuttoned to reveal a full expanse of white torso. The trousers were turned up at the calves to allow a better glimpse of a huge pair of red plastic boots with at least three-inch rubber soles . . .'

On and on the writer gushed, finally getting to the statement which would alter David's career irreversibly.

'David's present image is to come on like a swishy queen, a gorgeously effeminate boy,' Mick said. 'He's as camp as a row of tents, with his limp hand and trolling vocabulary.

'"I'm gay," he said, "and always have been, even when I was David Jones."

'But there's a sly jollity about how he says it, a secret smile at the corners of his mouth. He knows that in these times it's permissible to act like a male tart, and that to shock and outrage, which pop has always striven to do throughout its history, is a balls-breaking process.

'And if he's not an outrage, he is, at the least, an amusement. The expression of his sexual ambivalence establishes a fascinating game: is he, or isn't he? In a period of conflicting sexual identity, he shrewdly exploits the confusion surrounding the male and female roles.'

'Why aren't you wearing your girl's dress today?' Mick asked.

'Oh, dear,' David replied with a flick of his wrist, depositing ashes in an ashtray perched precariously on one knee. 'You must understand that it's not a woman's. It's a *man's* dress.'

As is so often the case, accidents have lasting impact. And this was no different.

The telephone at Haddon Hall rang constantly.

His record company was the first to call. 'They panicked,' says someone who was there at the time. 'They said, "Oh, my God, David, what've you done!" They wanted him to retract it. Of course he didn't.'

His friends, meanwhile, thought David had gone 'over the top'. His gay friends were not ready to expose themselves so cavalierly, so boldly, so *recklessly*. And his straight friends wondered what in the hell he was talking about. Many 'gays' had 'come out', acknowledging their homosexuality, at least to fellow homosexuals, as early as the 1950s, when many gay bars and ghettos were formed in major cities such as London and New York. In the 1960s the gay underground began to emerge, organizing into groups, publishing newspapers and offering, tentatively, to join forces with other protest groups. But by the early 1970s, the gay movement still had not acquired any real power although homosexuals continued to have a large impact on the world's art and culture, as they had done for two thousand years. The gaining of power wouldn't come until the late 1970s and early 1980s when, for instance, homosexuals would attain political office in California and begin to emerge as a large, well-defined 'market', and voter bloc.

In 1972, it may have been comforting to be involved with a small community of fellow homosexuals and perhaps promote the cause of gay equality, but the climate was far from conducive to 'coming out'. It just wasn't regarded as socially 'safe' yet. And most certainly not if you were an established entertainment personality. There had been several performers, such as Liberace and Alice Cooper in America and Marc Bolan and Gary Glitter in Britain, who had projected a queen image, but no one who was already established as a heterosexual performer had made a sudden and public switch when David stepped forward and did it. Even the gay community was stunned.

No one of course, was more surprised than David's heterosexual friends. 'He may have fucked the odd boy or two,' says Mary Finnigan, 'but he was basically heterosexual. David liked girls. I mean, I had a fairly intimate relationship with the guy and there's no question about his enthusiasm.'

No one was as shocked as his mother.

'I felt dreadful,' she told Charles Shaar-Murray. 'I mean, what's come over him! So I rang him up and I said, "What's happening, David? Are you changing your sex?" He said, "Don't believe a word of it, mum."'

The press, of course, descended on Beckenham from Fleet Street like a pack of dogs.

Journalists had watched the development of Glam Rock for nearly eighteen months, with Marc Bolan and Gary Glitter mincing around London's stages like a couple of drag queens. But never had anyone said anything about actually *being* gay.

With David sitting cross-legged in interviews, gesticulating grandly with his cigarette, and declaring to one and all that he *was* gay, homosexuality was no longer implied, ignored or dodged. Now it was out in the open. Now, according to the writers on Fleet Street, it was Fag Rock, and David was the King of the Queens.

While Cliff Richard blamed David for the disintegration of morality in all of Western society.

And so, in the blaze of publicity, David began his first tour in two years.

Orchestrating all of this was Tony DeFries.

'He was high-powered,' says Angela. 'Tony was interested in twenty *million* dollars, not twenty thousand. Tony DeFries had a very active mind and a desire to really *do it*! In the end, I found him exhausting. I could keep up with him for a while and then I'd have to stay at home in London for four weeks and recover. And he did this *all* the *time*! He never tired.'

Says RCA's Dennis Katz: 'DeFries was terribly difficult to work with, but great for his artist. He was very attentive to detail. He wanted to be in on the selection of the paper the album cover was printed on! He pushes and pushes and pushes. When I signed David, some of the RCA people in London wanted me fired. Two of them had been at Philips when David was there and they *hated* DeFries.'

In February, 1972, as David began his tour – fourteen shows in twenty-five days, stretching from London to Glasgow and back – notoriety already was his. But not, yet, the fame and fortune. The tour was exciting, mainly because David and the boys hadn't worked lately, and because finally they were getting some live reaction to the new 'Ziggy' material, but the money received was slight. In some venues, tickets cost as little as thirty pence which meant that, once again, David was performing at a significant loss.

By now, the RCA advance was disappearing quickly and payment of royalties due for *Hunky Dory* – which was selling only modestly – was nearly a year away. The single released from the album, 'Changes', was expected to be a big hit, but only went to No. 66 on the American charts and in England sank without a trace.

Worse than the lack of recording success was David's growing paranoia. Returning to London from a brief holiday in Cyprus with Angela the previous winter, David developed a serious fear of flying, when a stormy flight caused him to declare, 'I'll never fly again!'

It was on his British tour that he confided this and other fears to Mick Rock, a photo-journalist who soon became a friend. Mick interviewed David backstage in Birmingham and then during an all-night session at Haddon Hall.

David confided, 'I get worried about dying. At the moment it's this terrible travel thing. I keep thinking we're going to crash. Last month, it was being killed on stage. Not here so much. In America. I know that one day a big artist is going to get killed on stage, and I know that we're going to go very big. And I keep thinking – it's bound to be me. Go out on me first [American] tour, get done in at me first gig, and nobody will ever see me.'

David paused, theatrically.

'And that would make me *wild*!'

David may have tried to turn the confession into a small joke at the end, but the fear was real. He continued to draw and paint throughout his career and several of the sketches made during this period reflected the same theme. One shows a male figure, drawn in blue ink, with large, red bullet wounds in one arm, both thighs and groin. The facial expression shows pain and surprise and the caption reads 'The Entertainer Who Is Shot On Stage.'

Later, David would give such drawings to friends and to some of the people at RCA for souvenirs.

Tony DeFries had a plan and RCA made it theirs.

An American tour originally scheduled for March had been reset to begin in September and it was agreed that unless David somehow broadened his popular base in the US, he could fizzle out, winding up on the side of the road like so many other cult favourites. RCA's Herb Helman suggested flying some of the national press people to London to see David – to more or less preview the Ziggy show. After much discussion, RCA in America agreed to pay the air fare for a dozen writers from New York to London and RCA in London agreed to pay the cost of putting them up at one of London's finest hotels and to cover local transportation, food and drink.

As writers were being selected RCA began preparing the Ziggy album for release. Suddenly, a new song arrived: 'Starman', which virtually predicted the plot of *Close Encounters of the Third Kind* and offered the listener hope of salvation, the promise of contact.

Dennis Katz and the others in the A&R department loved the song and immediately suggested that it be inserted into the Ziggy album, replacing Brel's 'Port of Amsterdam', which didn't really fit. Dennis also insisted that 'Starman' be the first single released from the album, backed with 'Suffragette City'.

The Ziggy album was released on 6 June. David was still touring England – there were seven dates in May, another fourteen in June. In some of the theatres and clubs the crowds were disappointing, about half capacity. But the album sales were encouraging and when David appeared at London's Imperial College, the audience spilled on to the street outside the auditorium at the end of the show, and a group of London gays in drag carried David out of the hall on their shoulders as he sang another chorus of his encore song.

On 8 July David played the Royal Festival Hall in a benefit concert for the Friends of the Earth, proceeds going to the 'Save the Whales' crusade. David had appeared at this prestigious venue before for a similar cause, performing a mime act about Tibetan monks. How times had changed for David Bowie.

Disc jockey Kenny Everett was the evening's host. He

told the audience he had to fight his way through the feather boas to get to David's dressing room. Nothing but gays everywhere he looked.

'He insists upon introducing himself,' he said, 'so here is the second greatest thing . . . next to God . . . David Bowie!'

A single spotlight illuminated a thin figure with orange hair, white make-up, a green-and-salmon, Day-Glo pantsuit, and red, patent leather, lace-up boots with four-inch heels.

'Hullo,' David said. 'I'm Ziggy Stardust and these are the Spiders from Mars.'

The band began to cook, crashing into their three-and-a-half-minute warning, 'Five Years'.

Before the evening was over, David changed into a white satin suit and introduced his friend Lou Reed (who was dressed all in black). They sang several songs together, then Lou left and David sang his own apocalyptic vision, 'Suffragette City'.

The reviewers were effusive. 'T. S. Eliot with a rock and roll beat,' said the critic for the *Times*. 'A remarkable performer,' said the writer for the *Guardian*. *Disc*, one of the newer music weeklies, headlined its review, 'Bowie saves the Whale and Rock.' And *Melody Maker* began its story: 'When a shooting star is heading for the peak, there is usually one concert at which it's possible to declare: "That's it – he's made it."' Said the critic for *Music Week*: 'David Bowie will soon become the greatest entertainer Britain has ever known.'

Six days later, on Friday, 14 July, a diverse group of American writers gathered at John F. Kennedy Airport in New York for the flight to London. There was Lillian Roxon, the plump, gregarious columnist for the *New York Daily News* (also the author of the *Rock Encyclopedia*, the first volume of its type), and next to her Lisa Robinson, doyenne of the New York rock literati, representing *After Dark*. Nearby stood Henry Edwards of the *New York Times* (he later wrote the screenplay for the Beatles' *Yellow Submarine*), Bob Musel of United Press International, Alan Rich from *New York*, Lenny Kaye from *Changes*, Ellen Willis from the *New Yorker*, plus writers from *Creem*, *Playboy* and Andy Warhol's *Interview*.

The group had a day to recover from jet lag, to shop and see the sights, then they were taken by bus to the Friars Club in Aylesbury, stopping on the way for a traditional English supper of roast beef and Yorkshire pudding in a sixteenth-century inn.

The performance was in a working men's club with plenty of beer and no seats, leaving the American writers to wander freely among the two thousand or so young Britons in attendance -- including a preponderance of Skinheads with closely shaven skulls and heavy 'bovver' boots and a leavening of quiet, effeminate males who were at the centre of the Bowie cult and present at every show he gave, no matter where.

To the sound of the *alla marcia* of Beethoven's *Ninth Symphony* -- regarded by many in the audience as the theme from the film *A Clockwork Orange* -- David virtually catapulted on stage, wearing another of Freddie Buretti's creations, a green jumpsuit cut to the sternum, boots with four-inch risers, his hair a spikey carrot-red.

The Spiders behind him glimmered just as brightly -- Ronno in red and platinum sequins, everyone in knee-high, lace-up boots, skin-tight pants and shirts open to the waist.

The show included an acoustical rendition of 'Space Oddity' and Jacques Brel's poignant 'Amsterdam', as well as Lou Reed's song about heroin, 'Waiting for the Man' and the song David had written for Lou, 'Queen Bitch'.

None the less, the Ziggy Stardust songs prevailed and it was Ziggy who was the evening's star: outrageous and androgynous, angry and arrogant and having fun. David changed costumes twice, belted out the rockers in a macho voice while mincing around the stage, thrusting his skinny hips towards the audience, finally (during 'Suffragette City') dropping to his knees in front of Mick Ronson's guitar, to mimic fellatio.

The American writers had never seen anything like it.

Next day, Tony DeFries prepared another show, this one at the extravagant Dorchester Hotel. Tony's whole thing was to treat the person like a star before he'd ever made it, so that everyone would come to believe he *was* a star. So from Day One, it was always limousines and the best hotel rooms, champagne and crystal and available drugs. Angela backed him up and had a special wardrobe that was Ziggy or Spider in style, to be worn always, even when going to the supermarket. 'Every time you go out,' Angie said, 'it's a gig, it's a promotion!'

DeFries took a suite at the Dorchester and moved David into one of the rooms for a day of interviews, entertaining the writers in another room as they waited for their fifteen minutes with Ziggy Stardust. David, of course, wore a dress, cut practically to the navel.

There was free champagne and assorted drugs in both rooms, and, in the end, everyone wandered around, having a party. Lou Reed came in heavy eye make-up and told the press corps that David was producing his next album. Iggy Pop, another friend of Bowie's from America, who had made his first appearance in England the night before, was also there. DeFries hovered over David, who remained for most of the day on a settee which was positioned against a background of pink satin wallpaper. David smoked his incessant cigarettes and told lies about himself, while Tony played the traffic cop.

In the adjacent room, suddenly there was a scream.

David looked up in alarm, but was told it was nothing to worry about: Angela had merely bitten one of the press people (Lillian Roxon) on the breast. She said she did it because Lou Reed's manager had bitten *her* on the stomach.

Lou Reed interrupted one of David's interviews by going over to him and kissing him full on the mouth.

At some point, Iggy Pop – who was wearing silver eye shadow and a Marc Bolan T-shirt – talked about leaping out of the window, but apparently changed his mind.

The American press had never seen anything like this, either.

The stories that appeared over the next few months all struck a common chord. 'I Went to England and Saw the Queen' was the way Alan Rich headlined his story in *New York* magazine. *After Dark* went all the way: 'David's hand rests on his hip while he's belting out his tunes. The lights playing on his innocent, unlined face colour him an unearthly green . . . More unearthly than his face is his crotch, which seems unusually large, almost inhuman . . .'

To Bowie, it seemed so bloody odd.

From the Dorchester suite, where the champagne flowed and the caviar went warm, and everyone could have virtually whatever he or she wanted . . . David and Angela went home to their £7-a-month flat in Beckenham. It was like being rich for a day, and then it was back to 'reality'.

When his Aunt Pat came to visit, she went away thinking David was living in a pigsty; everywhere she looked there were discarded clothes and piles of paper and tangled recording equipment. When David's mother arrived, letting herself in with her own key, she was shocked to find her grandson walking around the flat in wellingtons, otherwise naked, his hair hanging down to the middle of his back, eating baby food from a tin.

The flat was messiest when David was at home, writing. At other times, David went out, making the rounds of Soho clubs and playing impresario with some of his musical friends.

This happened most notably in the summer of 1972, when he and Mick Ronson produced a single and an album for a band called Mott the Hoople, a group that had a loyal following among English folk-rockers, but had never had a hit. When David offered them 'Suffragette City', hoping they'd record it, he heard back that they were on the verge of retirement. Figuring he could 'save' the band, he now offered them Tony DeFries – who promptly took control – and then he wrote an original song for them which became the anthem for all glitter-rockers, 'All the Young Dudes'.

Unlike his earlier songs about the London mods, this one looked at the followers of glam rock sympathetically. While his older brother was at home with his Beatles and Stones, Billy (the Young Dude) dressed like a queen and kicked like a mule, picked painted stars off his face and contemplated suicide, while listening to records of T. Rex. Once again David was writing about the disconnected kids he saw in his audiences and on the streets, but this time not with sadness or maudlin sentimentality, but pride and soaring joy.

'All the Young Dudes!' he chorused. 'Carry the news!'

At the same time as he worked with Mott the Hoople, he and his producer Ken Scott went into the Trident Studio with David's favourite American composer, Lou Reed, to begin work on Reed's next album, *Transformer*. David was characteristically modest about his intentions. 'All that I can do is make a few definitions on some of the concepts of some of the songs and help arrange things the way Lou wants them,' he said. 'I'm just trying to do exactly as Lou wants.'

The first song recorded was Reed's next single, a bitter-sweet musical catalogue of some of the characters in the Andy Warhol crowd, called 'Walk on the Wild Side'. For added assistance on this one, David called Herbie Flowers, the bass player who had worked with him on 'Space Oddity'. Flowers thought the song needed a saxophone at the end and he suggested David's old teacher, Ronnie Ross who came in and did it.

When 'All the Young Dudes' and 'Walk on the Wild Side' were released a few months later, they would become major hits, in America and in Britain, changing the careers of the artists significantly.

*

David Bowie was hot again. *Hunky Dory* was, by now, temporarily history as the Ziggy persona emerged. By the first of July, the Ziggy album was in all the album charts in both America and Britain, and 'Starman' was on its way to becoming a serious hit, going to No. 65 in the US, and No. 10 in England.

At the same time, an album called *Revelations – A Musical Anthology for Glastonbury Fayre*, which purported to be a sort of soundtrack from the previous summer's organic free festival, was released containing David's song 'Supermen'. Like all the other material on the album (by a variety of artists ranging from Marc Bolan to Pete Townshend and America's Grateful Dead), it was recorded long after the 'fayre' in a studio, and the album quickly became little more than a curiosity item. None the less, when the album appeared – also in July – one more spotlight was turned on the Bowie camp.

The press continued its spectacular coverage. No one could have wanted more. 'David Bowie Is Gonna Be Huge,' said Charles Shaar Murray in the *New Musical Express*, after watching the Ziggy show. 'David's all right, you know. He may even be the shining genius his ads say he is. Whatever, he's a gas. Long live Ziggy Stardust! We needed him.'

Other British critics echoed the praise. And in America's top rock paper, *Rolling Stone*, Richard Cromelin reviewed the Ziggy album effusively, referring to a 'lusty – and forlorn bravado that is the first hint of the central duality and of the rather spine-tingling questions that rise from it: just how big and tough is your rock 'n' roll star? How much of him is bluff and how much inside is very frightened and helpless? And is this what comes of our happily dubbing someone as 'bigger than life''?'

In the rest of America the reaction was similar. Said *Boston After Dark*: 'Another exemplary album.' The *Philadelphia Inquirer*: 'David Bowie is one of the most creative, compelling writers around today.' *Crawdaddy*: 'David Bowie albums live in a state of perpetual tension.' *Phonograph Record* magazine: 'Perfection in popular recorded sound.' *Hartford Courant*: 'Polished, refined rock showmanship . . . Bowie writes some of the most solid, forthright rock being put out today.' And from the highly regarded *Los Angeles Times*: 'A strong, moving, powerful piece of rock 'n' roll.'

Simultaneously, David went back on the road and into rehearsals for his biggest show to date, scheduled for 19 August in what had become London's most prestigious rock venue, a spacious movie hall, the Finsbury Park Cinema, renamed the Rainbow Theatre.

By now, David's audience had broadened and solidified. The hard-core following of homosexuals was loyal to a fault; queens were now beginning to pursue him backstage, creating a transvestite groupie scene. At the same time, David was becoming an inspiration to thousands of sexually ambivalent youths, the ones who hadn't made up their minds yet (a significant crowd in any generation, perhaps especially so in England during the heyday of Glam Rock). And, most important, though his gay posturing surely must have alienated some heterosexuals, when parents began attacking him, many straight young men flocked to their neighbourhood record stores, thinking, 'If me mum and dad don't like the bloke, he must be a bit of all right!' Thus, David's audience now cut across all sexual boundaries.

The morning before the Rainbow show, David talked

about the Ziggy character, revealing how his personal view of rock theatre had changed. The lines separating what happened on stage and off were blurred now. 'I think what I do and the way I dress is me pandering to my own eccentricities and imagination,' he said. 'It's a continual fantasy. Nowadays there is really no difference between my personal life and anything I do on stage. I'm very rarely David Jones any more. I think I've forgotten who David Jones is.'

If true, this was a compelling admission. There were now, he was saying, at least two David Bowies, a split in the personality . . . and he was losing touch with the original.

Years later, David would say it was deliberate when he remained in character offstage. 'I took the character into the interviews as well,' he said. 'I would do the interviews in character, unbeknownst to most of the interviewers. The idea was that I was going to use myself as part of the production. I didn't want to stop when I got off the stage. I took the whole thing . . . any time I was in public, I was whoever I was at the time.'

*

On 19 August 1972, after touring on and off for four months David/Ziggy and his Spiders were capable of presenting a polished act, night after night after night. But for the Rainbow show that wasn't enough. So he called his old mentor, Lindsay Kemp, only two weeks before the date to help him with the choreography and to assemble a group of dancers who would be called the Astronettes. A set was constructed of scaffolding, to allow David to appear at various levels in different costumes throughout the show. Hundreds of pounds of dry ice were purchased to be dropped into containers of water to produce a clinging fog on stage. As David made his entrance, singing 'Lady Stardust', a picture of Marc Bolan was projected on a large screen, the first of several hundred images. It was, as one long-time pop writer-observer said, perhaps 'the most extravagant rock show ever produced in Britain.'

The critics were kind and sales of the Ziggy album climbed sharply, as David went back into the Trident to finish *Transformer* with Lou Reed. And then, in September, it was back on the road again, travelling to Bournemouth and Bristol, then north to Manchester, Sunderland, Sheffield and Liverpool.

On 1 September, RCA released a re-recorded version of 'John, I'm Only Dancing' (backed with the more recent 'Hang On To Yourself'), and one week later 'All the Young Dudes' by Mott the Hoople was released by CBS. Both instantly went into the British charts, David's record peaking at No. 12, the Hoople's at No. 3.

Then on 10 September, following a final performance in the Top Rank Suite in Hanley, Stoke-on-Trent, David boarded the *Queen Elizabeth II* for New York. Still afraid of flying, he and Angela left more than a week ahead of his band.

*

America.

The previous trip had been child's play. A folly. A public relations joke. A sales scheme that failed. In Britain, David was a major star. In America, he was a minor cult figure. In Britain, the Ziggy album had soared straight to the No. 5 position on the bestseller lists. In America it was languishing in the upper 80s.

Aboard the *QE2*, David had ample time to contemplate what lay ahead. To be sure, the initial reviews of the Ziggy album were excellent, but how would American audiences react to the Ziggy show? They'd already seen Alice Cooper. Would Ziggy Stardust be enough? Or, on the other hand, too much? Glam Rockers like Gary Glitter and Marc Bolan had never toured the US, were virtual unknowns in America and Alice Cooper's cross-dressing was regarded as a show biz joke. Was America ready for serious androgyny? Or would David be laughed off stage?

ALADDIN SANE

In New York, Tony DeFries met Timothy Ferris, a writer for *Rolling Stone*. DeFries had reinstated his no-interview policy, believing that by keeping David in reserve, he would increase David's American popularity.

None the less, DeFries agreed to meet the reporter himself. He did this because *Rolling Stone* had reviewed David's albums most favourably and because *Rolling Stone* was, in 1972, the single most important arbiter in rock. Ferris took an immediate dislike to DeFries, as was clear from his description: 'His long, pointed nose is out of Dickens. His complexion is an uneven white. He favours fat black cigars. When he smokes one, he resembles a ball of oatmeal on a stick.'

As Ferris pulled out his tape recorder, DeFries produced his own, which he said would allow him to check the accuracy of the quotations. There followed a carefully enunciated monologue about how big David Bowie was going to be – *the* star of the seventies.

'He is one person of many facets and many talents who can be and will be an industry on his own,' DeFries said. (A theme he would echo for as long as he managed David.) 'You see, I've always seen David as a building. I visualize him as a building. Something rather like the Pan Am building on Park Avenue [a massive 59-storey office building covered with mirrored glass which towers over the central Manhattan neighbourhood].'

*

While members of his band travelled by plane to the first date in Cleveland, Ohio, on 22 September, David and Angie – her hair now dyed white with streaks of purple and red – crossed nearly a quarter of America in a chartered Greyhound bus. David often sat alone in the back, writing songs or gazing out at the countryside.

From Cleveland, he went to Memphis – Elvis Presley's home town: David asked his driver to take him past Graceland on the way into town – and thence ultimately on to Carnegie Hall. The break-in shows seemed to work. David was happy about the audience reaction, although he remained somewhat stiff and anxious about New York, where he would meet the national media. A few of the influential writers were already on his side. Most were not yet convinced. In 1972, acceptance by the journalistic doyen of New York was more or less demanded for subsequent rock and roll stardom. Nothing beat massive record sales, of course, but in lieu of that, a rock act had to have the word-of-mouth that came with national publicity.

Outside Carnegie Hall a searchlight revolved slowly, slicing the sky with light. Outside the doors gathered a peculiar crowd, some looking like what one writer called 'Christmas trees on legs. There was much glitter and several men dressed as ladies.'

This was the Event of the Week. Bowie had been hyped solidly for more than three weeks by RCA. In the audience were Tony Perkins, Todd Rundgren, Alan Bates, Andy Warhol, Lee Radziwell, and all the rock writers living and working within 150 miles of New York. They were not disappointed.

The woman who had jumped naked from a birthday cake for Mick Jagger a week or so earlier, rushed the stage with an armful of gladioli. Angie jitterbugged in the aisle. The house lights dimmed. Beethoven's Ninth roared out and in a blinding flash of strobe lights, Ziggy Stardust made his/ her entrance to a standing ovation.

The show offered a little of everything in David's repertoire, emphasizing the Ziggy persona, of course, but also including an acoustical spot in the middle that featured 'Space Oddity' and a dramatic reading of Jacques Brel's 'My Death'. Then slam-bam-thank-you-ma'am, back into Ziggy, with David throwing in a little mime (using his flattened palms to create the illusion of imprisonment behind an invisible wall). As was his custom by now, he also fell to his knees and grabbing Ronno's buttocks, pressed his lips to Ronno's guitar to simulate fellatio. (The same act which got Jim Morrison arrested in Miami in 1969.)

For ninety minutes he performed, closing with his plea to the audience to 'Give me your hands!' The first ten rows complied.

Some of those present were not impressed. Bob Christgau wrote in *Newsday*, the influential Long Island daily, that David may have been prettier than his opening act, Ruth Copeland, but he wondered if winsomeness and songs about Andy Warhol from an 'English fairy are enough for the American rock audience.' Albert Goldman, there for *Life* magazine, wrote *nothing* afterwards. 'I must concede that the performance did not impress me at all,' Goldman says today. 'In fact, I told my assistant, who accompanied me, that I thought he was the classic example of the star established through hype. Obviously, I was wrong, but I wasn't wrong about that concert. It was nothing and the atmosphere was one of frenzied hype stirred up by RCA.'

Others reacted quite differently. Don Heckman in the *New York Times* called David 'a solidly competent stage performer who brings a strong sense of professionalism to every move he makes. As a performer, Bowie delivered. He understands that theatricality has more to do with presence than with gimmickry, and that beautifully coordinated physical movements and well-planned music can reach an audience a lot quicker than aimless prancing and high-decibel electronics . . .'

The writer for *Billboard* said, 'Bowie set himself a number of impossible requirements for the full success of this tour, and then, being Bowie, proceeded to meet all of them with grace.'

'A star is born!' cried Lillian Roxon, the *New York Daily News* columnist whom Angela had bitten on the breast a few months earlier in London. 'I have always wanted to write that in a review and now I can. English rock singer David Bowie made his New York debut in Carnegie Hall on Thursday night and took that sceptical, cynical audience by storm.'

And Ellen Willis of the *New Yorker* was one of those standing on their chairs at the end of the show.

As Ziggy and the Spiders moved from city to city – and eventually from coast to coast, arriving in California in mid-October, the album reviews offered more praise. *Circus* called it 'a stunning work of genius' and *Boston After Dark* called David 'the most important artist to have emerged in this decade.' And the *Village Voice* effused, 'The man is a stone genius and, for those who have been waiting for a new Dylan, Bowie fits the bill. He is a prophet, a poet – and a vaudevillian. Like Dylan, his breadth of vision and sheer talent could also exercise a profound effect on a generation's attitudes.'

At the same time, everywhere David went, he was greeted by hundreds of Ziggy clones – young men with their hair bleached white or dyed red, their faces painted a metallic gold.

In the face of this incredible acceptance, David's feelings were severely mixed.

Generally the reviews of the concerts were good and in most cities, the auditoriums were completely sold out. And everywhere, his management offered him comfort and security. Interviews were given selectively, photograph sessions rarely. The backstage area was kept clear of fans and hangers-on; even concert promoters were told to watch the shows from out front, rather than from the wings.

'It was the best in California,' says Mike Garson, Bowie's piano player. 'We stayed at the Beverly Hills Hotel, in the bungalows. I remember we had Perry Como on one side, Elton John on the other. And I remember that the bill for incidentals at the hotel came to $10,000! We lived in total, total luxury. When a date was cancelled in Arizona, we stayed in Arizona for ten days, lying by the pool.'

None the less, David said he did not enjoy the tour. As he cross-crossed America, he found the landscape disquieting. Even while still in New York, sitting in the early morning light in a suite in the Plaza Hotel, his thoughts were dark. There had been a party in the room the night before, where Angie danced with a Marilyn Monroe look-alike and the outlandish transvestite Wayne County danced with Cherry Vanilla. It all seemed, somehow, so decadent. 'If I'm in a very light mood, I find everything in America so kitsch,' David said. 'It's wonderful and I'd love to have it all hanging in my bedroom. If I'm in a bad mood, I find it terribly repressive and heavy.'

The mood in New York was heavy. Iggy Pop flew in from

Los Angeles for the show, then spent the night telling David tales of the Detroit revolutionaries he had known in his Michigan youth. David began to see his friend as a Che Guevara-like figure with a gun and a diesel truck, a member of 'the National People's Gang'. By the time David and his band arrived in Detroit, another song was written: 'Panic in Detroit'.

In Los Angeles, David was unimpressed by the lavish setting of the Beverly Hills Hotel and when he left the city, it was the sad, burnt-out cases he saw along Hollywood Boulevard who were most memorable. Here, con men, runaways and prostitutes roamed and occasional silent screen heroes and starlets – now in their seventies – drifted towards senility. These impressions became 'Cracked Actor'.

Another song, 'Drive-in Saturday', was the result of seeing the barren landscape of the American Southwest from a train window during nocturnal transit from Seattle to Phoenix. 'If you don't go to sleep when you're supposed to,' David said, 'you suddenly see the moon shining on seventeen or eighteen enormous silver domes. I couldn't find out from anyone what they were. But they gave me a vision of America, Britain, and China after a nuclear catastrophe. The radiation has affected people's minds and reproductive organs, and they don't have a sex life. The only way they can learn to make love again is by watching films of how it used to be done.'

One after another, apocalyptic visions of America were scribbled into David's notebook. By the time he returned to New York, in December, one song, 'Jean Genie', was finished and recorded (in a studio in Nashville) and on its way to England for immediate single release, and he had the tracks to several others recorded in rough form.

It was while sitting in an overstuffed armchair in his suite aboard ship returning to London, that he wrote the album's title song. He had been reading Evelyn Waugh's *Vile Bodies*, a novel written in the 1930s about a future world where 'bright young things' danced and gossiped and drank in the face of the holocaust: 'Battle cries and champagne just in time for sunrise.'

David called the song 'Aladdin Sane', a play on words

which later he told friends was inspired by his brother Terry, who remained in Cane Hill Hospital: a lad insane.

David returned to London a major star. As 'Jean Genie' sped up the record charts, peaking at No. 2, one of David's old record companies, Pye, re-released four six-year-old songs on an extended play record and RCA re-released his two albums from Philips/Mercury, *Space Oddity* and *The Man Who Sold the World*, the latter with contemporary (Ziggy) covers, giving some buyers the impression that the albums were new. All went on to the British bestseller lists.

On 23 and 24 December, David and the Spiders performed two holiday shows at the Rainbow Theatre. (At the Christmas Eve show, concert-goers were asked to bring toys, which were delivered by van the next day to Dr Barnardo's Homes, where David's father had worked for so long.) David took a week off after Christmas, then appeared in Scotland on 5 and 6 January. After that, he and the Spiders and Mike Garson, who had been flown over from New York, went into the Trident studios to finish the album.

Tony DeFries was pushing now. David was to begin a 100-day world tour on 25 January – starting again in New York – and RCA wanted a new album in the shops before that date. Consequently, production was hurried and the album was somewhat fragmented and poorly done.

None the less, there was still a commonality, a cohesion which transcended the lesser quality and divergent themes. *Aladdin Sane* may not have hung together musically in the same way that *Ziggy Stardust* did, but the record presented a single attitude – even the super-charged version of the Rolling Stones' 'Let's Spend the Night Together' fit the mood. And the visual imagery was no less stunning than Ziggy's was. The carrot-coloured brush cut remained, and the make-up was more extreme. On a magenta and pink base, David carefully painted a red-and-blue lightning bolt, which bisected his face from left forehead to right cheek, a symbol of schizophrenia.

When David talked about the Aladdin Sane character, it was clear that he identified with his brother's illness: 'Aladdin Sane was an extension of Ziggy on the one hand. On the other, it was more a subjective thing. Aladdin Sane was my idea of rock and roll America. Here I was on this great tour circuit, not enjoying it very much. So inevitably my writing reflected that. This kind of schizophrenia that I was going through. Wanting to be up on the stage performing my songs, but on the other hand not really wanting to be on those buses with all those strange people. Being basically a fairly quiet person, it was hard to come to terms. So Aladdin Sane was split down the middle.'

David completed the album on 24 January and the next day sailed again for New York aboard the *Queen Elizabeth II.*

David had been away from America for only six weeks and if *Aladdin Sane* reflected his impressions accurately, one had to wonder why he was going back. The answer was business, of course.

Rock's counterculture had lost much of its momentum by now. George Harrison's concerts for Bangladesh, Bob Dylan's 'George Jackson' concert, and John Lennon's 1971 benefits for John Sinclair (the Detroit White Panther locked up for ten years for marijuana possession) and Paul McCartney's 'Give Ireland Back to the Irish' in 1972 showed the lingering existence of a social conscience, but by early 1973, the war in Vietnam was winding down, ending much of the political or revolutionary commitment generally associated with rock music.

At the same time, many of the big groups were fragmenting. The Beatles went their separate ways in 1970 and, while the members of the Who would continue to tour and record together for many more years, by January 1973 Pete Townshend and Roger Daltry were paying more attention to their solo careers. Janis Joplin, Jimi Hendrix, Duane Allman and Berry Oakley (both of the Allman Brothers Band), Danny Whitten (of Neil Young's Crazy Horse) and Jim Morrison were dead, victims of life in the fast lane (motorcycle accidents, alcohol, and drugs). And Don McLean occupied the top spot in 1972 for eight weeks with the song, 'American Pie', a story about 'the day the music died.'

Tony DeFries was determined to successfully insert David Bowie into this picture of pop disarray. Despite the warm critical response, David's most recent album hadn't done as well in the US as expected, *Ziggy Stardust* had gone only to No. 75, and of the two more recently distributed by RCA, the re-released *Space Oddity* and *The Man Who Sold the World*, the first had gone to No. 16, the latter only to No. 105. The way RCA looked at it, David needed a hit desperately and finding nothing overwhelming in the new material, the company decided to re-issue 'Space Oddity' as a single. Strangely, it went right to the No. 15 spot.

With a song that was four years old becoming his first American Top Twenty hit, David and his band began two weeks of rehearsals, then opened their tour in New York's prestigious Radio City Music Hall.

The audience for the opening night (Valentine's Day) was David's flashiest yet – including Salvador Dali, Johnny Winter and Todd Rundgren; virtually everyone in Manhattan's rock elite; hundreds of youthful Ziggy look-alikes; and every drag queen from south of Fourteenth Street, wearing his most gorgeous gown.

David didn't disappoint anyone.

The lights dimmed as Walter Carlos' reverberating organ music from *A Clockwork Orange* echoed through the theatre and David descended to the stage in a cage, illuminated by a single spotlight, while to his right and left revolved two mirrored globes sending thousands of shards of light whirling dizzily over the audience, as the Spiders crashed into 'Hang On To Yourself'.

The show that followed was slightly faster than most of those that came after it. David was rushing now, pounding the songs out one after the other with only the briefest moment between the end of one and the beginning of the next, leaving the stage five times to change costumes, while Ronno and the boys maintained the pace. Even the Stones' 'Let's Spend the Night Together' was played so fast it seemed as if a 45 rpm record was being played at 78.

The first half of the show closed with 'Suffragette City'. And then there was an intermission, during which the colourful audience began its promenade.

The second half opened with David and his Spiders rising from beneath the stage through a trapdoor, as if they had been beamed down from *Star Trek's* Starship Enterprise. In this portion of the show, several of the old songs were changed – 'Space Oddity' was no longer an acoustic duet between David and Ronno, but was now a full production number – and several new ones, from the as-yet-unreleased *Aladdin Sane* album, were added. The show closed with 'Rock and Roll Suicide', and as it ended, a man leaped on to the stage and grabbed David, who fell to the stage.

It went very quiet in the big theatre. The sound of security people wrestling with the young fan could be heard in the last rows. David was carried backstage. Some of the band members and crew thought David was joking. Others recalled his fears of assassination. Mike Garson rushed to David's side and loosened his clothing and elevated his feet. A nurse appeared and after making her examination, she declared that David was suffering from exhaustion. (Although Mike believed it was the result of too little to eat, too much to drink and too much heavy make-up which didn't allow his face to 'breathe'.) That night, David slept for twelve hours.

Then it was off to Philadelphia by bus.

Tony DeFries was more in control on this second US tour. While still in New York he went to David and said, 'I want you to tell all the writers you're going to be starring in *Stranger In A Strange Land*'.

'Robert Heinlein's book?' David said.

'Yes. You know it, of course.'

'Of course. I didn't know they were going to make it into a movie.'

'Doesn't matter,' Tony said, pulling on his cigar. 'We're going to tell people you're going to be the star. Doesn't matter if it's true or not. People'll believe it. Word'll get out. It'll be in the press and first thing you know, the scripts'll come piling in and you'll be a movie star. I guarantee it, mate.'

David said he'd do his best, and for the rest of the tour he told every interviewer that he was going to star in *Stranger In A Strange Land* and they dutifully printed the news.

As predicted, the scripts began to arrive on Tony's Main-Man desk.

David had lost money on the first tour and Tony was determined to do better this time. So he cut corners whenever possible, putting David up in the best hotels – accommodation befitting a star – and the rest of the band in slightly cheaper places nearby. And where all incidentals, including room service and bar bills, were covered on the first circuit, the musicians now received a minimal per diem amount. And there weren't so many limousines. David always had one, of course, but the rest of the boys now travelled in station wagons hired from Hertz.

Even so, the costs were enormous. Besides David and the eight members of the band, there were three backup singers, a sound engineer, a stage manager, two equipment managers, a wardrobe mistress and hair stylist, a lighting director and two light men, a road manager, a tour coordinator from MainMan and a bodyguard.

The bodyguard, a large black man named Stuart George, earned his salary in Los Angeles, in March, when David and his travelling companion, Freddie Buretti (who had designed many of his costumes), were dancing together at the Rainbow Grill, one of the most popular bars on the Sunset Strip.

'Hey, look at the faggot!' a man with long hair said, pointing at David. He seemed drunk.

David ignored the remark.

'Wanna suck my dick?'

Suddenly the man lunged at David and tried to throw a punch. Stuey George moved in. Stuey literally picked him up and carried him outside and – as someone said later – 'took care of the situation efficiently.'

For the rest of the tour, David didn't move from his hotel rooms.

Another problem arose when David said in an interview that he wanted to expand the band to an eleven-man group. It may have been no more than a whim, said on the spur of the moment, but the Spiders were furious.

'They came to me and said they wanted to quit,' says Dennis Katz, who had left the RCA artists and repertoire department to practise entertainment law. 'They said they felt it was a four-man band and David was the vocalist. I told them they couldn't quit in the middle of a tour and they went ahead and finished the tour. But from that point on, it was never the same. They felt like they were being used.'

There were shows in Philadelphia, followed by more in Nashville, Memphis, Detroit, Chicago and Los Angeles, and then David sailed to Japan. David read, voraciously, and during the long voyage from California to Japan, he read books about *Kabuki* and *Noh* theatre, Zen and Japanese art, as well as some of the novels of Yukio Mishima, the three-time Nobel Prize nominee who had committed *seppuku* – ritual suicide – in 1970. Mishima was born into a samurai family and imbued with the code that apotheosized complete control over mind and body. For David, he was becoming a significant influence.

*

'Welcome to Japan!'

The mimeographed tour itinerary greeted the cast and crew: 'We sincerely hope that this visit to Japan will be an enjoyable one and especially a successful one. Please be advised that this itinerary has been planned for with extreme care and in detail, and we would sincerely appreciate your kind attention to the times mentioned in this itinerary especially when travelling to other areas in Japan as trains run on time here, and each and every individual seat has been reserved. We thank you very much for your close and kind cooperation and understanding. Please be advised also that space [time] has been provided after each date on the itinerary to make personal notes, etc . . .'

That meant everyone had time to go sightseeing, a factor that David appreciated. In the next seventeen days, David would experience Japan as only a few very special tourists do.

Going to Japan, for David, was like going to a 'source'. Although he was no longer a practising Buddhist – if ever he really was – the teachings of Buddha remained clearly etched in his memory, and the sexually ambiguous stance of Buddhism was still a large part of what made Ziggy and Aladdin go. So, too, the discipline and movement of the *Noh* and *Kabuki* theatre. David often said in interviews that Ziggy Stardust – and by extension, Aladdin Sane – was 'Japanese theatre meets American science fiction'. For many years, David had told friends he wanted to visit Japan. Now, finally, he was getting his chance. And according to the friends he had along with him, he was somewhat nervous about it.

97

'In a way it was a test,' one friend says today. 'David had been *using* Japanese culture for years in his act and now he was going to Japan to perform that act. So he was anxious about how the Japanese would react. At the same time, anxious to learn more, which he could then put into the act to keep the cycle going.'

David arrived in Japan on 5 April, Angela and Zowie came the following day, and together they met Kansai Yamamoto, a fashion designer who had given David a costume when David was in New York. It was snapped from stem to sternum and could be popped off with a single movement. David loved it and wore it in concert, commissioning the designer to create another nine costumes based on traditional Japanese dramas.

Some of the garments clung to his body, others engulfed him completely, and all were dramatic to the point of surprise. There was a striped, one-legged suit of beaded tights that came with a set of doughnut-like bracelets and a bright green feather boa. Others offered ballooning capes or brightly coloured bell-bottom pants on which the cuffs were fully three feet across. David wore the costumes during his ten performances in Tokyo, Nagoya, Kobe, Osaka, Hiroshima and, then again in Tokyo.

'In Japan we were faced with an audience that we presumed didn't understand a word of what I was saying,' David said. 'There I was more physical than on any other tour I've ever done. Literally, I activated the whole thing with my hands and my body. I needn't have sung half the time. In America, we'll just keep it down to simplicities. But Americans are very academic towards their rock and need to have a cultural stability. The Japanese are theatrical and far more aware than either England or America.'

Part of this theatricality and physicality David talked about came in the form of near-nudity, when he put aside Kansai's flashy wardrobe and performed wearing only an athletic supporter, which he insisted was what a proper Japanese sumo wrestler would wear. Whatever his reasoning, it made for an interesting sight: a red-haired, Caucasian 'sumo wrestler' who weighed only 118 pounds, screaming 'Rock and Roll Suicide' to an audience of young Japanese.

Another night, David climbed the scaffolding on one side

of the stage to a height of about fifteen feet and jumped.

'I thought, this guy thinks he can *fly*,' says Mike Garson. 'There may be some acrobats could've handled that. He's a pretty rubbery guy, but I knew it was too high. He went flying past me at the piano and just wiped out. He finished the show, but he was in pain and the next night he performed from a chair.'

David and Angela enjoyed Japan. Kansai had a son Zowie's age and the two played together. Between cities, the Bowies travelled into the countryside and attended performances of *Kabuki* theatre, where David learned new make-up techniques from Japan's most popular *Kabuki* star, Tomasu Boru.

With characteristic reserve, David told a newsman as he left the country, 'There is nothing about Japan I disliked at all.' And then he and his family and Iggy Pop, who joined David at the end of the Japanese tour, boarded a boat from Yokohoma to Nahodka, then took a train to Vladivostock to catch the Trans-Siberian Express, travelling 'soft', the Russian equivalent of 'first class'. Next stop: Moscow.

The band flew home to London, where Tony DeFries was preparing for the final leg of the tour, twenty-seven concerts in England and Scotland which were to begin in less than a month. Tony had recently moved his offices, taking a two-level flat in Gunter Grove, hiring his first full-time staff. Two of these employees would play a major role in David's life – Kathy Dorritie, the New York advertising executive's daughter who spun out of the Warhol factory scene calling herself Cherry Vanilla, and the daughter of an American photographer who, like Angela, had grown up all over Europe (and therefore was multi-lingual and multi-cultural), Corinne 'Coco' Schwab.

'It was a circus,' David said later. 'For a while, we worked on it together and it was fun. It was my idea to have people like Cherry Vanilla running around speaking for me, saying anything she wanted to say about me, and when it came back to me, I'd agree with it. It was bizarre. I asked some actors from Andy Warhol's factory to be my office and they said, "But we're actors!" And I said, "That's very good reason for you to be my office. You're going to be my accountants. You can handle my PR." For about a year I had actors pretending to be office people and it was just hysterical.'

'It was a totally outrageous group of people,' says one observer. 'Some of them were complete nut cases. And *everybody* wore costumes. I don't care how hot it was, DeFries had that bloody fur coat and all the girls – with the exception of Coco – were falling out of their dresses. Everywhere you looked, there were tits staring at you.'

DeFries was no fool. He was playing David's game, using outrageous appearance to attract attention and to keep those with whom he did business off-balance, on the chance that they might lower their guard. He was also very careful about *illegal* behaviour. DeFries had an absolute horror of anyone on the team getting arrested and drug use was forbidden. Any instance of possible drug abuse was checked so thoroughly that Cherry Vanilla was severely chewed out when DeFries caught her taking a vitamin pill. The Bowie camp was so outrageous that DeFries figured everyone in it was a target.

The major targets, David and Angela, were then moving slowly across Russia with Geoffrey MacCormack and Leee Black Childers. For eight days, the Trans-Siberian Express failed to live up to its name, giving them ample time to relax. David spent most of the trip wrapped in a kimono, sipping tea served by stocky, uniformed female attendants. Rarely did he leave the train.

However, once when he disembarked with Childers for a few minutes at Sverdlovsk, two uniformed guards approached the photographer. As they moved to take him away, David raised a 16 mm camera to film the scene. Two more guards moved towards David. The two female train attendants who by now were fond of this orange-haired Englishman literally picked up Childers and Bowie and carried them back to the train, which quickly pulled out of the station.

By the time David reached Moscow, he joked later, he was thinking about calling himself Ziggy Sootdust, because of the dirt that came in under the train windows. And however glamorous his car seemed at first, it didn't come equipped with a bathroom. David was also upset by the poverty he saw through the train windows, and by what he saw in the next car, which contained hundreds of Russian peasants, crammed into tiny compartments.

David and his friends arrived in Moscow on 1 May, the day when the Soviet leaders annually stage a May Day parade of military might – miles of tanks and missiles, and troops goose-stepping past the members of the Presidium, carrying huge pictures of Lenin and banners showing muscular field and factory workers.

David and Angela went to Gum's department store, the largest store in Russia, and found barren aisles, with few of the necessities available, and no luxuries. The only 'souvenirs' they found were Russian soap and underwear.

Before he'd left the country, he'd even had his *Playboy* magazines confiscated.

David was appalled. 'By the time I got to Berlin,' he said later, 'I was calling it the "Free World", and really meaning it.'

After some beer drinking in Berlin, the Bowie party trained to Paris, where they checked into the best hotel in town, the George Cinq. It was here that a small group of English pop journalists found them, joining a number of French writers at a hastily arranged press conference. France was regarded as a minor market for David's records, but his charm and affability was never on greater display. Of Russia, he merely said he found the people interesting. When asked if he had stolen much of his performance style from Iggy Pop and Lou Reed, he laughed and suggested the questioner talk to Iggy and Lou, although he was so angry he gripped the table edge in front of him so tightly his knuckles hurt.

The next morning, David took a train to the French coast where he, Angela, Cherry Vanilla (who had joined the group to assist with the press conference), Childers and a handful of London journalists boarded the hovercraft for England.

'He was scared,' says Roy Hollingworth, a writer for *Melody Maker*. 'These boats were enormous beasts and David had never been on one before.'

'Don't worry, David,' said Angela, 'it travels only one foot above the water.'

David looked shocked. 'One foot!' he cried. 'I thought it travelled *on* the water.'

David had been away from England for more than three months, had been travelling on and off for eight, completely circumnavigating the globe – covering 45,000 miles in all. David smiled wanly when he arrived by train at London's Charing Cross Station to be greeted by a hundred or so fans.

'I'm sick of being Gulliver,' he said. 'You know, after America, Moscow, Siberia, Japan . . . I just want to bloody well go home to Beckenham and watch the telly.'

And so he did.

There was a homecoming party in Haddon Hall on 5 May, when nearly everyone close to David and Angie gathered for an evening of talk and music. Then exactly one week later, on the 12th, the eight-week tour of England began with a performance in Earl's Court, a cavernous indoor stadium that never had been used for a concert before.

There was much publicity about David's return to England, about his new wardrobe from Japan, about his new character, Aladdin Sane. All seats were quickly sold, with some touts asking as much as £25, when the price for all tickets at the box office was only £2.

It wasn't even worth *two*! The stage was so low, several thousand people couldn't see the show. The sound system echoed ferociously. The audience rushed the stage and fights started after a group of fans stripped and danced naked in the aisles, provoking one woman to slap one of the dancers, who, in turn, tore off her blouse. The show was stopped and David had to tell everyone to 'stop being silly'. Ten minutes later the show resumed, but it was fruitless. Already people were leaving. David was so upset afterwards that he screamed at the promoter and at Tony DeFries and at everyone else he saw, then he calmly said, 'We are scheduled to come back here on 30 June. Cancel the fucking show. Now.'

The show was cancelled and three days later – with 'Drive-In Saturday' moving into the No. 3 spot on the British charts and the new album heading for No. 1 – David and the Spiders and their friends boarded a train for Aberdeen, where they began a sold-out tour that took them to thirty-seven cities in forty-five days.

If David survived the tour, some of the concert halls did not. In Glasgow, David later recalled, 'We had, I think, four couples making it in the back row, which was fabulous. It's the first time I've heard of that happening. There was also a whole row of seats physically torn out of the floor, which sounds like the fifties to me. Can you imagine how much energy has to be used to tear out a row of seats?' The next place that happened, in Brighton, the manager of the 2,000-seat Dome was not amused. He banned David from appearing there again.

'On that tour we lost three limousines,' says Barry Bethel, who travelled on the tour as compere. 'Ripped them to pieces. Can you imagine? I mean, what can kids do to limousines that can write them off completely?'

As one of the shows was starting, David answered the telephone in his dressing room. Barry Bethel says David was suddenly flushed and denying something furiously. He could hear a male voice on the other end, shouting threats. David cried, 'No, no, no!' Finally, David hung up the phone and burst into tears.

'It was Mick Jagger,' Barry says today, 'and he was accusing David of having it on with Bianca. David and Bianca had gone out the night before, when Angie went to London for a television interview. David said it wasn't true and he said Mick was going to kill him, was going to carve him up, was going to shoot him on stage. He threatened Bowie in every way. And David said, "That's it! The show's off!" There were two thousand kids out there and the Spiders were warming up. We pushed him on stage anyway.'

The next morning, David called Mick and still Mick refused to believe him.

'I'll see you in London!' Mick said.

The final two shows, staged on 2 and 3 July, were held at the Hammersmith Odeon and were designed to take the place of the cancelled second show at Earl's Court. To this one, David invited D. A. Pennebaker, the American documentarian who made *Don't Look Back* with Bob Dylan in 1967 and in 1969 produced and directed both *Keep On Rockin'* (with Jerry Lee Lewis and Little Richard) and the classic *Monterey Pop*. David wanted the same *cinema verité* treatment for Ziggy and Aladdin Sane.

'Concerts are easy to shoot,' Pennebaker says today. 'If it's a good show, it's a good film. But I felt that there were very few performers who could hold up for ninety minutes. Not that they aren't good enough. It's just that you lose something moving from live concert to film.'

The show was nearing conclusion when David paused and looked into the darkness of the vast hall before him. 'This show will stay the longest in our memories,' he said, pausing again, as the audience began to applaud and cheer. He waited a moment and then continued: 'This show will stay the longest in our memories, not just because it is the end of the tour, but because it is the last show we'll ever do.'

There was a moment's stunned silence. The last show? At the age of twenty-six, David Bowie was *retiring*?

HALLOWEEN JACK

Outside the theatre, hundreds of Ziggy look-alikes wandered around, confusion showing beneath the lightning bolts they had painted on their faces. A magic cárpet had been yanked from under their stacked three-inch heels. Throughout pop London this night, there was shock.

'All I can say is that at this time, I do not want to do live concerts again for a long, long time,' David said backstage, '– not for two or three years at least.'

An end-of-the-tour dinner party was held at the Café Royal, one of London's most expensive restaurants. Because of David's announcement, it came to be called 'The Last Supper', but it was a joyous event, none the less, although it didn't start out that way.

By the time David reached London, his concern about Mick Jagger's threats had softened somewhat. He no longer believed that Jagger would shoot him on the Odeon stage. However, when he again called Mick and tried, for the third time, to convince him he hadn't put the 'make' on Bianca, Mick only said he was coming to the party and watch out.

The party was one of the events of the year. White Rolls Royces and Bentleys with smoked glass windows delivered a rich and varied diet of American and British stars. Elliott Gould came with Britt Ekland and shared a table with his ex-wife, Barbra Streisand and with Lulu and Ringo Starr. Peter Cook and Dudley Moore were together at another table. Elsewhere in the big, candle-lit room were Sonny Bono, Tony Curtis, Cat Stevens, Keith Moon, Mac Rebbenack (better known as Dr John the Nighttripper), Lou Reed, Ryan O'Neal and D. A. Pennebaker.

Finally, Mick and Bianca arrived. David was standing near the entrance, talking with Lou Reed.

''Allo, mate!' Jagger called.

David looked up, his face an unnatural colour.

Barry Bethel moved in, stepping in front of Mick. 'I know why you're here,' he said.

'No, you don't,' Mick said, stepping around Barry and up close to David.

He then kissed David on the cheek and the two of them started to laugh. Before the party ended, David danced with Mick, Angela danced with Bianca, and they all sat in each other's laps.

During a moment of solitude, Mick and Lou Reed told David they were surprised by his early retirement.

'I've always said I would quit some day,' David said, 'but no one listened.'

He leaned over the table and looked intently at his friends. 'Don't you see I'm keeping myself from being stifled?'

He said he wanted to make movies. There were four scripts he was considering.

'But you're a musician,' said Jagger. 'Aren't you going to miss playing?'

'I'm not a musician,' David said. 'I'm a writer and if I kept touring, I'd soon be thought of as a rock and roll singer and nothing else. That's just a part of what I do. I never wanted it to become my whole life.'

For a week afterwards pop music journalists did little but wring their hands and offer pensive interpretation. The *Evening Standard* headlined its story 'Tears as Bowie bows out.' Roy Hollingworth assured everyone in *Melody Maker*, 'Don't worry, kids; it's just tactics.' And Rosalind Russell in *Disc & Music Echo* said, 'It'll take months to grow out that lavatory brush haircut and tomato-coloured hair dye. My dears, what will we do with our silver boots and outrageous robes if we can't wear them to Bowie shows any more? We can't even raise an eyebrow in surprise because many of us have shaved them off à la Bowie.'

David was paying no attention whatsoever.

The morning after 'The Last Supper', he boarded a train for the coast, took a boat to France and then continued by train to Paris, where he motored to the crumbling old Château d'Hérouville outside the city. It was here that he and several musicians planned to live for the next few weeks while recording his next album, a collection of British hits from the 1960s. Years later, David talked about how important it was to reflect on one's past, and to use the lessons learned from that reflection, artistically. In France, David was doing just that. Ziggy Stardust and Aladdin Sane were dead. Now David was paying tribute to some of the groups that he used to listen to at the Marquee when he was starting out.

David had wanted to keep the Spiders together for the new album, but his failure to warn band members Woody and Trevor that he was quitting live performances created a troublesome rift. Initially, both refused to accompany him, with quick replacement invitations going to Jack Bruce, a bassist formerly with Cream, and Aynsley Dunbar, who had played drums for Frank Zappa in America. Bruce did not accept, Dunbar did.

'It's easy to understand why the Spiders were upset,' says Ken Fordham, the saxophone player in the band who went on to France. 'We all expected to have another tour of the States. It was a bit of a disappointment. More so to the others. They put a lot into it and they hadn't had that much money out of it, really. We were paid a concert rate of pay. The others got a regular weekly wage and even that wasn't much. They weren't being paid well at all. They were living on the hope of more later and the promise of future fame. When David said he was quitting, we all thought, "My God, there goes all the money we were counting on." Believe me, that sort of thing can cause problems.'

'After the Hammersmith thing, it was getting a little hairy,' says Mike Garson, who continued to play piano for David. 'Woody wasn't there and we were both good friends. He was very upset, very upset. He decided not to go and Aynsley Dunbar took his place. Trevor also sensed that he was going to lose his gig and so he went along, holding on for as long as he could, when Jack Bruce said no. Mick felt the same insecurity. So there was tension between them and David.'

The château was perfect for recording. Originally Chopin's home, its fame had been renewed two years before when Elton John recorded an album there and called it *Honky Chateau*. Still, it was Marc Bolan, who recorded his *Slider* album there, who suggested that David try it.

The dozen songs that David selected for the album were a mixed bag. The only thing that held them together was nostalgia, plus the fact that all of them were 'rockers', more or less. It was also a British album, because only five of the songs had been hits in the United States – 'Here Comes the Night' (a hit for Ben E. King and for the Irish group Them), the Yardbirds' 'Shapes of Things', 'Friday On My Mind' by the Easybeats, the Animals' 'Don't Bring me Down' and the Who's 'I Can't Explain'.

Others, known only in England, were 'Where Have all the Good Times Gone' by the Kinks, 'Anyway, Anyhow, Anywhere' by the Who, 'Rosalyn' by the Pretty Things, 'I Wish You Would' by the Yardbirds, 'Sorrow' by the Merseys, 'Everythin's All Right' by the Mojos and 'See Emily Play' by Pink Floyd.

David's renditions did little to improve on the originals; it seemed only that he wished to sing the songs, as a tribute, no more, no less. In fact, the liner notes which he provided RCA not only included the names of the bands that first recorded them, but also the names of the London clubs which spawned the bands.

When David completed his album of oldies – to be called *Pin-Ups*, with a cover photograph of David and the popular sixties model Twiggy – at the end of July, David, Angie and Zowie left the château for a holiday in Rome. It was here that David created his next major stage character.

Just as Aladdin Sane was an extension of Ziggy Stardust, the decadent Halloween Jack was an outgrowth of Aladdin Sane. And once again, David moved closer to his personal – as well as his dramatic – apocalypse.

Actually it had begun years earlier, with David's utter fascination with George Orwell's novel *1984*, a stark, futuristic tale about a totalitarian society ruled by the omnipotent, but unseen 'Big Brother'. Written as Orwell was dying of tuberculosis in 1947 and published posthumously a year later, the book presented – or rather projected – the notions of Communist Russia, carried to the extreme, where individual freedom is crushed.

When David re-read the book in 1973 – by which time *1984* had been translated into sixty-two languages, selling ten million copies worldwide – David believed that Orwell was speaking the unwelcome truth, forecasting accurately the future of Western society, and he told Tony DeFries to purchase the performing rights to the book at any cost. He had an idea for something quite different from anything done before: a musical *1984*.

Orwell's estate was controlled by his widow. She hated a British film version made in 1956 and told Tony no. Tony indicated that he was not prepared to take that for a final answer. And then he told David he thought she might be holding out for more money. David continued to work on the show and invited Tony Ingraccia, who had directed the Warholian *Pork*, to come to London to help him stage the show.

While David was writing this new musical, he was enjoying spectacular chart success. By the end of July, 1973, all five of his available albums were in Britain's Top 40 and three (*The Man Who Sold the World*, *Ziggy Stardust* and *Aladdin Sane*) were in the Top 15, an unprecedented event for a solo artist in the post Beatles era. One of them, *Aladdin Sane*, was firmly entrenched at No. 1. Then, while he was recording in France, one of his old labels, Decca, pulled one of his most embarrassing singles from its files, 'The Laughing Gnome', re-released it. It went to No. 6.

The news was less thrilling in America. There, David's records were selling only modestly and several people at RCA were beginning to wonder if their belief in this peculiar British singer hadn't been misplaced. Apart from 'Space Oddity' (which was, by now, ancient history), David had not yet had a Top 10 single, and on the album charts, only *Aladdin Sane* had broken into the Top 20. *Space Oddity*, *Ziggy Stardust* and *Pin-Ups* had gone Top 30, but *Hunky Dory* and *The Man Who Sold the World* had barely gone Top 100. While there was nothing embarrassing about this, it fell far short of what everyone had expected, especially considering how big David was in England

RCA was also upset by the cancelled US tour. Pressure was applied and finally David agreed to allow a television show to be videotaped in London for broadcast by an American network show, *The Midnight Special*. Unwilling to unveil his new Orwellian character prematurely, David further agreed to bring Ziggy back out of the closet for a final appearance. This, of course, was exactly what RCA and Tony DeFries wanted.

But first came Ava Cherry, a thin, black model from Chicago, who remained in David's life for four years.

Angie was still Number One, of course, but the marriage was no more monogamous now than it had been before – if anything, a little less so. After all, Angie *had* caught David in bed with one of his backup singers during the *Pin-Ups* sessions and before that, he had had a brief fling with another singer, for whom he had written 'Lady Grinning Soul'.

At the same time, Angela, who was launching a career of her own in modelling, was talking openly about her own affairs. 'I don't understand this concept of faithfulness in marriage,' she said. 'I am not faithful in an old-fashioned way and neither is David. But that doesn't mean we are apart. I can see nothing that can break the marriage. If I am sleeping with someone and David phones because he needs me, I go right away.'

Angela and Zowie were present during the three days required to tape the television show. David selected the location, the Marquee Club, as well as his guest stars, Marianne Faithfull and the Troggs, who added even more to the nostalgic mood. Even some of the songs he picked came from the *Pin-Ups* album.

However, the costuming and audience came straight out of Ziggy Stardust.

For each song, there was a wardrobe change, each one more outrageous than the last. For the old Who hit, 'Can't Explain', he wore black plastic thigh-length boots with stiletto heels, a bright red plastic corset and two large black feathers joined somewhere around his waist and stretching past his ears. And for 'Jean Genie', he appeared wrapped in fish netting, his right forearm and left leg covered in gold lamé, two strategically placed gold lamé hands covering his chest. (A third hand was to cover his groin, but the NBC staff thought that too suggestive and it was replaced by tights.) A third costume, consisting of little more than a black jock strap, drew louder gasps because a thin moustache of pubic hair showed.

'Oh my God!' someone said after the first recording. 'He'll have to sew that up. We can't use that take.'

Then the director said to David, 'We'll have to do it

again . . . and, David, can you do something to hide your hair?'

David said of course he would and on the next take, every musician in the band deliberately played so badly, that the director was forced to use the original one.

Even Marianne Faithfull got into the mood, wearing a nun's cowl and black cape to sing her duet with David, the old Sonny and Cher hit, 'I Got You Babe'.

The audience, selected from a list of the most loyal Bowie fans, also went along, most of them appearing as Ziggy clones. Tony Visconti came to one day's taping, with his wife, singer Mary Hopkin, and so did long-time friends Lionel Bart and Dana Gillespie. And visiting from New York was that city's best-known rock and roll drag queen, Wayne County, who wore a skirt of inflated condoms in his stage act, but for the Bowie show dressed more conservatively, in thick white make-up, a red négligé and a candy-floss wig. Cherry Vanilla, who knew Wayne from New York, grabbed his fake bosom and shrieked in delight, 'Are they silicone, my dear?'

Wayne merely curtsied in response.

The MainMan organization was bustling. About the same time that David recorded his *Pin-Ups* album, DeFries hired Barry Bethel away from RCA to take over as general manager. DeFries was opposed to the *Pin-Ups* concept and thought it was a total waste of David's talent and time, believing it would set his career back, perhaps irretrievably. Then when David announced his retirement from the stage, forcing cancellation of the million-pound tour of America, DeFries threw up his hands, telling Barry, 'I want to leave. I want to get straight out of this.'

DeFries wanted David back on the road, and he wanted him in the studio, as did RCA. But all David seemed to want in the final months of 1973 was time to 'fiddle about'. He told DeFries he wanted to produce a record by the Astronettes, only one of whom – his old friend Geoff Mac-Cormack (who was now calling himself Warren Peace) – had any musical experience. And he talked incessantly about staging two theatrical productions, one based on the Ziggy Stardust character, the other based on Orwell's *1984*. The trouble was – from Tony's point of view – David wanted to put these productions into a London theatre or on television, neither of which would be very lucrative.

Meanwhile, the money was moving through the Main-Man organization in a torrent, and during the final months of 1973, David was enjoying every pound of it. He had moved out of Haddon Hall and was now living in a three-floor, ten-room Chelsea house owned by actress Diana Rigg, while waiting to move into a £400,000 Victorian mansion in Kensington owned by the actor Richard Harris. This was a house David had wanted for many years. Built by wealthy nineteenth century eccentrics, it had painted Venetian ceilings, dozens of stained glass windows, and Ruritanian turrets, a perfect successor to Haddon Hall.

David still had most of his Beckenham group with him, but now the little 'commune' was being conducted with swagger and style. When he attended plays in London's West End, he travelled in an American limousine. He drank only the best French wines. He planned elaborate practical jokes. For instance, when he was told he was going to win awards from *Melody Maker* magazine for his recording, composing and producing abilities, as well as the single of the year ('Jean Genie'), he sent two friends in his place, having them made over to look exactly like himself and Angela.

'It was what you Yanks call "piss-elegant"' says one who was in the Bowie entourage at the time. 'Angie was still planning a modelling career and calling herself Jipp Jones. So she was bringing in the top photographers. Mick and Bianca were coming over all the time. And so was Ronnie Wood (then with Rod Stewart in the Faces, soon to be with the Rolling Stones). It wasn't exactly a salon, but sometimes it looked that way, with David drifting about in his three-tone spaceman jodhpurs, shirts cut to the navel, serving wine in crystal and talking literature and art.'

Probably the most impressive, or unusual, guest to visit the Bowie flat was writer William Burroughs, who taxied down from his cluttered, two-room flat in Piccadilly in November. David admitted that he hadn't read any of Burroughs' novels except *Nova Express*, and that one just the week before. And Burroughs said he had heard only two of David's songs, both from the Ziggy album. None the less, the two got along famously.

Both admitted to feeling uneasy about the word 'love', said they got many of their ideas from dreams, and shared a common excitement about pornography. (David said he preferred the German films.) They agreed that Andy Warhol was probably alien, or reptilian, because his skin colour wasn't normal. When Burroughs compared some of David's lyrics to the poetry of T. S. Eliot, David responded by saying he was thinking about staging his Ziggy show by mixing up the forty or so scenes in a hat just before the actors went on stage, much as Burroughs cut up a manuscript and reassembled the lines randomly before having them set in type.

'Maybe,' David exuded during the two-hour meeting, 'we are the Rodgers and Hammerstein of the seventies!'

*

In the final months of 1973, David Bowie was being eclipsed by others in the glam or glitter rock genre. Within a month of his announced retirement at the Hammersmith Odeon, Queen released their first album and by Christmas it was on the American charts, the band's fruity costumes, elaborate production and the lead singer's blatently bisexual posturings contributing much to their success. At the same time, Elton John, already an established hit-maker, had crept closer to his own emergence from the bisexual closet by adopting costumes for his stage act which made Ziggy Stardust seem quite conservative (he also had a smash album, *Goodbye Yellow Brick Road*). For much of November and all of December, the No. 1 song in England was either 'I Love You Love Me Love' by the overweight, androgynous, lamé-clad Gary Glitter (a sort of rock and roll Liberace) or 'Merry Christmas, Everybody' by a band of glittery working-class rockers called Slade. (We don't do no rock operas,' they said. 'We're doin' a cock opera.')

In America, Richard Nixon told everyone in November, 'I am not a crook.' And his vice president, Spiro Agnew, practically admitted his own guilt by resigning in face of an indictment for taking bribes while governor of Maryland. The music, meanwhile, was not corrupt, but bland, with No. 1 hits by Ringo Starr ('Photograph'), the Carpenters

('Top Of The World'), Charlie Rich ('The Most Beautiful Girl') and Jim Croce ('Time In A Bottle').

Tony DeFries called David into the MainMan offices to tell him that Mrs Orwell just wasn't interested in selling the theatrical rights to *1984*, at *any* price. Several other projects had fallen by the wayside, too. The Ziggy Stardust show had been abandoned out of boredom and, at the same time, D. A. Pennebaker's documentary of the final Ziggy show, *The Last Concert*, was bogged down in bureaucratic infighting, as Jeff Beck insisted he should be paid a large sum for his two-song contribution and RCA and Tony DeFries squabbled over percentage points. No one was showing any interest in the Astronettes album, the television show taped in the Marquee was broadcast in America to a lukewarm reception, and David's latest single ('Sorrow' backed with Jacques Brel's 'Amsterdam') bombed in the US.

And the money was running out.

When David celebrated his twenty-seventh birthday on 8 January 1974, Tony DeFries suggested that it was time to record a new album and to think about another tour. They weren't broke yet, he said, but if David didn't do something pretty spectacular within six months or so, the chances were good that he would be and David could forget about the worldwide stardom he had worked so hard to achieve.

'Let's look at it reasonably, David,' Tony said. 'You're the biggest star in all of the United Kingdom. No one can touch you here. In America, you're still a minor attraction.'

David looked at his manager, puffing as usual on a Gitane cigarette. 'All right,' he said, finally, 'let's get after it then.'

Previously, David had told friends he had twenty songs for his Orwellian stage show. When he decided to 'go off on a tangent and produce [his] own idea of the story without infringing Orwell's too much,' he cut the number to fourteen, then to eleven, deciding to call the album *Diamond Dogs*, a title he took from the ominous opening monologues, which took the form of a catalogue of ugly images: corpses, fleas, and rats . . . packs of dogs and genocide.

Almost every day during January and February 1974, David was chauffeured to the recording studio in Barnes to flesh out his musical nightmare, working again with Ken Scott, who had co-produced his last four albums. Now, David said, he wanted to do practically everything himself musically, to play all the guitar and saxophone parts as well as the Moog and Mellotron. (Herbie Flowers came in on bass, Mike Garson continued on salary as David's pianist, and Tony Newman and Aynsley Dunbar played drums.) Later, David admitted that taking on so much musical responsibility was frightening. He missed the support of an organized band, he said, and never wanted to be in that position again. But, one by one, the songs went down and the bizarre and apocalyptic visions piled up, like junk left behind in an army's despairing retreat, or in the evacuation of a great city.

In the title song, David introduced his 'hero', Halloween Jack. He was a 'real cool cat', David said, only interested in the latest party. In another song inspired by Orwell, 'Big Brother', David sang about 'a glass asylum'. Even in the love songs, the mood was despairing: 'We'll jump into the river holding hands.'

In the end, Big Brother won, of course, and David closed the album with 'Chant Of The Ever Circling Skeletal Family'. The title said it all.

However grim the message, this was still doom you could dance to. Almost every song was a strong rocker, many of them openly inspired by David's friendship with and respect for Mick Jagger. David's guitar playing, rough as it was, conveyed much of the sinewy intensity of Keith Richard and several of the vocals were Jagger-like in their bluesy cynicism.

Six or seven hours a day, and sometimes more, David was in the studio and however danceable the songs, the overall mood seemed to affect him. 'In those days,' says Ava Cherry, who generally accompanied him everywhere, 'I was cheerful, whereas he could be very dark. If he was working and you went into the room and started talking, he'd scream, "Get out! Get out!"'

Ava says that letters from his mother arrived every week. He refused to answer them, refused to take her calls.

'I'd say, "Why don't you write to your mama?"' Ava says.

'I'll do what I want to do!'

'He complained about her asking for money,' Ava says. 'And he never talked about his brother, who was the subject of his mother's letters. With David, if you knew he didn't want to talk about something, you didn't bring it up. You walked softly. Or you were out.'

Finally the album was complete, except for the final mix. David never felt secure in this area and so he called his old friend Tony Visconti, who by now had left Marc Bolan and was building a recording studio in his home. When David saw the studio – and embraced his friend – he said he wanted to finish the album there.

'But I don't even have any furniture in it,' Tony said.

'That's okay, we'll manage.'

That first day, David and Tony sat in front of the sixteen-track board on carpenter's sawhorses, laughing and talking as they had four years before.

'The next day,' Tony says, 'this big van showed up in front of my house and out came tables, chairs and loungers and all that, and he completely furnished my studio. Plus, when we were hungry, he would send away for meals – and not Chinese or Indian takeaway, but proper steaks and salads and bottles of wine and tablecloths and all that.'

David's mood lightened. As Tony mixed the album, and assisted in the completion of the Astronettes' album, he began calling various Americans to London to discuss a summer tour.

One of the first to arrive was Toni Basil, a fast-talking brunette who had danced on 'go-go' shows in the 1960s and who had had small acting parts in two successful films, *Easy Rider* and *Five Easy Pieces*. She had also choreographed the George Lucas film *American Graffiti* and when David called her, she was leading a group of dancers called the Lockers. (Angela had seen the group and urged David to use her.)

'We talked about the Living Theatre,' Toni says (an improvisational group internationally known for its avant garde plays and ideas). 'We talked about mime. He told me he had wanted Michael Bennett (later the choreographer of *Chorus Line*) to do the show, but he said David was too far out. David had this idea about having ropes tied around the necks of some dancers. When I told him he could do it if he was careful, he yelled at Corinne, 'The Diamond Dogs number is back in!'

Another person called was Jules Fisher, a slender, balding man who had made his name in the theatre, first as a lighting director, then as a producer-director, with credits that included the first American theatrical tour of *Tommy* (using musicians other than the Who and starring Teddy Neeley) and *Lenny*, the Broadway drama based on the life of Lenny Bruce.

Jules liked David. 'He had an attitude,' he says today, 'a perspective of what he wanted, a very clear vision of what it should feel like. And that's what I liked the most, because when an artist can communicate what he really *feels*, he can then leave it up to other artists to execute. If he can express his emotions about it, a painter could give him a backdrop or a scenic designer can do a set, a costumer do costumes and so on. And for *Diamond Dogs*, he had an understanding of German's expressionistic art and film. He wanted that image and I'd seen all of those films. I also knew all the painters he could mention. I felt he was communicating ideas that could be realized on the stage. Very often, rock and roll performers are looking for flash, pizzazz and colour and size, but they don't have a concept behind it: just give me the most light or the brightest light, or the biggest speakers. David Bowie had a concept. He said, "I see a town, like the one in *The Cabinet of Dr Caligai* . . ."'

Another Fritz Lang film was mentioned when David met with a former student of Jules Fisher's, Mark Ravitz. He was called to design the set.

'David gave me three clues,' Mark says. 'Power . . . Nuremberg . . . and Fritz Lang's *Metropolis*.'

It was no mystery why David mentioned Fritz Lang and, especially, *Metropolis*, a film that the German director conceived in 1924 while being detained aboard ship in New York Harbour. Looking at the Manhattan skyline, he plotted a futuristic examination of a conflict between bosses and workers in a society ruled by fear and Big Brother's robots. The similarities to Orwell's novel and David's own vision of the future of western society were obvious.

Mark created three sets, showed them to Jules and then to David when he arrived in New York aboard the S.S.

France on 11 April. David selected the elements he liked. Mark designed a finished model and once David approved that, construction was begun in a warehouse in New Jersey.

What appeared to be tall buildings (done in an eerie sort of art deco style) formed the backdrop, the cityscape inspired by Fritz Lang. Some of the skyscrapers had paper walls, which could be ripped away during the performance (and replaced for the next show). One of them was rigged to 'bleed' large drops of red. A bridge that would lower David to the stage as he was singing connected the tops of the two tallest structures. Out of another wall a giant arm appeared, with a small seat at the end of it, where David was to sing 'Space Oddity' as the illuminated seat moved slowly over the heads of those in the audience. For another song, Jules and Mark were asked to create a remote-controlled, steerable device that looked like a jewel and moved from upstage, then opened like a flower, revealing an interior lit with black light and a giant hand: David wanted to sing while seated on the six-foot hand.

Jules says the set cost at least $250,000. Nor was that all. He says the remote control device that powered the moving jewel – originally designed for an industrial show in Las Vegas, where it was used to drive an empty Ford on stage – alone cost $2,000 a week to rent. Costs escalated far beyond what was planned – so far beyond, in fact, David agreed to abandon his plans to buy Richard Harris' mansion in London and instead use the money to pay for scenery.

None the less, David lived in New York in the style to which he had become accustomed. His suite at the Sherry Netherlands Hotel in midtown Manhattan – his home off and on for the next six months – had tile and marble floors, a fountain in the foyer, a grand piano in the living room, and three large bedrooms. And everywhere he went – to a Broadway play, to the Apollo Theatre in Harlem to see the Temptations, the Spinners and Marvin Gaye, to a rehearsal with his band, to look at the scenery under construction or to work with Toni Basil on the choreography – he travelled by chauffeured limousine. His companions were invariably a bodyguard, and a gorgeous woman – usually Ava Cherry, who remained on the MainMan payroll and now had her hair cut short and bleached white, so that she looked, as one writer put it, like a Negro tennis ball.

Diamond Dogs was released a week after David arrived in New York, two months before the start of the tour. David was proud of the album, telling friends that it was his 'protest', a 'supercool' statement of 'indifference'. It was, he said, 'more me than anything I've done previously.'

The critical reaction ranged from love to hate. Predictably, the British press was deferential. Chris Charlesworth, noting in *Melody Maker* that by now David Bowie albums were greeted 'with as much awe as a release by the Beatles in the sixties', compared the production to that of the American producer Phil Spector, noted for his 'wall of sound', and pronounced the album 'really good'. And the writer in *Sound* said *Diamond Dogs* was David's 'most impressive work since *Ziggy Stardust*.'

At the other extreme was Ken Emerson in *Rolling Stone*. He called it 'Bowie's worst album in six years', said David's guitar playing was 'cheesy', that David had lost his voice, and that his lyrics, once noted for their complexity and clarity, were now simplistic and murky. 'Most of the songs are obscure tangles of perversion, degradation, fear and self-pity . . . It's difficult to know what to make of them. Are they masturbatory fantasies, guilt-ridden projections, terrified premonitions, or is it all merely Alice Cooper exploitation? Unfortunately, the music exerts so little appeal that it's hard to care what it's about. And *Diamond Dogs* seems more like David Bowie's last gasp than the world's.'

Even the cover art was controversial. Painted by the Belgian artist Guy Peellaert, who had published a book of brilliant rock portraits called *Rock Dreams*, it showed David transformed into a dog. In the original, the dog was clearly male, but RCA blanched at the open display of a canine sex organ and had the offensive penis painted out. Of course this only served to fan the flames still warming the argument about David's sexual ambiguity. (The cover also fired a feud between David and his friend Mick Jagger, who had planned to use Peellaert for the Rolling Stones' next album and had told David about the artist in the first place.)

During the last week of April, all of May, and the beginning of June (as the album slowly climbed the American charts) David watched his show come together. With Toni Basil he improvized choreography, standing one day on the bridge holding two ropes which were tied to two men (Diamond Dogs) below. ('A lot of the choreography was geometry,' Tony says, 'using patterns formed by ropes.') Suddenly David got an idea. By using the same ropes in another manner, he could form a square and incorporate some shadowboxing.

'He was just extraordinary,' Toni says. 'I learned much more from him than he ever got from me. For one song, "Sweet Thing", I gave him an idea and *he* did the choreography. And on another song, "Suffragette City", all I said was "Let's do James Dean", and he took it from there, turning his back on the audience as he left the stage, to create the sullen, brooding Dean character.

'I've never met anyone who could think so fast on his feet. The bridge broke when he was on it. It was the first day of rehearsal with the set, a few days before the tour started. As the bridge was falling, he calculated precisely when it would hit, jumping into the air just before the crash to avoid the shock.'

For the first time, most of the band members were Americans. Herbie Flowers, who played bass on many of his records going back to 'Space Oddity', agreed to leave his lucrative London recording scene for the tour. So did Tony Newman, who had played drums on the album. But everyone else he found in New York – Michael Kamen (who had led an avant garde band called the New York Rock and Roll Ensemble, which mixed classical music with rock) as musical director, Earl Slick on guitar, Richard Grando and Dave Sanborn on baritone and alto sax, and Pablo Rosario on percussion. Gui Andrisano and his old friend Geoff MacCormack sang backing vocals and took the roles of the Diamond Dogs.

On 14 June 1974, the huge Montreal Forum filled quickly with thousands of Ziggy clones, young men and women with their hair cut short and dyed various colours, lightning bolts bisecting their faces, stacked heels and wearing gold lamé. None of them, nor the straighter, more conservatively dressed members of the audience, were prepared for what they saw.

The house lights went down and the stage lights went up, revealing Hunger City, as David's voice intoned the opening 'legend' from the *Diamond Dogs* album: 'And in the Death as the last few corpses lay rotting on the slimey thorough-fares . . .'

Then David appeared wearing flat shoes and a grey suit, his bleached blond hair parted in the middle and combed back in waves. He didn't exactly look like a businessman. More like a hipster in baggy, pleated pants. But nothing at all like what was expected.

The show itself was another shock, as the bridge rose and fell on cue, skyscrapers spurted blood, Major Tom zoomed slowly over the audience at the end of a pneumatic arm, and the mirrored, rolling jewel opened to reveal David descending on a purple hand. The Diamond Dogs allowed themselves to be tied up with ropes. Then David was wrapped in the same white ropes. It seemed kinky, but so well rehearsed it was emotionless. David moved from one song directly into the next. As the bridge reached the stage at the end of a song he went directly into 'Ch-ch-ch-changes!' And from that into 'Suffragette City', 'All The Young Dudes' and 'Will You Rock And Roll With Me Tonight'. Then David bowed grandly and the house lights went up.

Was this a rock and roll show, or what? Where was the band? (Actually they were on the right, labouring anony-mously in the dark much like a Broadway orchestra stuck somewhere in a pit.) During the intermission, the audience chattered. It was good, but what was it? And what was David doing in a *suit*?

The second act opened with 'Watch That Man', followed by 'Drive-In Saturday', David's only acoustic number in the show. After that came 'Space Oddity' with David pro-jected into the air over the audience, with multi-coloured flashing lights. The sado-masochistic rope routine illus-trated 'Diamond Dogs' and it was while singing 'Panic in Detroit' that he wore boxing shorts and stabbed at the air with big red gloves (his bodyguard Huey towelling him down between verses). 'Jean Genie', 'Big Brother' and 'Time' followed that – sung from the rolling jewel – and then came 'Rock And Roll Suicide' and it was all over. There was no encore. There wasn't even a bow at the end.

A few minutes later a voice intoned over the public address system, 'David Bowie has already left the auditorium!' Just like Elvis Presley.

The next day they were in Ottawa and after that in Toronto and then the caravan of limousines, buses and trucks moved south into the United States to perform thirty-three shows in thirty-two days throughout the Northeast and South.

By the time the group rolled into Philadelphia on 8 July, it all ran together: places, people, and scenes. Toronto? That was where one of the security guards tried to throw Angela out of the auditorium. Detroit? That was where the first night's show was cancelled because there was a high school graduation in the afternoon, which would have left the Bowie road crew only three hours to assemble a set which demanded twelve. Memphis? That was the city David had to hitchhike to reach, after his limousine broke down somewhere outside Nashville. Tampa? That was the show they performed without sets because a bee flew into the cabin of one of the trucks and the driver ran off the road and into a swamp.

The rest was a terrible, buzzing blur.

Part of it was the result of the exhausting, almost impossible schedule. To get from one city to the next, the stage crew had to tear down the set as soon as the show was over, load everything into trucks whose drivers then drove all night, delivering the pieces to a weary stage crew for reassembly the next morning. The musicians got only a little more sleep and David, still afraid of flying, travelled from city to city sleeping in a limousine.

With this sort of routine, uppers and cocaine – always available – were inevitable. And as the tour progressed, they were everywhere, and consumed in enormous quantity.

Initially on the tour, there were good times. Herbie Flowers remembers the practical jokes the band played on DeFries, calling room service to order a dozen cheeseburgers in his name at every hotel they stayed in . . . later calling him on the telephone and telling him to stick his head out of the window to see something very strange, then dousing him with a bucket of water from above when he did.

But soon enough the good humour was replaced with cocaine-induced paranoia. On more than one occasion, Herbie says, several members of the band insisted upon changing hotels because of the 'vibes' they felt.

'It got that ugly,' he says today. 'It got that oppressive. A lot of that was cocaine-induced.

The worst was in Philadelphia.'

CRACKED ACTOR

The show in the City of Brotherly Love was booked into the Tower Theatre for 14 and 15 June and on the second day it was announced that a live album would be recorded. That was when Herbie led a band revolt.

'Probably David asked me to do the Diamond Dogs tour because he knew it was going to be a long, long tour and he needed somebody he could socialize with,' Herbie says today. 'And we got on very well for a while, until through seniority I became like the trade union representative for the musicians. It was suggested that we should share rooms and I said no. Then when we heard they were going to record a live album, I confronted David about it.'

Herbie had talked with the other musicians. 'Herbie went nuts,' says Mike Garson. '"How can they do this without our permission! How come we're not getting paid? How come there's no contracts? We're not going on!" So we agreed that we weren't going on stage that night unless we got paid. We figured out how much the album was going to make. Minimally, we figured it out to be a million dollars. We said we're ten people, we want fifty thousand dollars – five thousand each.'

Herbie went to David's dressing room a half-hour before show time. DeFries was there, along with Pablo Rosario, one of the band members, and Corinne Schwab, who was now being credited on the show programme as David's personal assistant. Herbie asked DeFries what he planned to pay the musicians for the album.

'Well,' said Tony DeFries, 'you'll get the seventy dollars union rate for a live album.'

The tall, English bassist looked at DeFries, then at David, and back to DeFries again. 'No,' he said. 'We want five thousand dollars. Apiece.'

DeFries was aghast. 'Never!' he said. 'We're losing money

on every date. You saw the half-empty houses in the south! We don't have it! You'll bankrupt us! We'll have to cancel the tour!'

Herbie was unmoved. 'One other thing,' he said. 'We want the money now, or we won't go on the stage tonight.'

David had remained silent during the heated conversation. But suddenly he picked up a chair and threw it at Herbie. Herbie ducked and the chair crashed against the dressing room wall.

Herbie looked at David and then at DeFries and said, 'That'll cost you a bonus for the stage crew.'

Herbie and the band members won. Before they went on to perform that night, and record a double album for immediate RCA release, Tony DeFries wrote out ten cheques for $5,000, smaller cheques for the crew.

The show that began – thirty minutes late – was spectacular. It was as if all the pressure in the world was being released. 'I can claim to be a genius for setting up the tension before we did the show,' Herbie says, 'because when we went on stage, the feeling of liberation in the band was glorious!'

From Philadelphia, the caravan travelled north to Boston and Hartford and then back to New York for two nights at Madison Square Garden.

There was a six-week break after that, as RCA rushed the live album for quick release. The idea was that the new double album would then help promote the second half of the tour, set to begin the first week of September. Herbie says he didn't wait around. He went back to England instead.

'I'll be honest with you,' he says today. 'If I'd a done the second half of the tour, I'd a died. That was the one time in my life when I thought I could get by with artificial support [cocaine]. I mean, I'm not saying who did what, but it was the one irresponsible period in my life I was thankful to escape from. For a week I stayed locked in my room at the Gramercy Park Hotel with a married couple looking after me. Then they put me on the S.S. *France* with someone else travelling with me to look after me. I got home in one piece and my wife said, "If you ever do that again,

I'm leaving you." It was a weird one, I'm telling you. And I was not alone.'

*

The band scattered and David went into the late Jimi Hendrix's Electric Lady Studio in Greenwich Village in an attempt to salvage the live album recorded in Philadelphia. What had been considered a great performance had not made the jump from the stage to tape. Tony Visconti had wanted to be present during the recording, but his car broke down, so several of the instruments hadn't been miked properly. Worse, David's voice revealed either exhaustion or the effect of too much cocaine; high notes were missed.

'If you listen to the recording now,' Tony says, 'you'll hear that it's very brittle and lacks depth, and for the twelve or so musicians he had on stage, it's very puny. Also, it had to be put out, it was a contractual thing. RCA was crying for another album and they just threw it out. It was one of the quickest and shoddiest albums I've ever done.'

None the less, it was an honest album. Of the seventeen songs on the two-disc set, David refused to re-record a single note of his vocal parts. The only parts re-recorded were the backing vocals. Because Geoff and Gui were dancing as well as singing, generally when they reached the microphones, they were out of breath.

'We could have fooled the public by making it very glossy,' Tony Visconti says, 'but we didn't have the time.'

The photographs on the album sleeve showed David at his thinnest yet, cast in a sickly blue. 'God, that album!' David later exclaimed. 'I've never played it. The tension it must contain must be like a vampire's teeth coming down on you. And that photo on the cover! My God, it looks like I've just stepped out of the grave. That's actually how I felt. The record is called *David Live*, but it should have been called *David Bowie Is Alive and Living Only in Theory*.'

Making things infinitely worse was David's disintegrating relationship with his manager.

David was arguing openly with DeFries by now. Tony was telling David to go back to the Ziggy Stardust character.

'Look at the audience!' Tony said. 'They *want* Ziggy.'

David merely shook his head. Later he admitted to being

somewhat unnerved by the Ziggy clones. 'It was very odd to see quite a large number of young people following a theatrical character, adopting the stance of a character that didn't exist at all, and a lifestyle that hadn't been created, and developing one of their own. They created their own *lifestyle* for Ziggy. They'd write and tell me of their communications with Mars and stuff. It got quite far out. It got very bizarre.'

'Talk about rock and roll suicide!' DeFries cried. 'Bring Ziggy back, mate, or that's what you'll be doing.'

David still shook his head. Ziggy was a character that David had grown tired of, bored by and mad at. Surely there was more to life than Ziggy Stardust. And what about the music? What about what *David* wanted?

This was not the only field of conflict, although the others were related.

'Tony did a tie-up with Woolworth's,' says Barry Bethel, who had left MainMan the previous spring. 'It was for the official David Bowie bust. Tony went to Woolworth's and said, "You can have it worldwide, but we want a royalty and you must buy it off of us." And they signed a contract. Woolworth's bought the bust from DeFries, who had it manufactured, so DeFries made a profit from having it manufactured as well as on the sales. There were posters, T-shirts, photographs. The merchandizing became so big. And RCA never had the rights to anything. Even if RCA wanted to sell a poster of the album cover, they had to pay DeFries.

'DeFries treated RCA with complete and total and utter contempt. He renegotiated David's contract once a month. You could not beat DeFries when it came to the law. Because of his incredible memory, he'd find a loophole somewhere. And he'd made incredible deals for himself. The deal he made for Lulu's album was an amazing example' – of the half dozen parties involved (CBS, RCA, DeFries, Lulu, David and Lulu's manager), where one would normally expect a fairly equitable division of the income, it was DeFries who took the lion's share. 'He got RCA to put up the money for the recording. He got CBS to waive all royalties. He got Lulu's manager to do the same with his commission. The rest was divided between David Bowie and Tony DeFries and Tony got half of David's share as manager. It was very clever.'

Worse was the way Tony was promoting David's recent records. When *Diamond Dogs* was released, he invited writers into the MainMan office in New York and let them listen but refused to give them copies to take home. Said Chris Charlesworth, who was writing for *Melody Maker*, 'I was supposed to do a big review and I wanted to hear it several times, as any reviewer would. They let me hear it once and wouldn't give me a lyric sheet. They even took my tape recorder out of my pocket as I entered the office so I wouldn't secretly tape it. Some offensive, gay bloke with a moustache took it. They said they didn't want me to take it to a radio station.'

Others who wrote about the album worked under the same restrictive conditions, resulting in inaccuracies and great holes, or leaps in continuity.

Mystery was one thing, but now David wondered: wasn't the music suffering?

Perhaps worst of all was the money. The big money had finally begun to arrive in the wake of David's enormous success at home in England and also growing acceptance in Europe, Japan and America. Barry Bethel remembers seeing a cheque for more than a million dollars from RCA for record royalties. Other large cheques came in from the publishing company. DeFries owned half of the publishing company, so took 50 per cent of that off the top, *then* took 50 per cent of David's share as manager, *plus* expenses for administering the publishing company. This gave DeFries enormous amounts of cash to play with. Which he did, with great relish, Bethel says, spending days moving it from country to country, according to the fluctuating value of the American dollar, the English pound or the Swiss franc, sometimes making as much as fifty thousand dollars profit in a week. All of which went into his pocket. There was nothing illegal about this activity, but David never shared in the windfalls and because it was, in a sense, *his* money that Tony was playing with, close friends say David grew resentful.

When David signed away 50 per cent of his income to DeFries and agreed to pay for all expenses besides, he had no income. But now he had a significant income, and he really had nothing to show for it. True, he was living like a king, but it was in a rented hotel room in New York, after all. While in London there was only another temporary flat, and no property except for some cars and furniture in storage and a sizeable but largely unusable wardrobe.

David wondered where his half of the proceeds was going. DeFries told him that it cost a lot to keep an act his size and importance on the road or in New York. That was true, too, but David was hearing stories about extreme extravagance. By now, MainMan had become synonymous in the music business for lavish waste. There were more than twenty on the payroll, including artists who were waiting for their albums to be finished or released (Dana Gillespie, Ava Cherry), friends and regular sidemen (Geoff MacCormack, Mike Garson), and various senior tour commanders, plus all the freaky office staff.

Most of these individuals travelled by limousine everywhere, and there were trips back and forth from London to New York almost constantly. Sometimes there were trips to places as far away as Rio de Janeiro.

The offices, in London's Gunter Grove and on Manhattan's posh Park Avenue, were filled with expensive, flashy furnishings. Even the MainMan matches that Tony had made came with little gold striking heads.

And David was paying for all of it.

It was, he said later, a bad time for him. For the first time, he could see the day when he and Tony would separate, perhaps by the beginning of the following year, although he knew that it would not be easy; his contract had another eight years to go.

Aggravating these problems for David was his cocaine abuse. According to Ava Cherry and others around him, it was accelerating at an alarming rate, and with excessive cocaine use inevitably comes paranoia, as David and the others had discovered on tour when strange vibes drove them from hotel to hotel.

'Some of the concert promoters began talking to David, telling him how much he was making,' Ava said. 'There was one promoter that handled several shows and he got close to David and David was amazed when he heard the figures. He had no idea at all.' This, and the cocaine, convinced him. By the time he reached New York, it was very clear to him: DeFries was the only one getting rich. And it was 'his' money that was doing it.

None the less, it continued to be a creatively productive time. For David, cocaine was not a recreational drug. David was a workaholic and a man who insisted upon remaining in control. Thus, cocaine, and amphetamines, were used not for fun and games or escape (as they were used by many rock stars), but solely and exclusively for work, much as amphetamines first were used by German Luftwaffe pilots in the Second World War to increase mental alertness and the number of flights per week.

In the six-week period between halves of the 1974 tour, there were several pressing chores. As RCA moved the live album towards the marketplace, David began frequenting the New York clubs, looking for new sidemen for his backing band, to replace those lost to coke and the friction that had developed on the first half of the tour. He also had in mind another studio album, which he wanted to begin recording as soon as possible.

It was while appearing in Philadelphia at the Tower Theatre that David visited the Sigma Sound Studio, to watch Ava Cherry record a song for the still-in-progress album by the Astronettes. This was the studio made famous by Kenny Gamble and Leon Huff, producers of the 'Philly Sound', a blend of soul and funk. Still enamoured of black music, David decided he wanted to return to that studio to record an album, so while in New York, he began looking for musicians who fit the black/Latin sound that he nowadays heard in his head.

He and Geoff and Ava returned again and again to the Apollo Theatre, where he spotted Carlos Alomar playing guitar for a band called the Main Ingredient. (Richard Pryor was the opening act that night.) David went backstage and talked to Carlos about going on tour and recording with him. Carlos, in turn, suggested that David add his wife, Robin, to his backup vocal group, and he recommended a drummer, Dennis Davis (to take the place of Tony Newman, who had returned to England with Herbie Flowers).

At the same time, Mike Garson suggested another drummer, Andy Newmark (both drummers were eventually used), and he urged David to hire Willie Weeks, the black bassist. Then Ava Cherry introduced David to an unknown, 300-pound black soul singer named Luther Vandross. David was reluctant to hire Luther because he was so large, but finally agreed, recognizing the fact that a favourite singer of his, Barry White, was just as big.

David called Tony Visconti in London, told him he had a new band and wanted Tony to produce his new album. When Tony heard Willie Weeks was playing bass, he said, 'I'll be on the next plane.'

'The session was booked for four and I arrived at the hotel at five and just ran to the studio, really jetlagged,' Tony says. 'David arrived at midnight. He was very thin in those days and living sort of reversed hours. He was going to bed at about eleven in the morning and all that. However, on that very first night of recording, there was such an electrifying atmosphere in the air that we recorded, that evening, "Young Americans".'

Destined to be David's biggest American hit since 'Space Oddity', this was what David later described as a song about 'a newly-wed couple who don't know if they really like each other.' This was a perfect analogy, for David was, himself, unsure whether he really liked America. No matter what, or how, he felt, the song showed David at his most American, able to write American lyrics with American rhythms backing them. In the image-crammed lyric, there were references to the ghetto, to the bills that young marrieds pay, even to former President Nixon. And behind it and under it and surrounding it were the jazzy saxophone cries of David Sanborn, the Latin percussion of Pablo Rosario, the rhythm and blues voice of big Luther Vandross. Thus, David blended three distinctive American musical sounds. Later, David called it 'plastic soul', but there was no denying the exuberance and danceability.

Work on the album continued for two weeks, with most sessions starting about nine in the evening and lasting until the following afternoon. Usually, David was late and, according to the musicians, invariably he was stoned.

'I remember three things about the Young Americans sessions,' says one of the musicians. 'First, I remember

David waiting several hours for coke to be delivered from New York and he wouldn't perform until it came. The next thing I remember is everyone used to fall asleep in the studio, except for David, who stayed awake on coke. And third, I remember making a lot of money from being in the studio for hundreds of hours, but playing only fifteen minutes' worth. There was so much wasted time.'

None the less, an impressive body of work was recorded and sequenced and dubbed on to a handful of cassette tapes for David to take back on the road with him when the tour resumed.

The opening track was yet another version of one of David's older songs, 'John, I'm Only Dancing', edited from a two-hour jam – six minutes of solid rhythm and blues. All of the others were new, including two ballads, the autobiographical 'Who Can I Be This Time?' and 'It's Gonna Be Me'. All of this material would eventually be deleted from the album before its release. (David had also taped two songs by a young Bruce Springsteen, who had hitchhiked to Philadelphia from his home in northern New Jersey, to spend the night sleeping on a couch in the studio reception area.)

One song included on the initial tape which made it on to the final version took as its title a phrase familiar to most Americans as the title of the Rocky Graziano biography and film (starring Paul Newman), 'Somebody Up There Likes Me'. Showcasing some of his best Stevie Wonder vocal effects, David advised his listeners to 'keep your eye on your soul, keep your hand on your heart.'

Others that made the final cut included 'Win', in which David announced, 'I say it's hip to be alive' and a reworking of Luther Vandross's 'Funky Music (Is A Part Of Me)', retitled 'Fascination'. (Vandross shares co-composer credit on the song.)

Suddenly, Tony DeFries came down from New York and there was a loud unpleasant confrontation. DeFries didn't like David's new music and he was openly worried about his habitual use of drugs. David was going to throw his career away, Tony said, and, more immediately, David was going to be unable to go back on the road in September.

David told Tony to mind his own business.

DeFries said that that was what he was doing – minding the business . . . and it was about time that David started doing the same.

David told DeFries to go screw himself.

That ended it. The sessions were nearly over, and David was just fine-tuning the songs and having the musicians wait around until he decided the final sequencing. Tony Visconti flew back to England and the band members went back to New York to wait for a call, while David and DeFries continued to fight. Now DeFries told David he didn't want Ava Cherry to go on the tour, but wanted her to remain in New York instead, to work with a new producer. Again, David said no. David also said he didn't want to take the Diamond Dogs set on the road with him again. He said it was too expensive and that half of the time something didn't work.

Tony DeFries urged David to take it to Los Angeles at least, where David was expected to perform for a week at the Universal Amphitheatre, a 3500-seat concert bowl behind Universal Studios. This was a major venue, Tony said, a major media marketplace. David agreed, although reluctantly.

The new live album was not yet in the shops when David and his band arrived in Los Angeles on 1 September. Right away, David broke one of the cardinal rules of promotion: in talking with Robert Hilburn of the *Los Angeles Times*, he declined to talk about the just-released live album, but played *Young Americans* (which wouldn't be released for another six months) instead.

'My record company doesn't like me to do this,' David said. 'But I'm so excited about this one . . . and it can tell you more about where I am now than anything I could say.'

The album didn't have its final title – at the time it was being called *One Damn Song* – and within a few months, David would replace several of the songs, but it was clear to Hilburn that David, again, had changed. (A fact the writer also noted by describing what David wore that day: black tuxedo trousers, a blue-and-white checked shirt, bold white suspenders and black shoes.) David agreed. In his previous albums, he said he used 'science fiction patterns because I was trying to put forward concepts, ideas and theories, but this album hasn't anything to do with that. It's just emotional drive. It's one of the first albums I've done that bounds along on emotional impact. There's not a concept in sight.

'I think I always know when to stop doing something,' he said. 'It's when the enjoyment is gone. That's why I've changed so much. I've never been of the opinion that it's necessarily a wise thing to keep on a successful streak if you're just duplicating all the time. That's why I tend to be erratic. It's not a matter of being indulgent, I don't think. It's just a case of making sure I'm not bored, because if I'm bored, then people can see it. I don't hide it very well. Everything I do I get bored with eventually. It's knowing where to stop.'

Of course, there was no stopping the Diamond Dogs juggernaut yet, although after leaving Los Angeles, David completely abandoned the complicated lights and sets and began incorporating some of the songs from the new album. From this point forward, as he played well-scattered dates in San Diego, Tucson and Phoenix in September, and in Madison, Detroit and Chicago in October, the show was called, unofficially, the 'Philly Dogs' tour.

The week in Los Angeles was by far the most important leg of the tour, because it was here that his long-languishing film 'career' began to catch fire. In the audience one night was the film star Elizabeth Taylor and a few days later, David was invited to her home to talk about appearing in a film with her which was to be the first cinematic co-production between the US and the USSR. The collaboration, like so many in Hollywood, never happened. The film was made, after much difficulty, but David and Elizabeth didn't work together. David came away from the meeting impressed, however – in part because she compared him to an actor she had co-starred with many years before, James Dean.

More important to his potential film career was a documentary that was made in Los Angeles by the BBC. The producer, a twenty-six-year-old intellectual named Alan Yentob, wanted to explore David's influences.

'He was of the generation who borrowed a lot,' Alan says today. 'When I started, I wanted to make a film about him

The modest Bromley terrace house – David's home through adolescence and into early manhood

Bowie (*centre, second row from back*) in a class picture at Bromley Tech

A Beckenham 'arts lab' hippy, 1969

Trevor Bolder, Mick Woodmansey, Ziggy Stardust, and Mick Ronson – Ziggy Stardust and the Spiders from Mars

The Spiders in Japan, 1973

Angie Bowie at the premiere of *The Man Who Fell to Earth*

Zowie with Kansai Yamamoto's son in Tokyo

On stage, 1978

In 1980: *Ashes to Ashes* publicity shot

A still from *The Man Who Fell to Earth*

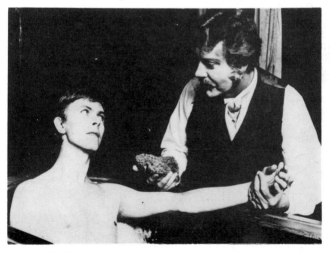

With Ken Ruta in a scene from *The Elephant Man*

In triple drag for a video

David at the US Festival in 1983, his first American
performance in five years

called *The Collector* – about this man who seemed to adopt other people's gestures, other people's presences or personalities. There he was, like a chameleon, changing shape, changing sound, and there were lots of allusions in his records, references to movies and all sorts of things that postwar children had been brought up with. It was a period when people were beginning to see all those Fritz Lang, Buster Keaton, and Judy Garland movies. So everything had to do with collecting things which belonged to another generation . . . and putting them together again. He was a very eclectic singer.

'Also, he was part of the art school movement. He was a bit arty. The dressing-up stuff. The costumes. The pretensions. He was rather pretentious, but always adventurous. He was always trying to get engaged with ideas. He absolutely and emphatically did not come out of the mainstream of rock and roll. He came out of something else. He came out of a side door.'

Yentob's observations were valid. David was all the things that the young producer believed he was, but in the end, Yentob made a different film. David wasn't prepared, or willing, to provide the sort of input Yentob felt he needed for *The Collector*. So in the end, the film was about a pop star in search of identity.

Yentob worked with a freelance film crew hired in Los Angeles and went backstage – capturing David while he applied his concert make-up – and then travelled with him in a limousine across the arid Southwest. David chatted amiably with the film-makers and with Coco, whose job it was to protect him from outsiders. David, of course, was very good at that himself, and in the BBC film – eventually called *Cracked Actor* and broadcast several months later – however fascinating he was, he revealed very little. Even the in-performance scenes filmed at the Universal Amphitheatre seemed almost stilted. The overall effect was somewhat mysterious, opaque, impenetrable.

Perhaps David was getting bored, as he had warned.

At the end of October, David was back in New York for a week in Radio City Music Hall and in November he was off again, performing another well-scattered series of one-nighters in Cleveland, Buffalo, Washington, Uniondale,

Memphis, Nashville, Atlanta and Tuscaloosa, three days in Boston and a week in Philadelphia.

There followed an appearance on Dick Cavett's show *Wide World of Entertainment*. Again, David seemed elusive, disinterested.

Cavett, appearing without a tie, asked, 'What kind of a person would you describe yourself as?'

'I'm a person of diverse interest. I'm not very academic.'

Cavett remained serious, almost intense: 'What does your mother think of you?'

'She pretends I'm not hers. We've never been that close, but we have an understanding.'

Almost all his answers were similarly brief and the image the viewer was left with had David poking the carpet with a cane and sniffing continually, a reaction, perhaps, to his continuing use of cocaine.

It wasn't *all* boring. On Thanksgiving Day, back in New York, David called a young recording engineer named Harry Maslin, who worked at the Record Plant, one of Manhattan's most popular studios. Maslin had worked with Bonnie Raitt, James Taylor, Carly Simon, Dionne Warwick and Martha Reeves. David told him he wanted to finish the *Young Americans* album, so he could go home to London for Christmas.

RCA had thought the album was complete, but when David met John Lennon one night at the Record Plant studios, things changed. It seemed logical that he and John Lennon record a song together about their respective hassles with managers. (Lennon was still reeling from the Beatles breakup and trying to disentangle himself from manager Allen Klein.) This was the song called 'Fame'.

'With John Lennon it was more the influence of having him in the studio that helped,' David said later. 'There's always a lot of adrenalin flowing when John is around, but his chief addition to it all was the high-pitched singing of "Fame". The riff came from Carlos [Alomar], and the melody and most of the lyrics came from me, but it wouldn't have happened if John hadn't been there. He was the energy, and that's why he's got a writing credit for writing it; he was the inspiration.'

The two singers also recorded 'Across the Universe', an

old Lennon composition originally released by the Beatles. Both songs were recorded quickly, in a single evening. Later, Lennon said he didn't even remember the sessions – he shared David's fascination with coke at the time, and in addition was drinking heavily – but for David it remained a peak experience.

'You know what Glam Rock is, doncha?' Lennon asked one day.

'No,' said David, 'what?'

'It's just rock and roll,' John said, 'with lipstick on.'

David loved that.

John's impact on David was significant. Until meeting John, David had believed there was somebody better at managing than he could be himself, that business and art never mixed comfortably or efficiently. John told David that that wasn't true, that artists *could* manage themselves.

'It wasn't until Lennon pointed it out to me that I realized maybe the artist is as good at managing as anybody else,' David said later. 'It was John that sorted me out all the way down the line. He took me on one side, sat down, and told me what it was all about, and I realized I was very naive. I still thought you had to have somebody else who dealt with these things called contracts . . .'

Within a few weeks of talking with John, David sent a telegram to Tony DeFries informing him that his and MainMan's services no longer would be needed.

'It was not a pleasant experience, the breakup,' says Ava Cherry, who lived with David during the last months of 1974 and the first of 1975. 'It got crazy. That was when David said we had to leave the hotel and move where Tony couldn't find us, so we moved into a town house on 21st Street. Every incident was a firecracker. David exploded with rage. He was very, very upset. He'd say, "This guy is embezzling my money!" He got hysterical.'

In the midst of all this, a quirky, intellectual English film-maker named Nicolas Roeg entered David's life, offering yet more change.

Nic was a cinematographer who had worked with a number of top directors, including David Lean (*Lawrence of Arabia*), Clive Donner (*The Caretaker*), François Truffaut (*Fahrenheit 451*) and Richard Lester (*Petulia*), before co-directing Mick Jagger and Edward Fox in *Performance* and making his solo directorial debut in *Walkabout*. *Performance* was a puzzling examination of identity, telling the story of a gangster-on-the-run (Edward Fox) who moved in with a reclusive, androgynous rock star (Mick Jagger) and what happened when their bizarre lifestyles were forcibly intertwined. It was an excessive, uneven film that verged on self-indulgence and pretentiousness, but one which virtually howled with ideas and had, in the end, enough style and excitement to make it an instant cult classic. *Walkabout* was a much simpler film, telling the story of two children lost in the Australian wilderness, dependent upon an aboriginal boy for survival.

Nic Roeg's second directorial assignment was the one David knew best. This was a supernatural suspense film based on the Daphne du Maurier story, *Don't Look Now*, starring Julie Christie and Donald Sutherland and released in 1973. The critics loved it. The audience did not.

David was one of the 'critics'. So when David was sent an early script of *The Man Who Fell To Earth*, which was to be Nic Roeg's third film (written by his friend, Paul Mayersberg), David read the screenplay instantly. Liking it, he agreed to a meeting in February.

Roeg was attracted to David through Alan Yentob's documentary, *Cracked Actor*, which had been broadcast by the BBC earlier that year. 'Watching that film,' Nic says today, 'he was my film's character, Mr Newton. My reaction was, "That's him all right, all wrapped up and done." I went to New York and David said, "Come round to the house." Coco let me in and said he was recording and would be back later, could I wait? So we sat talking and every hour or so he'd call in. Finally, after eight hours, he turned up. He was very bright, very charming, aloof but with good manners. We talked about the project. I like to do that. I thought I could get a good sense of what his feelings were. Dawn was coming up. I was anxious, I wanted him so badly, he sensed that. Towards the end of our talk, I told him, "You must . . . you *must* tell me."'

David replied, 'No matter what you hear, I will be there.'

*

It was January 1975. Gerald Ford was in the White House and four of Nixon's assistants had just been found guilty in the Watergate coverup trials. John Lennon, still fighting deportation, had released a new album and begun a five-year 'retirement'. *The Wiz* was a hit on Broadway and Elton John had the most popular song in America, 'Lucy in the Sky With Diamonds', as well as the bestselling LP.

David and Angela had drifted far apart. They had spent Christmas together in New York with Zowie, but that was about it. Except for her presence at the opening dates of the Diamond Dogs tour, they hadn't seen each other in nearly eighteen months. They talked frequently by telephone, but, as she told London's *Daily Express*, 'We're too much alike to be in love. We were only in love for a very short time. I don't understand the term "husband". I never really think of David as a husband. He's like my brother.'

Besides, Angie said, she had a career of her own to consider. She was being managed by Barry Bethel, who was sending her on interviews for acting jobs. She was also busy establishing a reputation for being as shocking as David was.

'We walked into the White Elephant restaurant on Curzon Street,' says Barry, 'and sitting at the table opposite me was a cabinet minister. Michael Caine was down at the other end. And I was there with Ken Glancey (RCA's head man in London), waiting for Angela. And she turned up. She had on the most beautiful gown, it was absolutely superb. Only trouble was, she was waring it back-to-front. She took off her coat and there were two Bristols glaring merrily at the cabinet minister.

'I mean, she just had to have attention. She managed that quite well over in the States. She went on the Dick Cavett show. She sat down for a little while and she started to get bored, which is the worst possible thing that can happen to her. So she took a tit out. And Dick Cavett said, "Ummm, well, Angela, guess it's hot in here, isn't it?" And she said, "No, you just weren't talking to me. You are now, though, aren't you?" This was live! It was headlines the next day!

'She was completely outrageous. She just didn't give a damn. But she had a heart of gold, an absolute heart of gold. I'll never forget when Barbara, my wife, fell very, very ill. This was when I was still with MainMan and there was no way I could go to work, I was going to stay home and look after my wife. Apparently Angela phoned up the office and said, "Where's Barry?" They told her and she phoned me at home and two hours later there's a knock at the door: "How dya do? I'm a private nurse. Angela Bowie has sent me round to look after your wife." The private nurse was costing £400 a day. Flowers arrived. Chocolates. I mean, she had an incredible heart.'

David's conflict with DeFries was getting worse. David handled the stress by *not* handling it, by running away to California, telling Ava that he would be gone for two weeks.

He called Glenn Hughes, the bassist for Deep Purple, and asked if he could stay with him in Los Angeles for a few days and then took a train to the West Coast. Five days later he was in a small recording studio with his long-time friend Jim Osterberg.

Jimmy, better known as Iggy Pop, had gone through a bad time that made David's seem tame. He was known at the time in Los Angeles for passing out every night, the result of too much to drink, or from the ingestion of too many Quääluds, then an increasingly popular social drug that made you trip over your tongue and knock over tables and relationships.

David believed in Jimmy, wanted to 'save' him, and in May 1975, at four o'clock one morning, himself quite high on coke, David was sitting at the mixing board, staring at his friend. David had spent the previous nine hours composing, producing and playing every instrument on the backing track. Now it was time for his friend to sing. Jimmy was shirtless, intense. The lyrics that followed were improvized, as was Jimmy's custom.

David beamed at Jimmy, telling the others in the booth that Jimmy was like James Dean and Lenny Bruce, a genius who merely needed discovering. Jimmy left the studio, accompanied by a young woman, and David picked up a guitar and for the next two or so hours he improvized a song called 'Movin' On'. And then he spun into dawn's early light, jumped into a friend's white Volkswagen Beetle and headed into the Hollywood Hills, past garish record company billboards, 24-hour supermarkets and sagging palm trees.

'Los Angeles is my favourite museum,' he said.

Nic Roeg's film, *The Man Who Fell To Earth*, had been delayed until June, giving David three months in which to drift. Ava Cherry, after a big parting fight, was holidaying in Trinidad and now David was seeing old friends again, including singers Jean Millington and Claudia Lennear. After a week or so, he left Glenn Hughes' rented home in the Hollywood Hills and moved into the Beverly Wilshire Hotel. From there he made plans to move into Michael and Nancy Lippman's place on King's Road in West Los Angeles.

Michael was a lawyer with a talent agency and David was thinking of asking him to be his manager, but then suddenly Ava Cherry arrived with a friend, a *Playboy* Playmate named Claudia Jennings and David decided instead to move in with them. They were living in a house owned by Bobby Hart, a songwriter who had written a number of hits for the Monkees ten years before. David asked if he could move in. Claudia was getting ready to move into Robert Wagner's Century City apartment, so Ava said yes, of course.

It was the run-of-the-mill Hollywood run-around, propelled by adrenalin and coke, and David was in the centre of the storm.

David recalled some years later that 'I was one of those people you see on the streets who suddenly stops and says, "They're coming! They're coming!" Every day of my life back then I was capable of staying up indefinitely. My chemistry must have been superhuman. I'd stay up for seven or eight days on the trot! The Stones would be absolutely floored by me. They'd see me days later and find out that I hadn't been to bed! It was unreal, absolutely unreal.

'Of course, every day that you stayed up longer – and there's things that you have to do to stay up that long – the impending tiredness and fatigue produces that hallucinogenic state naturally. Well, *half*-naturally. By the end of the week my whole life would be transformed into this bizarre, nihilistic fantasy world of oncoming doom, mythological characters and imminent totalitarianism.

'I was living in a house with Egyptian decor. It was one of those rent-a-house places, but it appealed to me because I had this more than passing interest in Egyptology, mysticism, the cabala, all this stuff that is inherently misleading in life, a hodge-podge whose crux I've forgotten. But at the time it seemed transparently obvious what the answer to life was. So the house occupied a ritualistic position in my life.'

It was during this frenetic period that David let *Rolling Stone* magazine's seventeen-year-old boy-genius Cameron Crowe follow him around with a tape recorder. The interview he got was staggering in its scope and during the week or so he followed David, he was never bored.

Sometimes David seemed in complete control, as when he said of his battles with DeFries, 'The split had been building up for some time. For the last year and a half, I've had no empathy with them whatsoever. It took me that long to stop touring and come back to finding out where the office was really at. I guess it was a bit hard for them to come to terms with what I wanted to do. A lot of people who I never even met got involved. I grew to dislike their attitude. So I just said goodbye. No, of course, it isn't that simple, but I'm going to *make* it that simple. It's not going to bother me. I'll survive. I'm far from broke. I'm free. I've never been so happy. I've got that good old "I'm-gonna-change-the-world" thing back again.'

Cameron Crowe had observed David in a meeting with RCA executives, moving from one to the next and then to the next, with charm and apparent care.

Cameron said, 'You have the ability to make a room full of people all feel that they are most important to what you're doing.' And asked what that ability meant to David.

David said, 'It's really difficult to answer because the person you've described is my dad. I think that's one reason why I'm so keen on being accepted and striving so hard to put my whatever it is up here to artistic use . . .'

He also was most candid about what he had done to rock and why: 'I already consider myself responsible for a whole new school of pretension. Really. I'm quite serious about that. The only thing that seems to shock anybody any more is something that's pretentious or kitsch. Unless you take things to extremes, nobody will believe or pay attention to you. You have to hit them on the head and pretension does the trick. It shocks as much as a Dylanesque thing did years ago.'

And then, right in the middle of a speech like this, David would suddenly leap to his feet and rush to a nearby picture window, where he quickly drew the shade. The *Rolling Stone* interviewer noticed a large Star of David had been inked on the shade, then circled. Underneath was the word AUM.

'I've got to do this,' David explained. 'I just saw a body fall.'

He then rushed to the dresser and lit a black candle, and immediately blew it out to leave a thin trail of smoke floating upwards.

'Don't let me scare the pants off you,' David said. 'It's only protection. I've been getting a little trouble from the neighbours.'

And then that would be followed by another long speech, this one more disconnected, using the Ziggy Stardust characterization as a takeoff point (something he still often did): 'It was quite easy to become obsessed night and day with the character. I *became* Ziggy Stardust. David Bowie went totally out the window. Everybody was convincing me that I was a Messiah, especially on that first American tour. I got hopelessly lost in the fantasy. I could have been Hitler in England. Wouldn't have been hard. Concerts alone got so enormously frightening that even the papers were saying, "This ain't rock music, this is bloody Hitler! Something must be done!" They were right. It was awesome. Actually, I wonder . . . I think I might have been a bloody *good* Hitler. I'd be an excellent dictator. Very eccentric and quite mad.

'I was thinking a few days ago that when I got bored with films and had far too many showings in art galleries of my paintings and sculptures, maybe I should be prime minister of England. I wouldn't mind being the first English president of the United States, either. I'm certainly right wing enough.

'Listen, I mean it! I'll bloody lead this country, make it a great fucking nation! I can't exist happily and make records and be safe, because, man, it's depressing . . .

'I have this dream. I'd like to host a satellite television

show and invite all the biggest bands on to one stage. Then I'd come out with a great big wheelbarrow of machine-guns and ask them, "*Now* how many of you are going to do anything? How many are going to pick up a gun and how many of you are going to cling to your guitars?"'

For two months, David practised occult rituals that made Michael Lippman's hair stand on end – one of which required David to save bottles of his urine in the Lippman family refrigerator.

He created huge, symbolic sculptures in his bedroom and painted all night in sprints of chemical energy. One sculpture had its vaguely human foot shoved through a world globe, a baby in its misshapen arms, a penis shaped from 3-D Hollywood postcards (a Mickey Mouse pencil sharpener on the end). Others were inflated with a bicycle pump.

Sometimes David disappeared for days. Geoff Westen and Patti Mitsui, who operated the small studio where David and Iggy recorded together, say 'Lippman was always calling the studio to ask if I knew where David was. Sometimes I did, sometimes I didn't. One time, four cars of us converged on this house where he was. He had to go to RCA for a meeting and he was three hours late already. Geoff MacCormack and Nancy Lippman went in to pour coffee down him to get him into shape. Apparently he was coming down off a coke high and just crashed.'

Then in June, Jimmy Osterberg failed to show up at the recording studio. David called everywhere, without success. Jimmy was his closest friend and David grew even more concerned. Finally, he found his friend at the UCLA Neuropsychiatric Institute, a voluntary patient. Over the next several days, David was Jimmy's only visitor.

It was with this warning experience fresh in his mind that David left Los Angeles in June to travel by train to New Mexico for the filming of *The Man Who Fell To Earth*.

David had a lot on the line in making this film, and so did director Nic Roeg, which made David's position more tenuous. Nic had directed three excellent films, none of which were hits . . . and they had been made at least two years apart, a long time by Hollywood standards. In between, he paid the bills directing television commercials – as many top British directors do, but this didn't make him a hero in Hollywood, either. He was just too damned obtuse for them, all wrapped up in unlikely sequence juxta-positions, jumping from one scene to another and then back and forth, back and forth, until some obscure intellectual point was made. Roeg was enamoured of props and symbols and a fierce exploitation of social and cultural rituals. Many called his movies 'art films', the kiss of death at the box office.

In Hollywood, Nic Roeg was particularly unpopular. The film he made with Mick Jagger, *Performance*, sat on a shelf for more than two years before it was re-edited without Nic's permission and released, reluctantly, by Warner Bros, who still had no idea what it was all about. The successor, *Walkabout*, did so badly at the box office, that some say it led to the eleventh hour cancellation of Nic's first studio assignment in Hollywood. (Of a film called *Deadly Honey-moon*.) Even *Don't Look Now*, which did well in England, was given minimal distribution elsewhere, leaving it relatively unknown in America even today.

The Man Who Fell To Earth initially seemed to have fallen under the same curse. Originally a project at Columbia Pictures, the American film industry again had backed away from the eccentric English director and now the film was being financed by British Lion.

David was aware of much of this as his train moved towards Santa Fe and he knew that Hollywood's perception of Nic Roeg would colour its perception and acceptance of him.

More important was the anxiety David felt about taking on a starring role in a major motion picture, one which had a budget of three million dollars. The small parts he had in films when he was being managed by Ken Pitt offered him minimal experience and *Cracked Actor* only a little bit more. Now he was going to be in a difficult film which demanded his presence in 75 per cent of the scenes.

Travelling with him on the train were three of his closest friends, the core of companionship and support which would keep him afloat for the next ten years. The first, and perhaps the most important, was Coco Schwab, his ever-faithful assistant who coddled and protected him. The second was Geoff MacCormack, who probably would not have killed for David, but probably would have died for him; he was David's gofer and constant sycophant. The final member of the protective triumvirate was Tony Mascia, a 350-pound New Yorker who served as David's driver and bodyguard. Among their other duties, these three were charged with providing David with the freedom and space to focus all his energies on making Nic Roeg's film.

It was a sort of thinking man's sci-fi film, unlike anything else in the genre, telling the story of an extra-terrestrial who falls to earth and who, soon afterwards, appears in a lawyer's office with a handful of 'inventions' (actually products from his home planet) of such originality that he is able to revolutionize America's major systems of communication and build one of the country's largest corporate empires. The object is to acquire sufficient wealth to launch his own space programme, an attempt to return to his wife and family in far-off space. Unfortunately for David (who adopted the name Newton), his other-worldly origins are revealed and he is kidnapped by mysterious establishment forces, who imprison him while conducting elaborate tests to determine who, or what, he is. In the end, Newton's rocket site is destroyed and he is turned loose, having achieved nothing but the frustration of his hope. And so, in the end, he turns to drink.

It was a foreigner's look at America, perfect for the age, because in the decade following the British rock invasion, many foreigners were looking at the United States from the inside for the first time and were coming away simultaneously rewarded and shocked. David loved America, was infatuated by its crass and temporary culture, its energy and size. In his songs, he had been remarking on America for years. To do the same thing in a film? It was glorious.

For three months in the desert, David daily underwent as much as five hours of unearthly make-up, but he was away from the stress of his fight with DeFries and immersed deeply in a film-making process unlike any he had experienced. Film-making had bored him previously, he said, but Roeg demanded too much to put anyone to sleep. When it was all over, David would praise Roeg and the film extravagantly. He would also be relatively free of drugs.

This does not mean it was an altogether pleasant interlude. Quite the contrary. Often he was paranoid, depressed and humourless, characteristics of someone who had been ingesting large quantities of cocaine and amphetamines and was coming down from these drugs. David told one story against himself regarding the crates and crates of books he had with him. (In itself an odd comment on his mental state.) 'I was going through all these books and they were pouring out all over the floor, there were just mountains of books,' he said. 'And Nic was sitting there watching me and he said, "Your great problem, David, is that you don't read enough." And I didn't even think it was funny until months later. I really thought he was serious. And I felt so depressed and I thought, "What else should I read?" It didn't occur to me at the time that it was a joke.'

During the eleven-week shoot, David visited some of the local sights, including the Carlsbad Caverns, the opera house in Santa Fe (watching a production of *Carmen*, with a twenty-year-old heir to the Guinness banking fortune as his date), and a Tibetan monastery near Taos. For most of the time, however, he stayed to himself in his trailer dressing room, reading, painting and beginning what he described as a book of short stories called *The Return of the Thin White Duke* – 'partly autobiographical, mostly fiction, with a deal of magic in it.'

Magic was a subject that intrigued him. Many of the books he brought with him were examinations of the occult and they began to colour his perception of those around him, especially Nic Roeg, who had a reputation in the film industry for playing unnerving psychological games with his cast and crew.

'He's a disturbing man,' David said. 'You see, Nic I love very much, but I think he's very dangerous. I think he's very hard to work with without being very affected by him. He is an old warlock. I mean, something magical happens on every film that he does and it's hard to live with.'

In September, David returned to his 'favourite museum', Los Angeles.

THE THIN WHITE DUKE

David had been seen drinking tequila straight from the bottle in New Mexico on more than one occasion, but it was true when Corinne told journalists in Los Angeles that he was the healthiest he'd been in a year or more. And to keep David healthy, she said, she had started stocking his refrigerator with gallons of extra-rich milk.

'I want to put some weight on him,' she explained.

At the same time, David's records were selling faster and in greater quantity. The 'Young Americans' single was released in February and it went on to the bestseller charts in March, the same month that the album of the same name was moved on to the marketplace. This, too, went on to all the lists in both England and the US.

Once again, as David experienced success, more of his earliest music was repackaged and re-released to capitalize on his new popularity. This time, twenty-one songs he had released on two albums for Deram eight years before were given a new cover (a current *Young Americans* era photograph) and a new price. Suddenly, David was faced with songs he had long forgotten: 'Little Bombardier' . . . 'Karma Man' . . . 'The Laughing Gnome' . . . 'Please, Mr Gravedigger'. The double album sold well.

As 'Young Americans' peaked (in America at No. 28, in England at No. 12), RCA released a second single from the album, the song David wrote with John Lennon. 'Fame' was their mutual complaint listing all the drawbacks of success, and was a remarkable song. David found Carlos Alomar at the Apollo Theatre in Harlem and this single sounded like it. The finger-popping rhythm, adapted for the disco market, owed much to James Brown. The lyrics were reasonably clever ('Hey, what you get is no tomorrow/Hey! What you need you have to borrow') but it was the infectious and compelling danceability that sold the record, making it David's first No. 1 hit.

*

By now, Corinne Schwab had been integrated into David's life in every way possible. She found a house in Stone Canyon, an exclusive section of Bel Air, and then ran it for him. She opened his mail, answered his telephone and made his appointments. She bought his books, paint supplies and groceries. She served as his liaison with Michael Lippman and his assistant, Pat Gibbons, who handled most of the day-to-day matters in Lippman's office. She introduced him to artists' and writers' work and sometimes to the artists and writers themselves. Most important, she protected him, providing a personal shield that had been missing since he had left DeFries and MainMan. She was, in the words of nearly everyone around at the time, impregnable. 'She was in love with him,' says Ava Cherry. 'She told me that. But I don't think the love was returned, so unable to be his love, she settled for being his governess.'

Soon after moving into the Stone Canyon house with Corinne and Tony Mascia, who continued to serve as his chauffeur-bodyguard, David called Harry Maslin in New York.

'Harry,' he said, 'I want you to come out here and find me a studio. I want you to produce my next album.'

Then he called Carlos Alomar, Earl Slick and Dennis Davis, who had worked with him on *Young Americans*. For two weeks, they worked together in a small rehearsal room and then moved into the Cherokee, a funky old recording studio in Hollywood.

Says Harry Maslin: 'I loved those sessions, because we were totally open and experimental in our approach. We weren't trying to create a hit single. He had just come off a couple from the *Young Americans* album and I think he felt this was a time to feel free. He wanted to do the music the way he heard it and we didn't worry about RCA.'

Earl Slick later said, 'He had one or two songs written, but they were changed so drastically that you wouldn't know them from the first time anyway, so he basically wrote everything in the studio.'

Maslin added: 'To understand the way David works is to know that you *can't* understand the way David works. He's always changing things – just changing completely, so it's hard to tell at times what he's talking about. Right before the *mixing* he would change the lyrics of a song.'

The album originally was to be called *The Return of the Thin White Duke*, after the character who appeared in his attempts at autobiography and in a song called 'Station to Station' – the title symbolizing David's personal and musical movement. In fact, the track opens with the sound of a train huffing and puffing from speaker to speaker, followed by the distant howl of Earl Slick's guitar. Then David came in, singing somewhere between a croon and a snarl: 'The return of the thin white duke/Throwing darts in lovers' eyes.'

The mood was somewhat lightened on the album's second song – actually the first recorded – 'Golden Years', in which he promised, 'Stick with me, baby, for a thousand years/Nothing's going to touch these golden years!' This one was funkier, more danceable, containing much of the Latin-soul feel of *Young Americans*. A perfect disco single choice.

Another romantic, disco tune, 'Stay', conveyed a sense of paranoia, or fear of love almost lost: 'Stay, that's what I meant to say/Stay, you can never really tell when somebody really loves you . . .'

More puzzling was 'TVC 1–5', a song inspired by David's friend Jimmy Osterberg. Here, David sang in a style reminiscent of his early Ziggy Stardust days, more strident than anything sung recently, yet the song was almost rollicking, and the lyric was incomprehensible, the result of his using William Burroughs' 'cut-up' technique where the writer mixed up lines randomly.

As was his custom, David included a song that was not his, this one, the title song from the movie *Wild is the Wind*, a virtuoso ballad written by a Tin Pan Alley songwriter (Ned Washington) and one of the most prolific movie soundtrack composers of all time (Dimitri Tiomkin, whose other credits included the memorable *High Noon*, *The High and the Mighty* and *Giant*). David sounded almost as if he were auditioning.

The most unusual song was 'Word On a Wing', which David called his 'hymn'. And so it was. During the filming of *The Man Who Fell To Earth*, and in the years following, David often wore a Christian cross – even had several publicity photographs taken while wearing it – and although he never talked publicly about this apparent swerve in his beliefs, the lyrics were quite blatantly those of an individual who had been 'born-again'.

The songs were long. ('Station to Station' ran ten minutes, David's most extended composition so far.) And complicated. And difficult. So it was nearly three months before David pronounced the sessions complete. Says Harry Maslin: '"Golden Years" was cut and finished very fast. We knew it was absolutely right within ten days. But the rest of the album took *forever*.'

The sessions themselves were long, usually lasting eight to ten hours. Harry remembers one that started at seven o'clock at night and ended at nine the next morning when everyone was asked nicely to leave the Cherokee so a session scheduled for another band could begin. David told Harry to find another studio and by 10.30 they were in the Record Plant, where they remained until midnight. Twenty-nine hours in all, with only a break to change neighbourhoods.

David was losing weight again. Gone now were the gallon containers of extra-rich milk. David was back on drugs.

'The drugs I was interested in then were amphetamines and cocaine, because I always lived with such a fast-event horizon, and those drugs seemed to keep things happening,' David said later. 'They kept me working well. If I had to stay up three or four days to finish something, they gave me the ability to do that.'

'David's pattern was he liked to work four days or so, very strenuous hours, then take a few days off to rest and get charged up for another sprint,' Harry says. 'Dealing with David because of the drugs was sometimes difficult, because he would stay up so much, he'd get exhausted.'

Three times in November, as the recording sessions neared completion, David taped television shows, lip-synching to 'Fame' and an early mix of 'Golden Years' on *Soul Train*, a programme that was aimed at the black marketplace; singing no less than ten songs with Cher on her network variety show (including 'Fame', 'Young Americans', the Beatles' 'Day Tripper' and Neil Diamond's

'Song Sung Blue'); and being interviewed by satellite by Russell Harty.

And the records continued to sell. In England 'Space Oddity' was re-released by RCA as part of a 'Maximillion' series which offered three songs for the price of two . . . and six years after its original release (when it went to No. 5), it went to No. 1.

Other news in England was not so good.

It was while David was still in New Mexico, filming *The Man Who Fell To Earth*, that his mother gave the first interview of her life. When David later received a copy of the story that appeared in the *New Musical Express*, he was appalled. 'A MOTHER'S ANGUISH', the headline read, 'DAVID NEVER COMES TO SEE ME'. Now, four months later, the sensationalist Fleet Street papers were running similar stories.

Peggy Jones was very candid when she talked with Charles Shaar Murray, admitting there was a distance between mother and son even as David was moving through puberty. But the estrangement she felt now was overpowering.

'Mind you, he was very good, he sent me a mink coat, a thing I've never 'ad before,' she said. 'I'll show it to you. I was chuffed with it. And then I thought afterwards, Well, it's lovely to 'ave a mink coat, but where do I go to wear it? No money in my pocket. I'm an old-age pensioner. I'm living on eleven-pounds-fifty a week! I mean, for the money I'm living on, God knows what's going to 'appen to me in a few years. I may end up on national assistance. I don't want that to 'appen. My husband will turn in his grave!

'I can't understand it. If Geoff MacCormack can ring his mother up, why is it David can't ring me now and again? I mean, it would give me a terrific boost if 'e rung me and said, "Hello, Mum, how you getting along?" I mean, look at Elton John, how good 'e's been to '*is* parents!'

David felt doubly wounded, unfairly attacked on two flanks. His mother badmouthing him for all the world to hear was bad enough, but now a singer for whom David had little regard musically (he thought Elton had ripped off much of his own Glam Rock image) was adding his own five pence worth. David had never liked Elton, and considered his costumes poorly motivated and badly executed, even if he, too, claimed to be a bisexual.

'Elton had been in Los Angeles,' says Cameron Crowe, who was back on the scene, now interviewing David for *Playboy* magazine, 'and he was telling people that David was weak, was getting fucked up too much, and was going to die before he finished the tour that he was planning for after the album release. He wasn't talking for print, but he was telling friends in Los Angeles and it was getting back to Bowie and Bowie was angry. He was railing at Elton John, cursing him.'

Some say David was cursing his mother along with Elton John.

David did what he always did when the heat was on. He took some more coke and buried himself in work. He was right back where he'd been four months before. Worse, David was also babbling incessantly, as many 'speed freaks' do. Mostly he was rambling on and on about some of the stage characters of his recent past, especially Ziggy Stardust. Everywhere he went in Los Angeles, when people related to him as Ziggy, or Aladdin Sane, he became lost in, or absorbed by, the characters, and became them over and over again, not in concert now, but in casual conversation.

Once the new album was finished – now entitled *Station to Station* and set for a January release – David and his producer and band returned to the studio to record a soundtrack for *The Man Who Fell To Earth*. Anything, however, approaching the magnitude of a movie soundtrack was, by now, a very lost cause.

'David was so burned out by the end of *Station to Station*,' says Harry Maslin, 'he had a hard time doing movie cues. The movie was complete and we had all the videotapes and that's what we were working with. We had about nine cues down – of the sixty that we needed – and David had a big blowup with Michael Lippman.'

What happened is not clear. Afterwards, Lippman expressed genuine confusion. He had given David everything, he said, not only exclusive management, but a room in his home. Some, including Harry Maslin, think the break can be blamed partly on David's excessive drug use but also on the opportunism of Pat Gibbons, a Philadelphia promoter who had been working with Michael Lippman. Harry says

Gibbons told David he had to finish the soundtrack recording before he went on tour in February and he blamed Lippman for the deadline. The final scene was played out in middle January, 1976.

'We'd been working all night long,' says Harry Maslin, 'and it was nine o'clock in the morning. David couldn't work because he was so tired. He was in bad shape. He had no concentration on the music. He would go off into conversations about things that had nothing to do with the music. It wasn't that he was incoherent. It was that he couldn't concentrate on what we were doing. He'd sit and talk about Ziggy for two hours and finally I'd say, "We better get back to the music" and we'd get back to the music and then he'd go off again and start talking about something else.'

Geoff MacCormack became so concerned about David he called Angela. David and Angela had separated permanently. It was only a matter of time before one or both of them filed for divorce. Still, Geoff thought Angie could talk some sense into David. She came to Los Angeles a few weeks before Christmas and moved David into a house on Doheny Drive, not far from the Sunset Strip.

Now David was in the recording studio, babbling to himself and to anyone who would listen. Outside, the dawn was a strange, grey yellow. Suddenly Angela entered the studio reception room. Harry saw her and left the control room.

'Angie,' Harry said, 'you better go in there and get David out of the control room. I'm really concerned. He's about ready to go over the edge.'

Angie was distraught. 'I can't,' she said. 'He won't listen to me. If I go in there and do that, he'll get angry with me.'

'Look,' Harry said, 'he's not going to leave if *I* tell him to leave. He'll just try to be macho. But if his wife goes in there and sees he's not looking well and shows some concern, maybe he'll listen.'

Finally, Angie agreed and went into the control room. David was looking pale, uncertain, frightened. 'There were,' he would say later, 'pieces of me laying all over the floor.' Angela talked to him quietly and took him into an office where there was a couch. David lay down to rest.

Just then, Pat Gibbons entered the studio and with

David's exhausted and somewhat scattered consent, Pat called Michael Lippman and fired him.

The movie soundtrack was abandoned, and given to John Phillips, the leader of the long-defunct Mamas and Papas. A few days later, David took a train to Florida, where he caught a boat to Jamaica, to begin rehearsals for what now was being described as a 'world tour'.

David left Los Angeles as if released.

'It got to a point where I was totally confused about my own identity,' he said later. 'And I was disgruntled with the way I was writing. I felt it wasn't reaping me any fulfilment. So I physically opened a wardrobe door one day and mentally put all my characters into the wardrobe and closed the door and locked the door and left Los Angeles.'

Of course, it wasn't all that easy . . . nor was it all that true, because when David left Los Angeles, he still had his drug problem and he was now embarking on a tour in another role. This tour would be referred to in many ways, as 'the *Station to Station* tour' and as 'the White Heat, White Light Tour' (so named for the starkness of the lighting), but the phrase most often used was the one that David kept using over and over, 'The Return of the Thin White Duke'.

David certainly fitted that description. Always a spindly creature with never an ounce of fat, he was now emaciated, nearly skeletal, his pale face appearing almost skull-like when he grinned. His now-yellow hair slicked back in a fifties hipster style, wearing a white shirt buttoned to the neck (no tie), black pants and vest, the pungent Gitane drooping from one side of his mouth, he epitomized, at least visually, the jaded urban decadent.

David hadn't toured in more than a year and his fans were unprepared for what they saw. The Thin White Duke was not especially 'likeable', and certainly alien from anything a teenager could identify or have fun with.

Gone was the make-up. Gone were the costumes and outrageous props (the skulls, the ropes). Gone were the elaborate sets. Gone was the bizarre choreography. Now the show opened not with an orchestral crescendo or the voice of impending doom ('This is the year of the Diamond Dogs!'), but with a strange, murky, black and white film from 1922, Salvador Dali's and Luis Bunuel's classic surrealist *Un Chien Andalou*, best known for the scene in which a human eyeball is sliced with a razor. Banks of 'pure white light' added to the starkness, giving the performance the look of a book of black-and-white photographs, snapped in pre-Hitler Berlin.

The thirty-five-city North American leg of the tour began a week after the album's release, on 2 February in Vancouver, then crossed the border for shows in Seattle and Portland. David was astonished by how many Ziggy Stardust clones remained in his audience . . . and he was harassed by roving bands of transvestites who chased him through the hotel hallways, as if he were some lipsticked English queen.

By 1976, the evidence pointed the other way. Cameron Crowe thought he was finished with his *Playboy* interview, when the magazine sent him back to ask David specifically about his homosexuality.

'Because in all this time he was still being characterized as this gay guy,' Cameron says today. 'But I had only seen him with beautiful women. And when he wasn't around, they would invariably talk about like what a sex machine this guy was, and about how they'd been up all night with David.'

Others confirm this report heartily and David himself told Cameron Crowe, 'Since I've come to America, girls have been presuming that I've kept my masculine virginity, so I've had the wonderful prospect of having girls trying to get me over to the other side again. Girls are trying to convince me that it isn't that bad being a heterosexual . . . and I play dumb.'

Somehow, the drugs and alcohol never interfered with his performances. He had learned his lesson in Los Angeles when he had lost control in the studio and forfeited the movie soundtrack. Now a great, natural coping mechanism and his uncanny ability to recover quickly from frequent debauchery was reinforced by a determination never to lose control again. Each day he renewed this resolve as he and his eight-piece band and thirty-five backup people headed across America.

The rainy winter of the Pacific northwest was replaced by the fog of San Francisco and the blah-ness of Los Angeles:

a coastline of grey and white skies. Perfect for the Thin White Duke.

David's most loyal and dedicated big-time journalist friend, Bob Hilburn of the *Los Angeles Times*, greeted David in San Francisco. He pointed out in the story he wrote that when David first appeared in the northern California city, in 1972, only 1100 people came to see him in a ballroom that held 5000. The turnout was so disappointing that David skipped San Francisco on his next tour.

Not this time. Hilburn reported: 'Boosted by the success of his "Fame" single and all the attention he has received in the past four years, Bowie played the 14,000-seat Cow Palace (the city's largest rock hall) and the response was phenomenal.

'Though his 90-minute set started slowly as Bowie concentrated on new material, he worked up such an enthusiasm in the arena with his versions of such early well-known work as "Changes", "Rebel Rebel" and "Jean Genie" that a rare thing happened after the first, rather obligatory encore.

'The audience continued yelling for Bowie long after the house lights – normally the sign that a concert is irrevocably over – were turned on. An excited, but apparently unprepared Bowie finally came back on stage to do a hastily assembled version of "Diamond Dogs".

'Though he messed up some of the song's lyrics, the audience continued to roar its approval and kept doing so for a full five minutes after the house lights were again turned on. One Cow Palace official said it was the strongest response he had seen a rock set receive there in years. Bowie, clearly, has arrived as a rock superstar in America.'

*

In the winter of 1975–76, in Los Angeles, celebrities moved from party to party ritualistically, as if survival depended upon the mysterious sustenance received at these parties; perhaps it was the comfort earned in playing out the ritual perfectly: with just the right amount of chic and just the right amount of panache. In Los Angeles, the 'best' parties are called 'events' and both hosts and guests are rated 'A' (Cary Grant, any ex-Beatle, actors and actresses and

157

directors who had just won Academy awards, Governor Jerry Brown and Linda Ronstadt and anyone related to a US president) and 'B' (Tony Curtis, the city's black mayor, Jackie Bisset and Cher). In the winter of 1975–76, David Bowie was on *everyone's* 'A' list.

Following his third and final appearance in the 18,000-seat Forum, he and Angela and Zowie – together again, but only briefly – attended such an 'event' backstage whose guests included Ringo Starr, Rod Stewart, Alice Cooper, Neil Sedaka, Lou Adler and the current US President's son, Steven Ford. This also was the night that David was introduced to artist David Hockney by author Christopher Isherwood, a meeting that was carefully arranged. David used such parties to meet the individuals he most admired.

'Look,' says one of his associates, 'David is basically shy and he never would have had the nerve to ring up people like David Hockney and Christopher Isherwood and casually say, "Let's 'ava cuppa, what do you say?" On the other hand, it's easy for him to have someone else arrange a meeting at a party. Usually, it was Corinne who arranged the meetings. No wonder he kept her. Can you imagine having an assistant who turns you on to people like Hockney and Isherwood?'

When David talked with Bob Hilburn, he made much of his own personal transformation. He said he was taking full responsibility for his business affairs (even though Pat Gibbons continued as a sort of interim business manager). 'Over the last year I've become a businessman,' David said. 'I used to think an artist had to separate himself from business matters, but now I realize you have more artistic freedom if you also keep an eye on business.'

Everything he said exuded awareness and confidence. It's possible to credit the cocaine for some of that confidence, but not much of it. David really *did* seem to be in control again, as he talked in revealing detail about his early days in rock and the self-doubt he had felt more recently.

From Los Angeles David went to San Diego to Phoenix to Albuquerque to Denver and then there were two days free to travel from the steely winter blue of the southwest to the below-zero blue of the awful Midwest winter: Milwaukee, Kalamazoo, Evansville, Cincinnati. Then north to

more snow in Montreal and Toronto, then back into the
Midwest: Cleveland, Detroit, Chicago, St Louis, where the
temperatures were more bearable, but the skies were just
as grey.

The records sold better in every city following one of his
concerts, proving, again, that personal 'promotion' helps
make hits. In the past few months, David had sold a *lot* of
records. In England as David was moving across America,
Station to Station was on the album chart, where it would
remain for 16 weeks and go as high as No. 5, and his most
recent single, 'Golden Years', had gone to No. 8. In the
US, where sales were reflected by his recent appearances,
'Golden Years' remained on the charts for twenty-one weeks
and went to No. 10. Following on the heels of a No. 1 hit,
this made it clear that it wasn't just John Lennon's presence
on 'Fame' that made him a talent to listen to.

From St Louis, David moved further into the cold grey
South and then back into the ice-blue North, to Memphis,
Nashville and Atlanta, took two days to reach Pittsburgh by
train, then travelled to Norfolk, Washington, Philadelphia,
Boston, Buffalo and Rochester.

The halls were big and draughty and the shows were
becoming repetitious, which David hated. It was well
known that he had a limited attention span, so by the time
he moved into the homestretch of the American tour, he
began changing things.

Then suddenly it stopped being boring, when soon after
midnight on 21 March (three days after *The Man Who Fell
To Earth* was premiered in London), in a hotel in Rochester,
New York, hotel security men and local police invited
themselves into David's room and arrested him and Jimmy
Osterberg and two others on marijuana charges which
carried a possible fifteen-year penalty.

By 1976, a marijuana arrest was virtually ignored by the
press, even when the subject was a pop celebrity. By now,
even heroin arrests were greeted with yawns when connected
to music personalities. By this time, the army of those
arrested for drugs – some of whom unfortunately died from
them – included all of the Beatles and most of the Rolling
Stones, Marianne Faithfull, Jim Morrison, Jimi Hendrix,
half of the Beach Boys, all six members of Grateful Dead,

Tim Hardin, Janis Joplin, David Crosby, Stephen Stills, Ken Kesey, most of Jefferson Airplane, Eric Clapton, Eric Burdon, Tim Buckley, Tim Leary, Waylon Jennings, Three Dog Night's Chuck Negron, Johnny Cash, Joe Cocker and Sly Stone, to name but a very few.

There was real concern in the Bowie camp, however. The US government had tried to throw John Lennon out of the country for a similar charge the year before and David and his management didn't want any hint of a similar action to arise in *his* career. Consequently, his lawyers in New York raised holy hell, saying David had been set up, insisting that he didn't even use marijuana, and never had.

There was an urgency attached to getting these charges dismissed or moved through the courts very promptly. David had talked candidly about his drug use, admitting to drug abuse, in his interviews with *Rolling Stone* and *Playboy*, and it was believed, rightly, that if they were published before the case was settled, it could go very badly for David.

EXILE IN BERLIN

A month later, when David's case was quickly taken to a Rochester, New York, grand jury, the jurors yawned and dismissed all charges and the pendulum of David's life swung again.

He had just completed his first real starring role in a major feature film and he was confident that this would alter his image and expand his future.

He also was getting some important national publicity – not from *Rolling Stone* and *Playboy* (Cameron Crowe's stories wouldn't appear for another five months), but from two of the movie industry's most influential writers, Joyce Baker and Rex Reed. Both of these interviews had been conducted while David was in New Mexico, and for the most part were comprised of old news and lies. (For example, David told Rex Reed that his father was 'a gambler and a drinker and a layabout for most of his life'; he also said he had seven thousand costumes in storage trunks and was moving to Bhutan to escape British taxes.) However, both writers were widely syndicated so, once again, he was experiencing massive public exposure, and now it was coming on hundreds of newspaper movie pages, where Bowie had never appeared before.

As David sat on the deck of the big ocean liner which took him back to Europe, he re-read the packet of reviews of *The Man Who Fell To Earth*, given to him by his publicist in New York.

When the film premiered on 18 March 1976 at the Leicester Square Theatre in London, the stars flocked. David was travelling from Boston to Buffalo that day, so it was by telephone that he was told who attended and how they reacted. Angela was there, representing him, and so were two of the film's co-stars, Rip Torn and Candy Clarke. James Coburn and Lee Remick were in the audience and so were some of David's friends, Rick Wakeman, John Peel and old girlfriend Amanda Lear among them. The audience roared its approval and the reviewers were, mostly, kind.

There were 'enough ideas for six films', according to the *Financial Times* and 'with his enamelled, bony features and his soft feminine voice, Bowie is ingeniously right as the alien, a still centre around which the more flamboyant supporting performances and Roeg's own pyrotechnic direction can whirl and spark to often thrilling effect.' *Screen International*, a trade journal for theatre owners, said much the same thing: 'Pallid and gaunt and required to give a low key performance, David Bowie makes a convincing alien life form whose loneliness is beyond human experience. The inherent pathos of the character gives heart and soul to the technical wizardry.'

The more intellectual critics fell all over themselves. The *Guardian* said, 'The story spreads itself into the realms of political and moral allegory, and much else besides since it is also a romance as much about the mystery of love as of the universe.' The *Times* called the film a 'parable' and listed a dozen influential works behind Roeg's inspiration, including *A Clockwork Orange, 2001: A Space Odyssey* and *Citizen Kane*. And the *Evening Standard* said the film was a retelling of the ancient Greek Icarus myth about the boy who flew too near the sun and fell to the earth in flames.

Others were totally confused by the film. The *Daily Express* said the story had 'more holes than a string vest'. The *Daily Telegraph* said Roeg lost his narrative thread about midway through the picture, 'providing instead a succession of often stunning pictures, rather precariously related to rock music, or by overrunning dialogue, but in themselves contributing more to our mystification than understanding.' While the *Spectator* called it 'one of the best bad movies I have ever seen'.

The bottom line? According to *Screen International* it was a film for the 'under 35s who do not demand a coherent plot, David Bowie fans, and others who will seek out any film that shows naked lovers'.

The business prediction, according to the same publication? 'Very good in selected popular and intimate cinemas, particularly where there is a university in the vicinity.'

What all that meant was that David had starred in an 'art film', one which probably would not bring him great success, but which could add dimension to his career and image in much the same way that dramatic films had changed the lives of Frank Sinatra, Dean Martin and Bing Crosby and only a few other singers before him. (Sinatra in *From Here To Eternity*, Martin in *The Young Lions* and Crosby in *Going My Way* and *The Country Girl*.) In recent years, other singers such as Elvis Presley, Mick Jagger and Pat Boone, had made the move to motion pictures, but either they always played singers (as Jagger did in *Performance*) or they sang.

Besides the reviews, David read books on the ship that took him to France, where he caught a train to Germany (where he began his European tour in Munich on 7 April). Many of the books were about Hitler and Nazism. This was a long-time fascination for David, going back to his days as a Mod, perhaps earlier. Many people he met on his first visit to America, in 1966, remember him talking about Hitler almost favourably, at least respectfully.

Often in his interviews he had talked about Hitler, or fascism, and what he perceived as the inevitable return to dictatorship in Europe and its imminent arrival in America. Many of his songs carried the same theme. At one point, David even described Hitler as 'the first rock star. The way that Hitler used to create enthusiasm . . . the wave of fervour apart from the very basics . . . the Anglo-Saxon kind of politics that were used about nationalism and the romance of the country . . . plus using a bit of the Catholic spirit, and the ghost of Germany and bringing up images of the early mythology of Germany, it was wonderfully conducted. He was not a politician. He was something else. I think he was a media artist. He used politics and he used theatrics and he created this show that ran for twelve or thirteen years. He would march down the middle through the tables and the lights would hit the stage and the lights would build at various parts of his speeches and it was rather like a rock and roll concert. And the kids would get very excited and girls would get very hot and very sweaty and guys would say, "Oh, I wish that was me up there". That, for me is the rock and roll experience.'

From Munich David went to Dusseldorf and then there

was a day free before he performed in Berlin. In his big Mercedes (previously owned by the President of Sierra Leone), with Corinne and his driver Tony Mascia, Jimmy Osterberg and the American photographer Andy Kent, he decided he wanted to visit East Berlin.

There were two notable incidents. The first came during a visit to a retired operatic singer who lived near the Berlin Wall. Inside her home, he saw a bust of Hitler and allowed Andy Kent to photograph him, looking at the bust as if meditating on the man's mystery.

The second incident, or moment, occurred after the limousine moved through Checkpoint Charlie and into East Berlin. The car cruised slowly along the streets, David peering through the darkened windows as the car approached its destination: the bunker where Hitler killed himself in the final days of conflict. The party of five disembarked. Andy took pictures of the other four in front of the bunker. Then, as the others drifted away, David remained in place and looked at Andy. He smiled. He turned towards the bunker and raised one arm in salute, holding it stiff and in front of him as the Nazi generals did in 1945. Andy clicked off several photographs, but afterwards agreed to David's demand that he would never use any of the Hitler photographs without David's permission.

A concert in Frankfurt followed, then after a show in Zurich, David joined Angela and Zowie, now almost five years old, in what Angie described as 'a big cuckoo clock chalet set amid snow-capped mountains' overlooking Lake Geneva. There, they relaxed – and quarrelled – for two days. Things were not good between David and Angela. The long separations had taken their inevitable toll, and now they were to be separated again. Angela was to remain in Switzerland as David resumed his tour.

In Zurich, Pat Gibbons got a call from David, who said he needed money. Gibbons turned to Andy Kent and said, 'David needs this, will you take it to him?'

Andy said, 'Yes, of course.'

The limousine sped the distance at 140 mph as Andy held a bag with $20,000 in Swiss francs in his lap.

'Would you like to go to Russia with me?' David asked Andy later that day.

Andy said, 'Yes, of course.'

David told Andy to return to Zurich to arrange all of the visas. They were to be travelling *through* Poland and the Soviet Union, not visiting, so Andy was to obtain 'transit' visas, easier to acquire on short notice.

David and Jimmy Osterberg and Andy left by train on 20 April.

'We got taken off the train in Brest at the Polish-Russian border by an albino KGB man,' Andy says today. 'David never travels light and he had this big trunk. Everything was in order, but the trunk and the luggage were taken off the train. What'd they do? They took my *Playboy* magazine and put us back on the train again, telling us that someone would meet us in Moscow.'

No one met them and after finding an interpreter, they taxi'd all their belongings to the Hotel Metropole, then went sightseeing – visiting Gum's Department Store, Red Square and St Basil's Cathedral – after which they boarded the train again and resumed their journey to Finland.

At the Russian-Finnish border there was another incident, as David and Jimmy were taken off the train, stripped and searched. Andy Kent says he thinks the Russians were looking for religious ikons, a popular item on the Russian black market, although that would not explain the strip-search incident. No ikons were found, but the Russians did confiscate some of David's books, most notably those about the Nazi propagandist, Goebbels, and the Nazi industrialist, Albert Speer.

'I'm working on a film based on Goebbels,' he said later, 'and they found all my reference materials.'

Helsinki passed without incident.

But in Stockholm, the next stop, David created an incident himself, telling a Swedish reporter, 'I think Britain could benefit from a fascist leader. I mean, fascist in its true sense, not Nazi. After all, fascism is really nationalism. In a sense, it is a very pure form of communism.'

'We couldn't believe he said that,' says Andy Kent. 'Barbara DeWitt and Corinne were there and they said, "Fuck! He said that?"'

Although the Swedish newspapers overlooked the remark, they didn't in England, where David got precisely what he wanted: big black headlines and public indignation. David was scheduled to perform six nights in a row at Wembley's Empire Pool, and many seats were as yet unsold. David knew that controversy always sold tickets. Besides, David hadn't been in England in two years. He didn't want to enter unnoticed. He wanted to enter triumphantly, noisily, blatantly.

On 2 May following concerts in Gothenburg, Sweden, and Copenhagen, Denmark, David returned to London, which was waiting for him to explain himself. David insisted on arriving by train at Victoria, one of London's busiest stations. As he disembarked, surrounded by hundreds of fans and dozens of nervous policemen, as well as a gang of pushing, shouting journalists, he suddenly threw up his right arm in what appeared to be a quick but definite Nazi salute.

Later, David, and others, would deny vehemently that it was a Nazi salute, or anything approximating it. But photographs and television newsfilm of the incident made it clear. So did the lyric of a song he wrote with Jimmy Osterberg shortly afterwards. This was 'China Girl', a song about heroin and fascism. 'I stumbled into town,' David wrote, 'visions of swastikas in my head.'

Of course, this infuriated nearly everyone, especially the old grey heads at RCA. Eight years later, Barry Bethel, who had left RCA but remained close to David and Angela, was so upset he still refused to discuss it. 'It was looking for outrageousness for the sake of outrageousness,' Barry says.

In the week following his arrival, David's name, picture, voice and music were everywhere. The day he arrived, BBC radio ran the first of four parts of *The David Bowie Story*, and nearly all the garish daily newspapers put him on the front page. By the end of the week, Alan Yentob's documentary, *Cracked Actor* was running again on BBC television, *The Man Who Fell To Earth* was, at last, on general release, and his records were all over the charts. (*Station to Station* was in the Top 10 and 'TVC 1–5', released the same week, was in the Top 40.) As a result, all six shows at the Empire Pool were sold out.

It wasn't exactly the Beatles and Beatlemania, but it wasn't bad, either. David had done it. He had returned to

London triumphantly. (One night at the Empire Pool, he introduced himself as David 'Winston' Bowie, a reference to Winston Churchill and his earlier remarks about wanting to be Prime Minister.) And his audience had embraced him.

Everywhere he looked in the big auditorium he saw himself in various permutations. Over there was a Ziggy Stardust, a boy of fifteen wearing a torn T-shirt and an old fox fur stole, his make-up wrecked from pushing through the crowd. Nearby stood a twenty-one-year-old chef from Liverpool, his two-tone hair slicked back, wearing a waistcoat, trousers and crisp white shirt.

'No, I don't always dress like this,' another fan said. 'It's just for the show, and to show everyone I'm a Bowie fan, and that I'm a bit unique, too.'

And that was David's point. He had, as one writer put it, 'connected with the mood of constant change which has characterized this decade and instilled in his fans a fervent and challenging appreciation of the necessity to confront the anonymity which contemporary society would seek to impress upon them by celebrating the notion of outrageous individuality.'

David himself said, 'If I have helped one person discover that he could be more than he thought he could, then I have been successful.'

After the final Wembley concert, David turned on a sharp heel to every side of the auditorium, combining the Nazi salute with the two-finger peace sign, then leapt for joy and ran off.

And then, following a show in Rotterdam and two shows in Paris, he did what he was best at: he virtually disappeared.

Behind the scenes, it was not good. David's use of cocaine had declined somewhat, but now he was drinking heavily. Worst of all, soon after Zowie passed his fifth birthday (28 May), Angela walked out of his life. And it's clear that, as far as Angela was concerned, one of the reasons was Corinne.

'Our lives fell into a familiar pattern where we tried hard to keep harmony,' she later wrote in her memoir, *Free Spirit*, 'but things were not helped by the constant aggravation that Corinne caused between us.'

Angela says Corinne was 'asserting her "indispensable"

167

role' and blocking important telephone calls, including one from Ken Glancey, the president of RCA. Angie says she confronted Corinne in France, shortly after the Paris concerts. They argued and Angie went to David.

'David,' she said, 'you should call Ken Glancey. The man wants to hear from you. No matter how you're feeling at the moment, some responsibilities just have to be carried out. And for that matter, it would make everybody's lives a lot easier if you would prevail on Corinne to be more polite on the phone.'

That did it. David exploded and told his wife to leave the room. After that, Angela said, 'there was no turning back.' She called a taxi and left.

'What a wonderful time it was for me,' Angela says today of her years with David. 'It was such a *great* learning experience. What an *opportunity* it was: 22, 23, 24, 25, 26 years old, jumping on airplanes, going back and forth to Los Angeles, to New York, to Paris and the South of France, to Rome. Everywhere I went there was work that I could *do*. What a college! What a wonderful way to grow up, to learn about business first-hand. Not to have to study it in books. Just *do* it! I got to go out and *do* it! And I *loved* it! That's what I was so upset about when David and I split. I was so hurt. It was the best job in the world and someone had taken my best job away from me. I was just there, thinking, everything I know, everything that I'm good at, I can't do. 'Cause that was my job. That artist was my *job*.'

The pop world had changed greatly during the years of their unusual marriage and responsibility for much of that change could be laid at David's feet. Disco was all the rage in the summer of 1976, especially in America, where the big hit singles included Johnny Taylor's risqué 'Disco Lady' (the first single in recording history to be certified platinum by the Record Industry Association of America, signifying sales of over two million copies) and 'Love to Love You, Baby' by the Queen of Disco, Donna Summer. David had been in the disco vanguard a year before with *Young Americans* and was staying current with *Station to Station* and 'Stay', his new single release.

Another thing: the latest trend in British pop was something that label-mad journalists called 'punk', a primitive movement in rock that was more offensive socially than musically; in fact, musicality had little to do with 'punk', where style was everything. The movement was epitomized by a young group of Londoners who called themselves the Sex Pistols, a band whose lead singer insisted his name was Johnny Rotten. Here, again, David was a sort of godfather, a role that David himself acknowledged. 'When Ziggy Stardust fell from favour and lost all his money,' David said in an interview, 'he had a son before he died, Johnny Rotten.'

As one part of the population disco'd the night away and another, smaller group began emulating the most upsetting band in rock (EMI paid the Sex Pistols £40,000 to go away after the musicians used obscene language on a live Thames TV programme and publicly vomited at Heathrow Airport; another record company, A&M, paid them nearly twice that amount when they announced their first single would be 'God Save The Queen'), David went into the recording studio with Iggy Pop at the Château d'Herouville. This was where David had recorded his *Pin-Ups* album. Now he was producing, and co-writing, an album for Iggy called *The Idiot*.

Over the years, David had worked with many performers, as producer and coach and entrepreneur, but never with anything other than one-hit successes such as he experienced with Lou Reed, Mott the Hoople and Lulu. Others, including Dana Gillespie and Iggy Pop, had so far failed to experience *any* success.

The Idiot was David's first complete album collaboration with his friend and was a raucous, inharmonious yet compelling collection of songs which reflected the electronic direction in which David himself was travelling.

It was almost predictable that David was shooting off in another direction. It was obvious that he had hit upon a winning formula in disco (combined with a somewhat aberrant and decadent visual imagery), one which probably he could have carried on for several years at least. But David was easily bored; his attention span was short, even for the fast-changing world of pop. As Charles Shaar Murray said, 'David has a pathological dread not only of simply repeating himself, but even of appearing to have squeezed an idea dry.'

Now David was determined to work with Brian Eno, whose band Roxy Music had opened David's Ziggy Stardust shows at the Rainbow Theatre four years before. Since then, Roxy Music had recorded half a dozen hit singles and as many hit albums (all in England; nothing in the US) and Eno had left the group to explore his electronic inventiveness in experimental but unsuccessful solo efforts. David said Brian gave him a 'totally new way of looking at it [his music], another reason for writing. He got me off narration, which I was so intolerably bored with. Narrating stories, or doing little vignettes of what at the time I thought was happening in America . . . Brian really opened my eyes to the idea of processing, to the abstract of communication.'

The album David and Brian produced, working, first, at the Château at the same time David worked with Iggy Pop and, later, in Berlin, was as experimental as anything David had done – but a natural outgrowth, none the less, of what he had begun in *Station to Station*, when he filled up twenty-four tracks with assorted sounds and tricks and longed for twenty-four more.

Tony Visconti, who returned to David's side and entered the project as co-producer (and whose wife Mary Hopkin sang backup on one song), said David was determined to surprise everyone with the new album, out of a fear of seeming predictable.

'To promote the last two albums, he must have done more than 200 shows,' Tony said. 'He was absolutely tired of being RCA's sure thing, and he also felt he was losing his pioneer spirit.'

One of the many ways he tried to offset this feeling was to experiment with new instruments. On one track or another, before the album was finished, David provided nearly all of the vocals and played the Arp, tape horn, brass, synthetic strings, saxophones, tape cellos, guitar, pump bass, harmonica, piano, prearranged percussion and Chamberlain.

One of the most interesting aspects of the album was the element that was missing on many of the tracks: the lyrics. Traditionally, David created lyrics for his songs *after* composing the music, often after recording the music, and this is what he tried again. But this time, according to Tony

Visconti, David hit a writer's block and failed to come up with more than one verse for some songs and no lyrics at all for others. Thus, one side of the album was largely instrumental, with the voice used 'texturally' or 'phonetically'.

An example was 'Warszawa', David's quasi-Gregorian picture of the countryside viewed during his recent journey by train through Poland. David said, 'Look, Brian, I want to compose a really slow piece of music, but I want a very emotive, almost religious feel to it. That's all I want to tell you at this point. What do you suggest as a start?'

Brian said, 'Let's go lay down a track of finger clicks.'

'And he laid down I think it was 430 clicks on a clean tape,' David later explained. 'Then we put them all out as dots on a piece of paper and numbered them all off, and I picked sections of dots and he picked sections, quite arbitrarily. And then he went back into the studio and played chords and changed the chord as he hit that number, and went through his piece like that. And I did a similar thing on my areas. We then took the clicks out, heard the piece of music as was, and then wrote over the top of that according to the length of bars we'd given ourselves.'

David was now doing musically what he had done lyrically, using the William Burroughs 'cut-up' technique, allowing music to create itself, randomly, or accidentally.

At the end of September, David, Iggy, Tony Visconti and Corinne abandoned the Château and went to Germany to finish the album in a studio close to the Berlin Wall. It was there that Corinne told David to take an apartment, to go into seclusion and rest.

David and Corinne – with five-year-old Zowie now in their care – found an apartment in the Schoenberg district, near the centre of the city. For David's tastes, it was a modest flat, large and airy and elegant in a 1940's way, but located over an automobile spare parts shop in a neighbourhood with a large number of Turkish refugees. Nearby were several bars, which David visited regularly.

Angela says she visited David in November, soon after he wrecked his Mercedes in an underground parking lot while drunk. He was smoking four packs of cigarettes a day, she says, and was still suffering from 'all sorts of people in the pop world who have been winding him up'.

Angela described the apartment as 'old-fashioned . . . brightened by David's musical instruments and Zowie's toys in tidy disarray'. But soon after she arrived, she said, she found David 'writhing about all over the place'. She called for a British military ambulance. She, David and Corinne were convinced: David was having a heart attack.

David remained in the hospital for 36 hours, where no coronary trouble was diagnosed. 'He'd just overdone things,' a hospital spokesman said, 'and was suffering from too much drink.'

When they'd returned home again, Angela says they talked about reconciliation. However, she said, if they were to resume their relationship, Corinne had to go.

'Angie, how can you ask that?' David said. 'You know how much I rely on her. She's part of the organization. She knows everything about my business. Who else could run it the way she does?'

'I could,' Angie said, angrily.

David made no reply.

A few days later David went out and Angie and Corinne argued. Finally, Corinne stalked out and Angie went into her bedroom, where 'amid tears, I seized every dress, coat and garment I had given her over the last six years and dumped them in a pile in the centre of the room. I grabbed a bottle of vodka from somewhere and poured it over them and then I struck a match . . .'

Angela left for London the same day.

*

Thirty-one years had passed since Hitler's death and the conclusion of the Second World War. Yet in Germany the war was a constant presence, especially in West Berlin. Russia and the United States sliced Germany in half in the postwar occupation days, and the capital city of Berlin was left isolated in the middle of Communist-held East Germany. Berlin was similarly cut in half, with East Berlin going to the Soviets and West Berlin to the Western nations. Running down the middle of the city was the dreaded Berlin Wall.

David had crossed over, driving through Checkpoint Charlie as a tourist. He had seen the bleakness of the East. As a visitor and then a resident of West Berlin, he also had seen, and enjoyed, the plenty of the West. Not far from his apartment were many of Berlin's most infamous clubs, where naked women wrestled in mud, sex was sold in and performed in the booths, and men dressed as women most convincingly.

David loved Germany, was an avid student of its culture, both artistic and political. He adored the films of Fritz Lang and was influenced by them in the staging of his last two tours. His painting and drawing was similarly much influenced by German expressionist artists, especially George Groz. And he revelled in the Germanic tradition of decadence, as described by Christopher Isherwood in his book *I Am A Camera* (later adapted for Broadway and Hollywood as *Cabaret*) and the music and plays of Brecht and Weill.

On the surface, it seemed an odd place in which to seek spiritual and physical salvation. In a similar situation, an American rock star would go to a rural environment, as so many were doing in the mid-1970s in northern California and Oregon, in Woodstock, New York, and in Canada. Some, including John Lennon, were buying or retreating to remote islands.

Not David Bowie. He was in full flight from the 'vile pisspot' (his words) called Los Angeles and finding renewal in West Berlin. From Sodom he had gone to Gomorrah and somehow he made it work.

'I felt like I'd fallen into the bowels of the earth,' he said later. 'It took me two years, at least, to shake off the depression. I switched to drink to compensate, and it was a bottle of whisky in the morning just to get rid of the depression. So I moved to Berlin and just went crazy. And it's a great place to go crazy. Nobody gives a damn.'

'It was the antithesis of Los Angeles. The people in Berlin don't give a damn about your problems. They've got their own. They're not sycophants. They're tough and cynical. At the beginning of Hitler's rise, he knew Berlin was the one place he had to keep his thumb on, because it was so radical. There were so many left-wingers there, he really had to come down heavy. That same cynicism and radicalism are still there, and that was what I thought I had to put myself through. I thought, if I could survive in Berlin without being mollycoddled, then I had a chance of surviving.'

The recording continued with Brian Eno at the Hansa Studios and the result, delivered to RCA in time for 1976 Christmas release, was called *Low*. The title seemed appropriate. In the past, David had introduced his audience to the disintegration of all of society. Now he was asking that same audience to witness his own disintegration.

RCA was totally confused. The year had begun with a Top 10 hit, 'Golden Years', the disco song from the *Station to Station* album. This was followed by David's first 'greatest hits' anthology, *Changes One Bowie*, a collection of eleven songs that spanned the years from 'Space Oddity' and 'John I'm Only Dancing', through the Ziggy Stardust and Diamond Dogs era, up to 'Young Americans', 'Fame' and the recent 'Golden Years'. This album went to No. 10 in the US as well, and to No. 2 in England.

And now *this*? RCA were totally mystified by the lack of hit potential.

Some of the familiar disco rhythms were there, but there were eleven tracks in *Low* and only *five* of them had any lyrics, most of which were mumbled or incomprehensible. Side one *opened* and *closed* with instrumentals and side two was *entirely* instrumental (ignoring the vocal sounds which came off more or less as chants)!

One of the 'vocals' had only two lines, repeated several times. In still another, one of the lines was so derivative ('I'm in the mood for your love') it was embarrassing.

Did Elvis Presley, RCA's other big act in the mid-1970s, turn in instrumental albums? Did John Denver, another RCA act who was fading but still popular, sing two lines and quit?

Release of the album was delayed while the executives at RCA tried to figure out what to do. They needed a new single for release in January at the latest and David's career had already been marked by too many re-issues and re-releases to try that tactic again.

Finally, the second week of January, a week after David celebrated his thirtieth birthday (quietly getting drunk with friends in Berlin), RCA released 'Sound And Vision'. It was a peculiar choice, because basically it was an instrumental and what little lyric there was revealed David's floundering state perhaps more clearly than any other song on the album. He sat behind drawn pale blinds, he said, 'waiting for the gift of sound and vision'. For RCA, neither sound nor vision was forthcoming.

As the album hit the record stores, there was a predictable flurry of interviews, not with David this time – who was not interested in spending any time with the press – but with Eno and Visconti and others who tried to explain the confusion away. No, they said, David hadn't abandoned the pop mainstream; he had never been in it.

It was 'drifting' music, Eno said, a kind of 'new muzak, with synthesizers,' the sort of music popularized in Germany by bands such as Kraftwerk and Tangerine Dream. 'Drifting' music, he explained rather dodgily, was the opposite of rock, which had a lot of 'anchorage'.

The critics were only slightly more helpful. Mick Watts, who had conducted the infamous 'bisexual' interview for *Melody Maker* five years before, was one of the first into print, calling *Low* 'a remarkable record and certainly the most interesting Bowie has made. It's so thoroughly contemporary, less in its pessimism, perhaps, though that's deeply relevant to these times, than in its musical concept: the logic of bringing together mainstream pop – in the album's disco bass-and-drums and conventional lyric – and experimental music perfectly indicates what could be the popular art of the advanced society we are moving into . . .'

Others came right along. Bob Christgau, who wrote for a number of American publications and graded albums as if they were high school history tests, called David's line 'Such a wonderful person/But you've got problems' a 'love lyric for our time' and gave the record a B+. While a writer for *Creem* magazine, Simon Frith, called the album 'such a fun record, such a refreshing *jeu d'espirit* . . . *Low* made me laugh a lot.'

Not everyone agreed. The critic for the influential *Boston Phoenix* said *Low* was a 'schizoid production' marked by 'experiments in drone, repetition and time annulment'. And while the reviewer for *High Fidelity Magazine* generally

praised the work for making 'no compromises towards commercial accessibility,' he also said the album was marred
by 'stylistic inconsistency' and 'robot-like rhythms'. The
overall effect, he said, was 'distancing'. Still another writer
for *Creem* called the album 'inaccessible' and 'confounding'.

As these writers fell all over themselves trying to explain
to others what it was they thought they heard, David
watched the album climb the English and American record
charts. By the end of January, only a week after its release,
the album was headed for the No. 2 spot in England, No.
11 in the United States, while the single, 'Sound And
Vision', one of the disco songs, was almost as successful
(No. 3 in Britain though only No. 69 in the US).

In America, single-oriented disco music kept on growing,
assimilating everything in its mechanical but danceable
path, and the top albums in the first three months of 1977
were Stevie Wonder's *Songs In The Key Of Life*, the Eagles'
Hotel California and the soundtrack to *A Star Is Born*, the
Hollywood remake that starred Barbra Streisand and Kris
Kristofferson.

In England, a small revolution was brewing as the punk
movement spread like an angry yeast. Besides the Sex
Pistols, London now had its first all-girl punk band, the
Slits, and the politically focused Clash. And the bestselling
albums were by a Scandinavian vocal group (Abba), an
American country singer (Slim Whitman), and the Shadows
band that had made its name in the 1950s backing Cliff
Richard (the album was a collection of hits).

Germany was so far away.

In February, David and Jimmy Osterberg went to London, where on 1 March, Jimmy began his first British tour
at the Friars' Hall. The room was not sold out and the piano
player in the band was not noticed. At his own request,
David was not lit.

David played piano behind Jimmy for the rest of the tour,
including three shows at the Rainbow, where David had
staged his first Ziggy shows. All three shows were sellouts,
largely because Jimmy was being described in the British
press as the 'founder of punk rock'.

A writer in the *Evening Standard* said, 'He has been noted
over the years for bizarre stage appearances that have

included antics like vomiting over a member of the audience, smashing his teeth out with a microphone and smashing a broken glass against his chest. Iggy's new record, produced by Bowie, is simply entitled *The Idiot*.'

The same week, a single was released from Jimmy's album, *The Idiot*, one of the songs he wrote with David, 'China Girl'. Jimmy flew to America for the next, larger leg of his album promotional tour.

'David,' he said, only two days before leaving, 'will you come with me? Tour with me in America?'

Jimmy knew that if David said yes, David would have to fly. There wasn't enough time for David to take a boat.

David stood mutely for a moment. He, too, knew what an affirmative answer meant: flying.

David smiled at his friend and said, 'Yes, of course. No point in breaking in another piano player.'

In New York, David went to the Manhattan office of his interim manager, Pat Gibbons, who tentatively told David that he felt he hadn't had enough to do since taking over from Michael Lippman. He'd stayed in constant communication with RCA's New York offices, of course, but with David not wishing to talk to the press and no tours planned – and tours were Pat's forte – he told David he felt David's career would benefit if he were given more responsibility. Also, he said, David's playing piano for Iggy Pop was fiscally irresponsible. David said he'd think about it and then gave Pat a list of books he wanted delivered to his hotel suite.

From New York, David and Jimmy travelled to his first North American date, in Montreal, and then they went to Toronto, Boston, New York, Philadelphia, Cleveland, Chicago, Pittsburgh, Columbus, Milwaukee, Portland, Seattle, Vancouver, San Francisco and Los Angeles. Fifteen cities in thirty-four days. For David, this was a month of good hotel rooms, bottles of Moët et Chandon, endless Gitanes cigarettes and comforting anonymity. For David it was an interesting tour, different from all the rest. Finally, he was given a chance to look at America without pressures. Now he was not required to sell himself. Now he could sit back and watch.

Much had happened in America in the year since he left Los Angeles, seeking refuge and recovery in West Berlin. For one thing, the political atmosphere was more hopeful now; Nixon's pleasant but bland successor Gerry Ford was gone and the new president was a fundamentalist peanut farmer named Jimmy Carter, whose only sin, apparently, was having lust in his heart (or so he told *Playboy* magazine) and who loved the music of Bob Dylan (or so he told *Rolling*

Stone). Other new heroes and heroines included Woody Allen and Diane Keaton (for their on-and-off-camera relationship), John Belushi and Dan Akroyd (whose smash hit television show, *Saturday Night Live*, revealed an offbeat irreverence that reminded David of the comedy of Monty Python), the Eagles (for their No. 1 album, *Hotel California*), and Werner Erhardt, a former used car salesman who invented a popular self-help seminar called *est*.

Good old America. Still crazy after all these years.

However much David enjoyed the journey, he was glad to be back in Berlin. Even in exile in Berlin, remaining in the shadows – usually refusing to give interviews, playing anonymous backup piano for Jimmy Osterberg, declining invitations to perform – David's career remained in full and prosperous swing. Despite the song's obvious shortcomings, 'Sound and Vision' sold well in England, though was less successful in the US. At the same time, David continued his work with Brian Eno in the recording studio and kept trying to get something happening in film.

It was a time of great change for David. He had given up taxis and was bicycling from his flat to the art galleries, where he spent more and more of his time. Inspired afresh by the German expressionists, he painted almost every day, producing portraits of Jimmy Osterberg and scenes from his neighbourhood.

At the same time, he began to look at Berlin with a more distanced perspective. Berlin, he told one interviewer, was a city 'made up of bars for sad, disillusioned people to get drunk in. I've taken full advantage of living there to examine the place quite extensively. One never knows how long it's going to remain there. One fancies that it's going very fast. That's one of the reasons I was attracted to the city.'

In another interview, he spoke of the 'friction' he found in Berlin. 'I've written songs in all the Western capitals,' he said, 'and I've always gone to the stage where there isn't any friction between a city and me. At the moment, I'm incapable of composing in Los Angeles, New York or in London or Paris. There's something missing. Berlin has the strange ability to make you write only the important things . . .'

This positive attitude was reflected in his next album, *Heroes*, which again was recorded with Brian Eno in West Berlin's Hansa Studios.

'It was more expansive,' says Tony Visconti, who again sat in the control room as co-producer. 'He used a bigger studio. Just 500 yards from East Berlin, from the Wall, and every afternoon I'd sit down at that desk and see three Russian Red guards looking at us with binoculars with their Sten guns over their shoulders and the barbed wire, and I knew that there were mines buried in that Wall, and that atmosphere was so provocative and so stimulating and so frightening that the band played with so much energy, I think they wanted to go home, actually.'

None the less, Tony insists, the songs that came out of the sessions were more positive than those on the previous album. During the recording of *Low*, he said, David was depressed about his continuing fights with Angela and his two former managers, and it was 'only the album, making *Low*, that was taking the edge off his depression'.

'When he made *Heroes*,' the producer adds, 'he conquered that low period and he felt like a hero every minute of the day he was in the studio. He got up and sang in the microphone at the top of his lungs. You can hear on *Heroes* what he calls his "Bowie histrionics", his own peculiar style of yelling and screaming. And *Heroes* was a very positive version of *Low*. It was such a positive period of his life. He was, in fact, a hero. We all felt like heroes. It was a heroic album.'

The title track was one of David's most romantic songs for some time. Every day during the sessions, David noticed a young man and woman meeting beside the Berlin Wall. There were many lovely parks in West Berlin, David said, and it was apparent – to him, anyway – that this couple chose a less attractive meeting place not just because it was near where they worked, but because love blooming next to the heavily mined wall was symbolic of a greater power. In fact, David so liked this song, and its message, that he recorded and released it not just in English, but also in German and French.

Even so, there was a sense of claustrophobic panic in the song, and in others on the album's first side there were scenarios on a somewhat bleak and uninviting future. 'Beauty and the Beast', 'Joe the Lion' and 'Sons of the Silent Age' all flirted with themes of social disintegration, macabre dreams and endless sleep, and although the final track, 'Blackout', was purportedly about the great blackout in New York, it seemed easier to read into the lines some of David's reaction to his own alcoholic blackout which recently had been mistaken for a heart attack.

The second side resembled *Low*'s second side and was largely instrumental, with songs again taking their inspiration from David's travels. David played his beloved saxophone on 'V–2 Schneider', inspired by the German V–2 rockets of the Second World War, played a Japanese stringed instrument called a koto on 'Moss Garden' while 'Neuköln' was his Berlin neighbourhood and the last track was titled 'The Secret Life of Arabia'.

The *Heroes* recording sessions stretched through all the summer months, ending in September. By then, David had gone to Paris several times: in June for several interviews – he was now becoming less inaccessible – and in July to attend the French premiere of *The Man Who Fell To Earth*. He also travelled to Spain for a holiday with Bianca Jagger and to London, in the first week of September, for television appearances with Marc Bolan and Bing Crosby.

The show with Marc was the last in a series of six hosted by Bolan, and David was a special guest. (Another act on the show was a band called Generation X, featuring a singer named Billy Idol.) Bassist Herbie Flowers was in the backup band and he says that the sense of competition between David and Marc remained strong, even after the passage of so many years and no personal contact.

'David's appearance on the show proved Marc was a mentor to David,' Herbie says, 'but David arrived with his entourage – the limo, the secretaries, his publicist, the media. So if he was acknowledging his debt to Marc, at the same time he was demonstrating his greater success. Marc was the star of the show, but he didn't have an entourage and he didn't have any hit records and David did.'

During the numerous breaks in the videotaping, Marc got very drunk. 'David overshadowed him,' says Herbie Flowers. 'It was that simple. And at the end of their song together, Marc fell off the stage. It was at that point that the director cut and when the show was broadcast later that month, that was what ended the show.'

Marc Bolan never saw the show. He died in an automobile accident on 16 September.

By then, David had appeared as a guest on Bing Crosby's *Merrie Olde Christmas Show*, singing the title track from *Heroes* and, with Crosby, 'Peace on Earth' and 'Little Drummer Boy'. That was Crosby's last performance as well. He died three months later of a heart attack.

The same week Marc Bolan died, David's record company released 'Heroes' as a single and Iggy Pop's *Lust for Life* (which included seven songs that David had co-written). *Heroes*, the album, was scheduled for release a week later. With so much new product in the marketplace, David went for the media's jugular, giving interviews to almost anyone who asked and giving the writers exactly what they wanted. In the case of the music press, all he had to do was talk and let the hungry puff press lap up every word. The national press demanded a little more and David was prepared to give it to them. If it was headlines they wanted, it was headlines they got.

The headline in the *Evening News* was typical: BRITAIN IS READY FOR A NEW HITLER, SAYS BOWIE.

After making it clear that David lived in Switzerland as a 'tax exile', the tabloid (which had a circulation of four million) quoted David as saying, 'Personally, I'm closer to communism than fascism. That at least has some saving graces. In Britain now, there are parallels with the rise of the Nazi Party in pre-war Germany. A demoralized nation whose empire has disintegrated. People are losing their dignity, which is dangerous. All the National Front needs right now is a leader, which they haven't at the moment. But one will come along.'

David was also quoted as saying he believed in Cabalism, a form of religion based on numerology and the 'missing scrolls of the Old Testament'. These missing scrolls, he said, were being held by the Russians, who used them in an attempt to bribe the Pope to stop the spread of Catholicism.

Swinging in another direction, a week later, David made a successful bid for national sympathy by setting up a trust fund for the 'love' child of his late friend Marc Bolan. Two-year-old Rolan Bolan was Marc's only child by his common-law wife, black American singer Gloria Jones. The headlines for this story were as big as the ones for his Hitler speech.

David received his worst treatment at the hands of Barry Cain in *Record Mirror*. The appraisal went on for thousands of words, most of them negative or cynical. David was called fickle . . . being apart . . . out of touch with the man in the street . . . condescending . . . distrusting . . . isolated . . . without depth or soul, . . . a man of little faith.

David's continuous role changing intrigued the *Record Mirror* writer, who said, 'See, Bowie uses the ultimate aegis to protect his oh-so-obvious vulnerability. And that's a diversification, a constant stream of guises epitomized in his music that tell us nothing about the guy.'

Other music publications were more tolerant, regarding David as a kind of saviour, or at least someone who was clearly ahead of the musical pack. *Melody Maker* was typical, calling David's two Berlin albums 'among the most adventurous and notably challenging records yet thrust upon the rock audience. Inevitably controversial, these albums have combined the theories and techniques of modern electronic music with lyrics that have found Bowie dispensing with traditional forms of narrative in pursuit of a new musical vocabulary adequate to the pervasive mood of despair and pessimism that he has divined in contemporary society.'

For a week, Barbara DeWitt, David's publicist, ran writers through David's hotel room, granting carefully prescribed interviews as if they were audiences with a pope or a king. David was always most gracious and seemingly very candid. The only reason he was ending his moratorium on interviews, he said, was 'to prove my belief in the album. Both *Heroes* and *Low* have been met with confused reactions. That was to be expected, of course. But I didn't promote *Low* at all, and some people thought my heart wasn't in it.

'This time, I wanted to put everything into pushing the new album. I believe in the last two albums, you see, more than anything I've done before. I mean, I look back on a lot of my earlier work and, although there's much that I appreciate about it, there's not a great deal that I actually like. I don't think they're very likeable albums at all.

'There's a lot more heart and emotion in *Low* and, especially the new album. And, if I can convince people of that, I'm prepared to be stuck in this room on the end of a conveyor belt of questions that I'll do my best to answer.'

The effort paid off, at least in England, where *Heroes* went to the No. 2 spot and the title song to No. 24. In America, the reception was considerably chillier. There, the single bombed completely and the album sold far fewer copies than any since *The Man Who Sold the World* (although it went to No. 35). According to the pop writer for the *New York Daily News*, David was suffering from 'a terminal case of cool'. Certainly the market was cooling.

So, too, were the executives at RCA. The legal war between David and Tony DeFries had not cooled at all and RCA was in the middle. 'It was bad enough that David practically refused to return any phone calls,' says a former RCA employee, 'worse than that, we had DeFries on the horn almost daily, making sure he was getting his contracted share of the gold. RCA was beginning to grow tired of David Bowie and flagging record sales didn't help a bit.'

None the less, in December following a holiday in Kenya with Zowie – visiting and posing for photographs with primitive Maasai tribesmen – David flew to New York to record for RCA the narration for a version of Prokofiev's *Peter and the Wolf* (as performed by Eugene Ormandy and the Philadelphia Orchestra). At the same time, he agreed to sit in his Mayfair Hotel room and be interviewed by anyone and everyone whom Barbara DeWitt could again coax into his proximity. To each he was charming – sitting cross-legged on a couch as was his custom, wearing a short-sleeved silk shirt and slacks, sipping a Coors beer and smoking the incessant Gitane cigarettes as he explained over and over and over again the meaning of *Low* and *Heroes*, the reason he went to Berlin, the plans for a tour the next year.

Why do you bother with concerts?, one of the writers asked. You've said you really don't enjoy touring . . .

'I can't live on the amount of money one would get for doing two or three shows,' David said. 'Not the way I want to live anyway. It costs a hell of a lot to get to the places I've been going to lately.'

How is your business and financial situation now? Are you in control?

'A lot better than it was. It's pretty steady,' he said. 'I'm absolutely in control of it, all the way down. I've only got three people working for me and everybody's on salary.'

Do you trust them?

'I don't have to trust them. Everything's in my name. *I* get the money.'

Then, his interviews over, David served as best man at the wedding of his bodyguard Tony Mascia and flew home to Switzerland for Christmas with his son. It was not David's most placid holiday. In fact, for the next two weeks, David experienced one of the most tumultuous periods of his personal life.

It started two days before Christmas in Montreux. Angela had been staying at David's home with Zowie again, but when David returned, they argued fiercely and Angela flew back to New York. Angela failed to call Zowie on Christmas Day. By 2 January 1978, when Angela returned to Switzerland, David was in Berlin with Zowie and his nanny.

Now it was Angela's turn to explode emotionally. With her was a boyfriend, a fellow American who called himself Keeth Paul, and Tony Robinson, a reporter from the *Sunday Mirror*, one of England's more sensational national newspapers. Robinson said Angela called him and asked him to come to Switzerland so she could tell her side of the story. She was, he said at the time, 'furious, almost hysterical' and planning to divorce David to gain legal custody of their son. When Robinson arrived, he said later, Angela was 'nearly senseless' (having taken a heavy dose of sedatives).

A few hours later, at about four in the morning on David's thirty-first birthday (8 January), Robinson said Angela locked herself in one of the chalet's nine bathrooms and took another massive dose of barbiturates and tranquillizers, then roared through the big house, smashing glass and crystal everywhere. When Keeth Paul tried to calm her, she hit him with a rolling pin. She then rushed into the kitchen, grabbed a large knife and threatened to throw herself on to it. Finally, she went to bed and fell into a coma.

Later that day, Paul and Robinson were unable to awaken Angela. They left her unattended to discuss whether or not they should take her to the hospital nearby and during that time, she roused herself and either fell or threw herself down a flight of stairs, blacking both her eyes, and breaking her nose.

Discharged from the hospital a day later, Angela returned home to the rented chalet where, according to Tony Robinson, she lay wrapped in a blanket, murmuring explanations: 'I just couldn't take it any more . . . I just wanted to top myself . . . I thought what the hell . . .'

David was not thrilled. At the time, David was giving her £17,000 ($40,000) a year and paying her rent and travel expenses as well as numerous other bills. The previous year, Angela spent more than $35,000 on taxis alone, using them even when she wanted cigarettes. In all, David figured he had given her $125,000 in 1977.

A week later, David filed for a divorce.

By then David was making a film in Berlin. It had been more than two years since he finished *The Man Who Fell To Earth* and during that time David had probably read thirty scripts and announced half a dozen 'sure things'. Most recently, he had told reporters that he was going to star in a film biography of the German expressionist painter Egon Schiele, a script brought to him by the English director, Clive Donner, who had directed both *The Caretaker* and *What's New Pussycat*. David planned to make the film with the American actress Sydne Rome, with whom he shared a European agent, and when that project was delayed, Sydne and their agent suggested David for the lead in Sydne's next film, to be made in Germany.

This was *Just a Gigolo*, a wry tragi-comedy which told the story of a shell-shocked young Prussian officer (David Bowie) who returns to Berlin after the First World War to find that the life he knew there has vanished for ever. He cannot adjust and drifts along until he becomes one of the gigolos employed by Baroness von Semering, a role to be played by Marlene Dietrich.

The director of the film, and the man who convinced David he should take the role, was David Hemmings, the English actor who had made his reputation as the mod photographer in Antonioni's pop classic *Blow Up* (a film which featured music by the Yardbirds, from the period when David was performing with the Lower Third at the Marquee, in 1966). Hemmings had also appeared in more than a dozen other, mostly forgettable, films since then, including *Barbarella* and *The Love Machine*. Hemmings was a classic: a great story-teller with one of those boozy baritone voices that make English actors sound so irresistible. He and David got on famously the night they talked at David's house in Montreux, and once shooting started in Berlin in January, the relationship developed most happily.

'David has a very special quality,' Hemmings says today. 'A quality of natural elegance. The camera *adores* him. You can't shoot him and lessen his attractiveness. The nature of the character he played demanded that I shy away from this. We took him into the worst shop in order to find the filthiest clothes and the real down-and-out look that was necessary for the character, and everything that David put on, it looked as if he'd just created a new fashion. It was absolutely extraordinary, and very funny. We laughed all the morning. Because he and I fantasized about creating the "gardening look", which was heavy wellingtons and old corduroys. If I put on heavy wellies and old cords and a sweater and a cloth cap, I'd look like a gardener. David looked like he'd just been asked by *Vogue* to do a cover!'

Hemmings said in an interview at the time that David had caught perfectly the 'intelligent helplessness' that his part required. 'The character David plays makes things happen by default. His presence is always there in the action, but he never quite gets it right, he always slightly misses . . .'

In the end, in a sequence that pre-dated the rise of Hitler, David is killed by a stray bullet from a fight between the Nazis and Communists. Both parties try to claim his body, and the Nazis win, burying him as a hero to a cause he never espoused.

David said he took the part because he believed in the ideas and issues, in the film. He hated politics, he said, and every time he said anything political in an interview, it was only to get a reaction. In *Just a Gigolo*, everyone political looked foolish; even the Nazis marched out of tune with the background music. Also, David said, 'I've tackled a subject

I'm fascinated with: that of gigolos, male escorts and male hookers for women. I've known various individuals in those professions, yet I've found they're rather inscrutable and difficult to get to know; therefore, the role was that much more of a challenge . . .' He paused, then added: 'It also allows me to display a more sensual, sexual side of myself that was totally lacking in *The Man Who Fell To Earth*, where I didn't even have any genitals.'

During the filming, there were wig-pulling rows between some of the actresses and there were enormous tensions and disagreements, many of which were blamed on communication difficulties between German- and English-speaking crew members. Adding more pressure was the uncertainty about Marlene Dietrich, who refused to leave her Paris apartment, where she said she was busy writing her memoirs. Dietrich was not essential to the film – after all, her part had originally been written for Trevor Howard – but there had been much publicity about her appearance, her first speaking role in seventeen years, since she appeared in *Judgment at Nuremburg* in 1961. With the exception of the screenwriter, who brought her into the film, no one had met her; not even David Hemmings had been granted more than the briefest telephone conversation. With a production cost in excess of five million dollars, executive tempers were fraying visibly and no matter how hard Hemmings tried to insulate his people from it, the tension was being felt.

Despite this, overall David thoroughly enjoyed making the film. He learned to dance the samba with his leading lady, Kim Novak, and shared scenes with two contemporary European greats, Maria Schell and Kurt Jurgens. And although he never actually appeared in a scene with her – the film was edited to make the opposite seem true – he adored the idea of being co-starred with Marlene Dietrich.

While filming, David continued to give lengthy interviews. Probably the most revealing of these was the one he gave Michael Watts for *Melody Maker*. In this story, David remained, as always, in complete control. When asked about his feelings about Tony DeFries and MainMan, he said only that he was grateful for all he had learned and let it go at that. When pushed, David even seemed amused when the interviewer asked him about Cherry Vanilla, who apparently said that MainMan 'peddled David's ass [in the gay community] like Nathan sells hotdogs'.

'Good Lord,' David said. 'Chronic, isn't it? I hope she meant it tongue-in-cheek. I know what she meant, yeah. She worked very hard at pushing that side of me, because it gave her very easy access to headlines. And all the time that that was going on, of course, I was in another country, so it was hard for me to keep any sort of control.

'My compromise at the time was to live with it. When I got to America and found out how I'd been set up over there, I thought, "My God, I can't fight this enormous snowball. I'll have to work with it and gradually push it back down to something more manageable".'

More revealing was David's forceful renunciation of rock music. He felt 'incredibly divorced' from rock, he said, 'and it's a genuine striving to be that way'.

Was that, perhaps, why *Low* and *Heroes* strayed afield? Possibly, he said. 'I felt I was very predictable, and that was starting to bore me. I was entering an area of middle-of-the-road popularity which I didn't like, with that disco soul phase, and it was all getting too successful in the wrong way. I want and need creative artistic success. I don't want, need or strive for numbers. I want quality.

'There comes a time when you go through the most ridiculous posture of saying, "I'd be really pleased if everybody stopped buying my records, so I could go away and do something else".

'You see,' he added later, 'the only way to remain a vibrant part of what is happening is to keep working anew all the time. For me, it always will be change. I can't envisage any period of creative stability and resting on my laurels.

'I think for what I do and what I'm known for, it would be disastrous. So that's *my* predictability.'

If he didn't want to be recognized as a rock star, what, then, did he wish to be?

A generalist, he said.

'A generalist?' he was asked. 'What was that?'

'It encompasses anything I wish to do, really,' David replied. 'I find, for instance, that I really want to paint seriously now, and not toy with it, and I am painting very seriously now every available moment. And I'd like to be known as a painter one day when I get up the nerve to show them. But I want at the moment to be known as a generalist rather than as a singer or a composer or an actor. I think a generalist is a very good occupation to have.'

So saying, David returned to the set and resumed acting.

'Not too shabby, not too shabby,' said David Hemmings at the end of the shot. 'Let's commit this to celluloid before it gets any better.'

BOWIE BOWIE

As soon as David finished his final scene in *Gigolo*, and Hemmings and the others moved one of the sets to Paris to accommodate Marlene Dietrich, David flew to America where on 16 March he began rehearsals in Dallas for what would be the biggest concert tour of his career, a sixty-five-city sweep of not just the US and Canada, but Europe, Japan and Australia as well.

Because he wished to perform much of the material from *Low* and *Heroes*, and because, he said, Brian Eno and Robert Fripp wouldn't join him (or *any* tour; they both hated touring), he changed the musical lineup – adding a synthesizer (Roger Powell) and electric violin (Simon House) to his standard rhythm section, Carlos Alomar on rhythm guitar, George Murray on bass, Dennis Davis on drums, plus two newcomers, Sean Mayes on piano and Adrian Belew on lead guitar.

Eleven months had passed since he finished his tour as the anonymous piano player for Jimmy Osterberg. In that period much had changed, again, in the US. In fact, some said that 1977 was the year 'the music' died. When David arrived in America in mid-March 1978, the Sex Pistols had self-destructed on their first and last tour of America . . . the heavy metal group Kiss, known primarily for its circus clown make-up and its lead singer's extra-long tongue, had been reduced to a Marvel comic book . . . the all-time hit song of the era was a saccharine, off-key 'You Light Up My Life' by Pat Boone's daughter Debby . . . and Martin Scorsese had produced a film of the Band's last concert called *The Last Waltz*. This was also the year that Elvis died, bloated and alone on his bathroom floor, ten different sedatives, tranquillizers, and painkillers taking final control of his heart.

The wave of popular culture in America, and perhaps in

all of the Western world, seemed to be crashing on to a different beach. For twenty years, the focus was on rock and roll. Now the tide was moving towards film. Rock music played a role in the transition with 'music movies' of course. Besides being the year of *The Last Waltz*, 1977 was the year that John Travolta and the Bee Gees made *Saturday Night Fever* a household phrase and the soundtrack from that film remained lodged in the No. 1 position in America for a staggering twenty-five weeks.

Even so, 1977 was a 'movie, movie' year – the year that saw America embrace two powerful anti-war movies, *The Deer Hunter* and *Coming Home* (both multiple Oscar winners) and two science fiction films that together changed the history of movie-making for ever, becoming two of the biggest grossers of all time, *Close Encounters of the Third Kind* and *Star Wars*.

It seemed a perfect time for Ziggy Stardust and the Man Who Fell to Earth (the two of David's characters that were most remembered by the American audience). How many scripts had David received over the years, with stories of guitar players who fell to earth from elsewhere to save the earth or ruin it? David sighs: 'I mean, you wouldn't think that many people *wrote* about Martians who play guitars, would you?'

By 1978, Ziggy and the eerie alien in Nic Roeg's film and all the rest of the characters were long dead, at least as far as David was concerned.

'I care an awful lot about the characters I created,' David said. 'Ziggy and Aladdin were nice – quaint, but nice. Lord, people saying, "Do you remember the old rock and roll with lipstick on?" I say, "Let it rest in peace."'

'I'm going out as myself this time' he said of his spring tour. 'No more costumes, no more masks. This time it's the real thing. *Bowie Bowie*.'

There were many who once thought David was ahead of his time who now thought he was dangerously behind it. His time, finally, had come, they said. And he had gone.

The tour was prepared quickly and fairly inexpensively. The lighting was adapted from that used on the previous tour. Again, David wanted to project a stark, black-and-white look, with only a little colour to soften it, so he dusted off the old fluorescent tubes and added some coloured gels for the spotlight. Rather than have just one costume this time, however, he decided to have two entire racks of them, a different outfit, perhaps, for every show. To design them he hired an old friend from his days with Lindsay Kemp, Natasha Kornilof, meeting with her for an hour while he was shooting *Gigolo*.

'We had torn bits out of magazines and we did small drawings and we had lots of ideas and wanted trousers that were kind of big and we also wanted to combine them with Hawaiian jackets, you know, those funny shirts that they used to wear in the forties, the ones with strange prints on them?' Natasha says today. 'We had also seen a funny mess jacket in another photograph and I went off and combined the large trousers with the mess jacket. I made him a series of tracksuits in velour. I made a snakeskin jacket to go over the tracksuits. I made loads of things, corduroy suits and sailor suits and hats. He was briefly in London, so I sent some stuff up, I didn't even see him that time, and he tried them on and said more of this and more of that and I went away and made more. Then he asked me if I would go to Dallas, where we had a grand try-on. Then he took me to San Diego, so I could finish buying him shoes.'

More attention was paid to the music, of course, as David led his seven musicians through a disciplined series of rehearsals aimed at reproducing the songs from *Low* and *Heroes* as closely as possible to the versions on the albums. (Given the changed instrumentation, naturally.) Then, deciding not to turn his back on his past entirely, he expanded the show's repertoire to include several songs from the Ziggy period.

By the time David and his band and road crew of twenty-five arrived in San Diego for the first show on 29 March, modest but impressive press kits had been distributed – including a reprint of the Michael Watts story and interview from *Melody Maker*, a biographical sketch (which, again, emphasized the promise that this new 'character' on stage was the real thing), and a charming, boyish self-portrait.

By now David was playing only in the largest arenas, coliseums and convention centres – 18,000 seats and up. These were the venues reserved for the biggest acts (Led

Zeppelin, Elvis Presley, the Eagles, the Rolling Stones), but which were mostly used for sporting events and circuses. These monstrous rooms were not designed for musical performances; consequently, the acoustics were usually mediocre and beyond the first twenty or thirty rows visibility was reduced rapidly until the performers became tiny specks. It was for this reason that David Bowie, and most others, had made their acts more and more visual and why David, with his mime background, generally performed with an advantage others didn't have.

Yet, in San Diego David performed a subdued opening set. Only 45 minutes in length, he appeared in front of a veritable 'prison wall' of stark, white fluorescent tubes, wearing ballooning white pants and an open-neck, short-sleeved white shirt, rarely moving from the microphone. And except for 'Jean Genie' and 'Fame', everything he sang or the band played was from the *Heroes* and *Low* albums. The audience seemed disappointed.

Following a long intermission – during which everyone was urged to fill up on junk food, alcohol and Bowie souvenirs – the mood changed, as David sang seven songs in a row from his classic 1972 *Ziggy Stardust* album. The audience responded with a series of standing ovations.

'As he went through such provocative, new-age rock tunes as "Five Years", "Suffragette City" and "Rock 'n' Roll Suicide", it was easy to see how deep Bowie's impact on rock has been,' said Robert Hilburn a few days later in the *Los Angeles Times*. 'The first great rock star to emerge in the 70s, Bowie didn't turn out the most hits, write the largest batch of noteworthy songs or necessarily draw the biggest crowds, but he shook the rock 'n' roll epicentre more than any other single figure in that period.' Hilburn concluded that although David may not have regained the compelling, celebratory heights of his Ziggy Stardust days in this show, 'he remains a towering figure in rock, one whose side steps are more interesting than most lesser artists' biggest leaps forward.'

Hilburn was a known and predictable Bowie fan; from David's earliest appearances in America, he had offered only praise. None the less, the *Los Angeles Times* was prestigious and Hilburn's reviews were being read with greater respect within the industry than they had been a few years earlier.

Everywhere David went, the reviews were adoring.

'Bowie is uncanny in his ability to pick musicians,' said *Variety*; 'Belew's lead guitar was a riveting and pivotal force . . .'

'A superb live show,' said the critic for the *New York Times*, 'and the enthusiasm at the end of Monday night's concert at Madison Square Garden – the first of two there – was a genuine attestation to excellence.'

The shows *were* excellent. Opening with the languid yet haunting, quasi-instrumental, 'Warszawa', then crashing into the rollicking disco rhythms of 'Heroes' (which gave Adrian Belew a chance to show off his glittering lead guitar as Simon House's swirling violin joined George Murray's fluid, bouncy bass), the shows seemed to rise and crash and rise again, like the sea when the surf is strong and rough. As soon as David had the audience on its feet, he went into something more subdued, like the gloomy 'Blackout' from *Heroes* (David's 'heart attack' song), and then when the audience was quiet again, he wheeled into an instrumental and then changed the pace another time, pounding into the 'Speed of Life' and 'Breaking Glass'.

After eleven songs, he spoke to the audience: 'Hello.'

The audience cheered its hello to him.

'We'll see you again in ten minutes. Will you be here?'

David, being coy. The audience cheered again.

'Thank you for coming.'

During the intermission there was recorded music by the Rutles (a send-up group, parodying the Beatles), Iggy and Lou Reed – David's choices.

And then the lights went down again as David and the band returned to the darkened stage.

David told the audience, 'The next guest on the show is . . .'

There was a long pause, followed by David's painful, plaintive, familiar cry:

'FIVE YEARS! FIVE YEARS! . . .'

And David was Ziggy Stardust again.

The Ziggy material held up, was as strong in 1978 as it was in 1972, and the audience responded noisily. The fluorescent tubes were flashing now as David sang the explosive 'Suffragette City': 'Wham, bam, thank you, ma'am!'

Next David performed another instrumental from *Low* and then sang the only non-original piece of the show, Bertolt Brecht and Kurt Weills's best-known song, 'Moon of Alabama' (also known as 'The Whisky Song' and popularized a decade earlier by Jim Morrison and the Doors). The closing number was a massive version of 'Station to Station'.

Then: 'Thank you very much. Thank you.'

The band disappeared, as the audience roared. And then the band reappeared for two encores, disappeared again and then reappeared for a final time for 'Rebel, Rebel'.

The next thing the audience heard was: 'David Bowie has left the auditorium . . .'

Through April and early May, there was hardly a major American market that David didn't work, from Phoenix to Fresno to Houston and Baton Rouge, from Kansas City to Milwaukee, from Nashville to Detroit, from Pittsburgh to Montreal, from Boston to New York. There were thirty-one performances in twenty-four cities in forty-one days. It was, as David so often put it, 'soul-destroying', but it provided the money he needed to continue. Even with many of the venues running 20 per cent behind the 1976 attendance figures – promoters generally blamed flagging record sales – the gross receipts at the end of the American leg of the tour went well beyond the three million dollar mark.

David played Madison Square Garden on 7, 8, and 9 May and five days later performed in Hamburg, Germany.

Back in Europe, David was 'home' again. However popular he was in America, here he was much *more* popular. For example, album sales of *Low* in England alone exceeded those in all of America. And with David's frequent and sometimes lengthy stays in France, Switzerland and Germany, he had built considerable local constituencies. The French and German versions of 'Heroes' had also endeared him to his European audiences.

Moreover, he was a much more controversial figure in Europe than he ever was in America, especially because of his outspoken views about fascism and Hitler; whether or not he believed those views, the emotional response in

Europe understandably was more emotional than reaction elsewhere. Consequently, security was tighter here. Tony McGrogan, who had taken Barry Bethel's place at RCA as director of artists' relations, was given the job of coordinating David's visits and tours. 'We always stayed in big hotels,' Barry says today, 'so it was no problem for fans to find out which one. That meant we had to register David under a false name. I was a fan of the Arsenal football team, so I used all the names of the Arsenal players. I gave all the names to the travel agent up front, so even they didn't know. I started with the goalie. David came to me when he got his hotel assignment sheet for the first city. "What sort of name is Jennings?" he said. I said, "Don't worry, it'll change tomorrow."'

David's bodyguard, Tony Mascia, and Coco also changed their names from hotel to hotel as the tour crossed the continent, moving from Hamburg to Berlin (where David halted the show when he noticed a steward manhandling a fan in the audience and called to the steward in German to stop), to Zurich, to Essen, to Cologne, to Munich, to Bremen (where the full concert actually was performed in a television studio for immediate broadcast), to Vienna.

David had a day free before going on to France, so while his band and stage crew travelled to Paris, he went to Cannes for the annual International Film Festival to appear with David Hemmings at a preview screening, a 'teaser', for *Just a Gigolo*. Editing of the film was not complete, but Hemmings and the film's backers felt it would be helpful if David were present to assist in marketing.

David also went to Cannes to advance his own film career. After more than a year of discussion, David still hoped to star in the film based on the life of Egon Schiele. He was also talking with German director Rainer Werner Fassbinder about a movie version of Brecht and Weill's *Threepenny Opera*. David had aspirations to be a film director eventually, but he wanted to proceed carefully, particularly after the recent lukewarm response to modest films directed by such rock stars as Neil Young and Bob Dylan.

After staying up all night in Cannes, meeting with people he hoped would make those dreams come true, David rushed to Paris and then to Lyons and Marseilles, and then on to Copenhagen, Stockholm, Gothenburg, Oslo, Rotterdam and Brussels. And each night he slept under the name of another Arsenal football hero.

On 14 and 15 June, David Bowie made his triumphant return to England. It was his first time in concert there in two years. RCA marked the event by releasing *Peter and the Wolf* (which by now had gone to No. 136 in America, nothing to celebrate, but surprising none the less), the BBC re-ran Alan Yentob's documentary *Cracked Actor*, and the still-breathless London pop music press flocked to interpret every note of music, every flick of David's Gitane ash.

The thirteen-concert, four-city British tour climaxed in London on 29 and 30 June and 1 July, when David played Earl's Court – five of David Hemmings' 35mm cameras trailing him for the production of another documentary. (The previous documentary by D. A. Pennebacker still sat, uneasily, upon a shelf.)

The reviewers were unanimous. The *Financial Times* called David a 'confident, happy Bowie, finished with excess and quite content to sing through his songbook to his very faithful fans', while the atmosphere was 'more exciting than for Bob Dylan a fortnight earlier'. The *Evening News* called him 'a totally controlled performer . . . one of the few singers in the world to use theatre effectively to augment rock music.' The prestigious, usually very stuffy *Times* said, 'Predictably the audience went wild. Less predictable was the warmth, even affection Bowie showed for them. A change for him, for us and, one might add, for the better.'

'It would be foolish,' said the *Evening News*, 'to dismiss him solely as a rock star. He is an interesting painter, an innovative lighting expert, an actor and an artist.'

David had scheduled four months of free time before his world tour resumed in November, and it was during this period that David's career went into a serious slump. Recent concert grosses and reviews were bigger and better than ever, but on other fronts, the news was all depressing. Record sales had been dropping and by summer 1978, there weren't any of his records on any charts, anywhere in the world, and, besides that, the première and distribution of *Just a Gigolo* was postponed when the film went into re-editing . . . the David Hemmings documentary filmed in

Earl's Court was shelved . . . and David added to all his other legal problems with an open fight with RCA.

The circumstances surrounding *Gigolo* were becoming increasingly confused. In September, a full month before the scheduled premiere in Berlin, *Melody Maker*'s Michael Watts wrote a story predicting the film would be the 'movie bummer of next year'. (It was scheduled for release in England in February, 1979). Watts said the film 'looks a total mish-mash from which no one emerges with much credit. David Hemmings has directed without any flair, the script is abysmal, and the acting (with the exception of Bowie's co-star Sydne Rome) is as stiff as a morgue.'

Watts went on to say that following the Cannes film festival, *Gigolo* had been turned down by every major British distributor. Finally, he reported, it was accepted by Tedderwick, a new production company financed from the Middle East whose only previous experience was in distributing *Death Trap*.

Hemmings tried to re-edit the film to suit the new distributors, but ran out of money before he could complete the job 'appropriately'. So, he says, 'I walked off the picture three-quarters of the way through the process. Someone else finished the cut and butchered it. The music by Manhattan Transfer was cut to ribbons. Women in the film who gossiped all the way through the picture to provide a narrative sense were cut out for the most part. In all, twenty minutes of the film was removed, including all the humour and irony.'

At the same time, David dropped all interest in the Hemmings' documentary. 'Dave came down to Spain to see my cut,' Hemmings says today. 'He decided at the end of the day that he didn't want to release it.'

But David's biggest problem was with RCA, to whom he was contracted for another five years.

'There were a number of reasons why David was getting forcefully and finally, very, very fed up,' says someone who was at RCA at the time. 'For one thing, I think he heard that he wasn't the first to be asked to narrate *Peter and the Wolf*. In fact, RCA hadn't wanted David to do it. RCA wanted Peter Ustinov or Alec Guinness, both of whom said no. David apparently didn't like being third choice.'

Besides that, says Herb Hellman, RCA's director of publicity, 'David's ego wouldn't allow for the possibility that we couldn't sell *Low* and *Heroes*. He resented the fact he wasn't on the charts.'

In London, Tony McGrogan tells other stories – about David's paranoia and secrecy.

'When David toured England that summer,' he says, 'we switched from using football names in hotels to staying in private homes. David didn't want to stay in hotels under *any* name, so I suggested finding some residences. He liked the idea and from that time on, whenever David came to London, he stayed in an estate house or big flat somewhere. I hired the flats and RCA always paid for them, but an address wasn't put on the rental contract until after RCA signed it. David didn't want RCA – didn't want *anyone* – to know where he was. I had an assistant at the time. He was with me *two years* before Coco would let him know where she and David stayed. On the way to the flat, I'd have to drop off John at a pub and pick him up later, after dropping David and Coco off. She made that a rule. I had the managing director [the boss of RCA in London] ask me for David's phone number and I refused to give it to him. Then he wanted the address and I refused again. My job was on the line, but I knew that if David thought I'd turned against him, it was all over. When the managing director demanded an audience with David, it was like waving a red flag at the bull.'

McGrogan sighs and says, 'I'm afraid that David was on an ego trip.'

One final irritant, for David, came in the way that RCA regarded the tapes for a live album he turned in after completing the American leg of his tour. Again recording in Philadelphia, David submitted approximately an hour and a half of music, which was to be released on a double disc set and called *Stage* (the same name he had planned for the documentary). When an artist released a live album, it was generally expected that many of the songs would be old favourites, but usually new ones were included, too. Or the versions of the old ones were different, or at the very least, more exciting because of the live ambience. None of that applied to the tapes that Tony Visconti rushed to New

York. It was as if David didn't want to give RCA *anything* new.

In addition, David wanted to count the double album as two records, to satisfy his legal obligation to provide RCA with two albums a year. RCA insisted upon counting it as only one album. David instructed his manager, Pat Gibbons – still hanging in there in New York – to cancel his contract with RCA. Pat told David that Tony DeFries had negotiated an unbreakable contract. And that's why David cancelled release of the documentary. 'DeFries may get 50 per cent of my live album royalties,' he reportedly told a friend, 'but he won't get a farthing from my film.'

It was with all this hissing and popping by long-distance telephone that David went into a studio in Montreux, Switzerland, to record another album with the balding cerebral Brian Eno. Tony Visconti, again retained as co-producer, says that it was in this album of 'David's triptych' with Eno that Eno 'came to the forefront. The first two, *Low* and *Heroes*, were a delicate balance,' Visconti says. 'But on this one, Brian was very much in control. He made a chart of his eight favourite chords and stuck them on the studio wall and he had a teacher's pointer and he pointed, he told the band, "Just get into a funky groove, boys". He was telling these three black guys who came from the roughest part of New York, "Just play something funky". So Dennis [Davis] goes [MUTTERS SOUND EFFECTS] and then Brian pointed to the chord of B-minor and Carlos [Alomar] and George [Murray] would play around in B-minor, then Brian would point at A-7 and then they'd play, and the whole album had that stifled, constricted feeling.'

David seemed, as far as the band were concerned, to be experimenting again for the sake of experimentation. On the song that eventually was released as the album's first single, 'Boys Keep Swinging', everyone in the band swapped instruments (Carlos played drums instead of guitar, George Murray piano instead of drums, etc.), giving the track a rough, 'garage band' sound. In recording 'Red Sails', David tried to create a 'very Germanic background' and on top he recorded a Chinese melody. In 'Yassasin', a song about his Turkish neighbours in Berlin, he used a Turkish melody line against a Jamaican reggae beat. And the mid-section of 'Move On' is 'All the Young Dudes' played backwards.

Lyrically, the album (to be released as *Lodger*) was a mixed bag, including a fervent anti-nuclear plea in 'Fantastic Voyage' ('Dignity is valuable/But our lives are valuable too!'), a sad appraisal of disc jockeys (in 'DJ'), a rollicking pirate epic in 'Red Sails' and a song about wife-beating in 'Repetition'. There also was a song inspired by recent visits to Kenya called 'African Night Flight' (a poignant narrative telling of German pilots who lived in African bars for years, swearing every night to return to civilization 'one of these days') and a song which captured some of David's own rootlessness, 'Move On'.

The final mix of these disparate songs was not completed for several months. In the meantime, at the end of the first week of November, David flew to Australia to resume his world tour. Consequently, he again missed the premiere of a film. *Just a Gigolo* opened in Berlin on 16 November, with nearly everyone in the cast in attendance. The film was badly received in the German press and David Hemmings immediately returned to the project, having negotiated the right to edit the film again before its premiere in London two months hence.

There were seven concerts in David's first tour of Australia, called 'The Oz Tour' – in Adelaide, Perth, Melbourne (where torrents of rain soaked the crowd and put the fear of on-stage electrocution in the minds of most of David's band), Brisbane (where the local government's Minister in Charge of Noise Abatement complained of David's decibel level), and Sydney. Then David and seven semi-trailer truck loads of equipment were flown to Japan for the final stops. Planning to spend the Christmas holidays in Tokyo, David made arrangements to have Zowie and his son's nanny fly in from Montreux for the start of the tour.

David was an absentee father most of the time, but maintained legal and physical custody. None the less, whenever Zowie was with him, he tried very hard to make it up, taking him to Kenya so the boy could see animals in their natural habitat and now to Japan. He also was very protective. He wouldn't let photographers take pictures of Zowie and when interviewers asked about him, David said only that he was seven and a half, blond and very lively and not interested in music at all, and then he changed the subject or shut up.

'It was a natural thing, what David was doing,' a close friend says. 'His father had shown him attention, had supported and protected him when *he* was little and now David was doing the same for Zowie.'

After the Christmas holidays, David flew to London to work on the mix of his album – now called *Lodger* and scheduled for a May release – and to help promote the long-delayed British release of *Just a Gigolo*, which was now to be premiered on 14 February at the Prince Charles Cinema in Leicester Square. Those attending the premiere were asked to wear 1920s style dress or black tie. David and his date for the evening, actress Viv Lynn, wore kimonos and wooden clogs. They should have worn suits of armour. Rarely has a film been so thoroughly panned in the press.

There were a few favourable reviews, but not many. *Films & Filming* magazine called it 'an original and often deeply moving movie' and said David's 'essentially filmic features are convincingly Aryan and his little-boy lost air admirably conveys Paul's [the character's] naiveté and inborn idealism.' While the American weekly, *Variety*, opened its review saying, 'Those who dug *Cabaret* [starring Liza Minelli in 1972 in what is regarded as the definitive musical look at decadent 1920s Berlin] probably will also admire *Just a Gigolo*.' The film, said the reviewer, 'delivers a lot of bittersweet entertainment and is never less than engrossing,' as 'Bowie goes through his tumbleweed paces with engaging appeal.'

As for the rest, it seemed, in the end, like overkill. The film was 'all show and no substance,' said the *Sunday Mirror*, and Bowie was 'completely miscast'. The *Financial Times* said David and all the others in the cast 'fall like ninepins before the hamhanded staging and the choppy, frenetic, try-anything editing.' The *Morning Star* said David 'exudes about as much warmth as a fridge' and the *Sunday Telegraph* fired away with an entire fusillade: 'The dramatic ability Bowie possesses is less enshrined as a living fact, than embalmed as a dead talent. Bowie's anaesthetized features worked well enough in his first film, *The Man Who Fell to Earth*. But then he played a man from outer space. Now he's supposed to be one of us; an occasional inflection of face or voice would have helped that illusion.' As for the film, well, it was 'an absolute mess'. Even the *New Musical Express*, which might have been expected to be more charitable, said David's 'dramatic ambitions obviously far outweigh his abilities. Bowie might look the perfect part as a foppish Prussian gentleman turned gigolo traipsing through 1920s Berlin, but he can't *play* it. An illusion is burnt to a crisp every time he opens his mouth or tries to convey any depth or detail of character. Bowie's efforts throughout are comically inept.'

David was shaken by the barrage. It was true that he didn't like the film. In time, he would even go so far as to refer to it, with an embarrassed laugh, as 'my thirty-two Elvis Presley films, all rolled into one'. None the less, in February and March 1979, as the reviews came pounding in, one friend says he was 'stunned first, then defensive, then appalled, and finally completely crushed'.

Fortunately, David didn't have to rely upon movie reviews and subsequent box office grosses for survival. (And in the case of *Gigolo*, distribution was spotty at first, then quickly non-existent, as the film was withdrawn due to a lack of public support.) In recent months, David's record sales had improved somewhat. His second live album, *Stage*, had, in spite of its lack of new material, done well, especially in Britain where it was a No. 5 hit. This didn't mean that David was out of the woods. In the US, the live album peaked at No. 44 – which meant it was profitable, but not a 'hit' – and although the single from that album 'Breaking Glass', limped to No. 54 in England, it failed to make the Top 200 in America.

With sales so erratic in Britain and dwindling again in America, it was time to pull out the stops, to take another page from Antonin Artaud and outrage with purpose and effect. He decided, this time, to do it with 'video'.

Musicians and singers had been appearing on television since Kate Smith and George Gershwin performed on the first experimental broadcast in 1930. In the decades that followed, music was a staple in television programming and with shows like *Your Hit Parade* and Dick Clark's *American Bandstand*, television came to be recognized as a potent medium through which a lot of records could be sold.

It wasn't too long before record companies, and individual bands, began to produce short promotional films with that specific goal in mind. In America in the mid-1960s, dozens of popular bands were featured in such films for something called Scopitone: put a quarter in the juke box and you got to *see* the performers as well as hear them, so long as you were within eyesight of the 'box'. This was a short-lived fad, however, and it wasn't until 1967, when the Beatles produced videos for 'Penny Lane' and 'Strawberry Fields Forever' to send to Ed Sullivan for broadcast on American television, that the concept was solidified.

It was that same year that Jim Morrison, who was a graduate of the UCLA film school (along with Doors keyboardist Ray Manzarek), produced what may have been the first 'artistic' promotional film, for a song called 'The Unknown Soldier'. In it, Morrison was tied to a post on the beach and executed, blood splashing out of his mouth at the moment of cinematic death.

After that, it was anything goes and by 1977, an unrecorded band called Devo was making highly polished, conceptually complete and somewhat bizarre videos instead of the conventional audition audiotape. This was part of what attracted David Bowie to announce that he would produce their first album. (He later changed his mind.)

David had been making impressionistic films of his own songs since 1967, when for Ken Pitt he acted out several songs for the self-produced television special, *Love You Till Tuesday*. Since then, he had produced other videos of 'John I'm Only Dancing', 'Golden Years', 'Wild Is the Wind' and 'Heroes', none of which had attracted much attention.

RCA agreed to underwrite the production of videos for three of the new album's songs – the three which were regarded as most likely to be released as singles, 'DJ', 'Look Back in Anger' and 'Boys Keep Swinging'. A young British director who had worked in America in television and who had produced an unlikely album of rock with Mae West was elected to put Bowie on tape.

For the first video, the slapstick tirade against radio, 'DJ', the director, David Mallet, positioned David behind radio turntables, which as the song progressed, David proceeded to smash, sparks and then flames leaping from the machinery. There was also a sequence in this three-minute film where David strolled along Earl's Court at eleven o'clock at night, attracting a crowd of passers-by, one of whom, a large black man, spontaneously treated David to a sloppy, tonguey kiss.

'Look Back in Anger' was the song created, in part, when Brian Eno pointed to chords written on the wall. Lyrically and visually, it made only slightly more sense, as David, while writhing rather ecstatically in a garret somewhere, slowly assumed the features of the Angel of Death. In one scene, he caresses a portait of himself, transferring some of the paint to his suddenly aging face. The allusion to Oscar Wilde's *Portrait of Dorian Gray* was obvious.

The third video had the greatest impact – an impact that would last for several years. This was for 'Boys Keep Swinging', a throwback song to David's Ziggy Stardust days, a mixture of macho and camp, somewhat reminiscent of the contemporary gay American group, Village People, a quintet of apparent homosexuals who dressed in various costumes and looned their way on to nearly everyone's hit parade with the overt 'YMCA' and 'In the Navy', Top 5 hits in both the US and England at the same time that David was mixing 'Boys'.

The videotape opened conventionally, with David wearing a suit and tie and executing some of his fastest dance steps, as if he were back on the *Soul Train* television show in America. Then there was quick cut to a trio of female backup singers.

'See those girls?' said an executive from RCA the day he previewed the video for the press.

'Absolutely goddess, the one in the middle,' said the writer from *Melody Maker*, referring to a figure in clinging gold lamé, the face reminiscent of both Vampira and Raquel Welch.

The man from RCA laughed. 'They're all Bowie,' he said. 'All three of them!'

The camera moved in for a close-up of a figure in a black wig, a flared polka-dot dress and a top that plunged to the waist. The figure strutted down a catwalk, long earrings swinging, and suddenly whipped off 'her' wig. David then dragged the back of his hand across his lipsticked lips, smearing it across his face like blood (a gesture he borrowed from the stage act of his friend, transvestite Romy Haag). Then the Vampira figure did the same thing. Finally the last figure, looking very much like Marlene Dietrich, came forward. This time the wig stayed on. The hand moved to the mouth. A kiss was blown and David mimed a sultry goodnight.

When the album *Lodger* was released in May, the 12-minute videotape of all three songs was offered to major television programmes and to select discos and clubs in England and the US. For the time, the 'Boys' portion was considered too blatantly gay, so most American television shows rejected the offer (years later the videos surfaced on MTV), but clubs in twenty major cities, from New York's chic Studio 54 to Chicago's Park West to Studio One in Los Angeles began screening the videos regularly.

The unusual and, to David infuriating, thing was that RCA in America refused to release 'Boys Keep Swinging' as a single (preferring 'DJ' and, later, 'Look Back in Anger' instead) even *after* 'Boys' went roaring up the British charts to No. 7, giving David his first Top 10 single there in two years. In America, 'DJ' went no higher than 106 and 'Look Back in Anger' didn't even make the Top 200.

Again, David began grumbling about RCA in America.

'It was different here, in England,' says Tony McGrogan, who was still RCA London's head of artist relations and looking after David whenever he was in town. 'In fact, we didn't have to go to him with ideas. He came to us. He suggested a contest for Capital Radio: the listeners were asked to write about "Bowie the Traveller" and the twelve best would join David in Tony Visconti's studio for an advance listen to the *Lodger* album. We treated him right, like the star he was. In America it was a different story.'

(The winning contest entry, selected by David, concluded, 'My portrait is of an empty room, a broken lipstick, a nomad in a journey of time, the last cigarette. The artist haunted with time.')

The contest theme was appropriate. For the remainder of 1979, David was on the move, criss-crossing the Atlantic repeatedly. He was in New York in March, in London in

April, and back in New York in June and July (when he was seen with his Swiss neighbour, Oona Chaplin, the widow of Charlie Chaplin). Then in August it was back to London again. During this visit, David attended the Edinburgh Film Festival for the first public screening of D. A. Pennebacker's long-lost documentary, now titled *Bowie '73*. Although the film was well received, again it was withheld from general distribution because David was unhappy with the soundtrack and, again, because he didn't want to see Tony DeFries profit from what he regarded as his film.

The reviews of *Lodger* were mixed. The critic for *Rolling Stone* said it was 'just another LP, and one of his weakest at that: scattered, a footnote to *Heroes*, an act of marking time.' And the *New York Times* called it the 'most eloquent' that David had produced in years.

Disagreement by now was predictable. Some liked David Bowie and others did not, and that was the way it was. However, what made the release, and critical acceptance, of *Lodger* unusual was the fact that in 1979, a David Bowie album was used as an excuse by several publications to print serious retrospective analyses of David's career.

Thus even the disgruntled *Rolling Stone* writer (Greil Marcus) could grudgingly extend praise, noting that David 'never has shied from pretentiousness; still, his pretensions – to grandeur, of course, but also to genius, wisdom, supermanship – have been thought out and musically supported. If he uses his body or his face as icons, he also makes his albums with a care that can only be called extreme. No matter how bloated or irrelevant his pose, the wit and resignation persist, just below the surface if not on it. The aesthete's narcissism has come to seem like a form of introspection – a means to will, knowledge, creativity.'

And the *New York Times* man (Ken Emerson) could eloquently say of 'rock's cunning chameleon' that 'David Bowie sloughs off musical styles and theatrical personas like a snake sheds its skin. The fascination his zig-zagging music has exerted for a decade now has always been somewhat reptilian: it glitters with a cold cunning that is spellbinding, but also a little bit repugnant.

'And yet this cunning has never been crass, commercial

calculation. To the contrary, Mr Bowie is extraordinary above all else for the alacrity with which he abandons a style – be it the fey, futuristic "glitter rock" that he launched in the early 1970s, or the disco funk he recorded in the mid-1970s before the Bee Gees, the Rolling Stones and Rod Stewart had even heard of disco – the moment it catches on. As far as triple-platinum stardom is concerned, Mr Bowie has thrown it away again and again.'

In October, David was in Switzerland with Zowie and his nanny and Corinne. (Angela was in New York, living with a punk rock singer who called himself Drew Blood, and being represented in her countersuit against David by Beverly Hills divorce lawyer Marvin Mitchelson.)

In November, David went to Kenya again. In December he was in London, in Brixton with David Mallet, filming for a special New Year's Eve television show. And then it was off to New York with Zowie for an appearance on *Saturday Night Live* and a trip to the Broadway theatre, where he saw a play that would alter the direction of his career unmistakeably.

THE ELEPHANT MAN

David Bowie never moved through major cities heedlessly. He *used* them. Cities were where he did business. New York was where his record company had its headquarters, and Manhattan was the centre of the world's communications industry. New York also was a cultural centre, where he could visit great art galleries and the trendiest nightclubs within walking distance of his fashionable East Side hotel. New York also contained the heart of American theatre and during Christmas week, 1979, David attended a performance of *The Elephant Man* on Broadway.

This was a play about a grotesquely deformed man from 19th century England, who was rescued from a carnival sideshow and sheltered for the final years of his life in a London hospital. There, under the sponsorship of a sympathetic surgeon and with the encouragement of eminent Victorian socialites, the Elephant Man (whose name was John Merrick) found a sense of personal dignity before dying at the age of twenty-seven.

The play was written by an American, Bernard Pomerance, and was first produced at the Hampstead Theatre in London in 1977, where it was not very successful. None the less, it attracted the attention of American producer Richard Crinkley, who cast an English actor named Philip Anglim as Merrick and took the show to New York, opening to great acclaim off-Broadway and winning a number of prestigious awards. By the time the show moved uptown to Broadway, the show, its director, cast and author had won so many Obies and Tonys that the director says today, 'For two months, all I did was say "Thank you".'

So the play was a big hit when David saw it. He was impressed. The title role was played without make-up or padding and nearly nude, as Anglim distorted his body and speech to convey the *impression* of great deformity, while the story itself was one of triumph of the human spirit over adversity.

David said later that he 'liked it as a piece of writing and for myself, I thought I would have loved to have had the part if it had been offered – but it hadn't been. And that was the last I thought about it.'

David had other things to think about. His divorce from Angela was scheduled to become final the first week of February. Angela was still threatening to write her memoirs, which might damage David's career or at the very least embarrass him, if he didn't provide her with $1 million in cash. David finally had answered her through his attorneys, asking if perhaps her memoirs might not also embarrass little Zowie, who was now nine? David's attorneys also reminded Angela of her widely publicized suicide attempts – to which she actually invited a Fleet Street journalist. What of her outrageous behaviour with a succession of younger men? As evidence, newspaper clippings were produced, some dated as recently as November 1979, in which the latest of her escorts, 'Drew Blood', was quoted as saying, 'When I found her, she no longer cared. She had let herself go completely. You would not have recognized her. She was carrying around a plastic bag full of syringes. Another day and she might have gone right over the top.'

Angela's attorneys then responded with their *own* packet of clippings and interviews, in which David admitted to his own mistakes involving drug abuse in Los Angeles.

And so it had gone for months, as accusations and demands went back and forth, with Angela asking for money and custody of their son, and David saying no to everything.

In the end, David won virtually everything. As a resident of Switzerland, and with Zowie in his physical custody, Angela had no legal claim. And as for the cash settlement, she abandoned her demand for $1 million, accepted $50,000 and was told she could go ahead and write anything she wanted.

The final decree was issued on 8 February. At the time, David and Zowie – who was now telling his father he wanted to be called Joey – were skiing in the Alps.

A week later, David was back in New York to begin his sixteenth album.

David always was one to take a deliberately variant view of things and the album eventually called *Scary Monsters (and Super Creeps)* was no departure. The dadaists had pronounced art dead in 1924, he said, 'so from there on, what the hell can we do with it?' He answered his own question: 'One keeps trying to readdress the thing, looking at it from a different view.' And so it was in creating the songs for *Scary Monsters*. Constantly, he took a 'different view'.

When he recorded the album's opening track, 'It's No Game', he used a Japanese friend Michi Hirota, to sing the lyrics in Japanese (as counter-point to his English) because he wanted 'to break down a particular kind of sexist attitude about women and I thought the Japanese girl typifies it where everybody sort of pictures her as a geisha girl – sweet, demure and non-thinking. So she sang the lyrics in a macho, samurai voice.'

'Scream Like a Baby' told a grim Orwellian story that David called 'future nostalgia'. Listen to almost all of his albums, he said, and you'd find a song that takes 'a past look at something that hasn't happened yet.' (A staple device in science fiction.)

'Ashes to Ashes' picked up the story of Major Tom from 'Space Oddity' of a decade earlier. After all those years of drifting in space, Major Tom had become a junkie.

Brian Eno was gone for this album, replaced by another musician with an intellectual bent, the guitarist Robert Fripp. David had been a fan and friend of Fripp's since hearing his band King Crimson at the Speakeasy the same night, in 1969, he met Angela. Like Eno, Fripp had left his band to make solo albums. Like Eno, his cult status grew and his record sales dwindled.

Others on the album were by now regulars: Carlos Alomar, George Murray, Dennis Davis and Roy Bittan, with Tony Visconti at the control board. Another guitarist showed up for one track ('Because You're Young'). This was Pete Townshend of the Who.

'It was a very bizarre session,' says Tony Visconti. 'Pete's from the old school of breaking the guitar against the amplifier, playing loud chords and getting extremely drunk on a session. Now, he didn't *do* that. He wasn't rowdy or anything, he was extremely polite. He probably knocked off one bottle of wine while he was there, but he didn't get drunk or belligerent. But he couldn't quite understand what we were about, because we're not, David and I are not rock and rollers.

'When we're just having a drink together, David and I, we're just like two little old men, I swear. We just talk about the planets and speculate about whether there is life on Mars or not, and talk about profoundly religious subjects. Or we go skiing together and all that, and Pete was very surprised to see us two sober, little old men sitting in the studio. And he was ready for a right rave-up and he felt like playing guitar all day and night.'

It was while David and Tony and the band were recording the instrumental tracks, in February, that David was introduced to the twenty-nine-year-old director of *The Elephant Man*, Jack Hofsiss. They took to each other immediately.

'He'd seen the play and we talked about it,' Hofsiss says today. 'His perceptions were right on the money. I began to think about David Bowie filling the role when Philip Anglim went into the road company. I wanted someone who would generate more interest in the play. I also wanted someone I'd find interesting. I saw *The Man Who Fell to Earth* and I knew of his stage presence, his sense of theatre in rock. He saw the larger elements of rock songs. The isolation he experienced in *The Man Who Fell to Earth* was similar to *The Elephant Man*.

No commitment was made. When Philip Anglim went on the road with the play, other professional actors took his place on Broadway as David went about his business.

In February, RCA released David's version of 'Alabama Song', the Brecht-Weill tune sometimes known as 'Whisky Bar' that did much to set the stage for an American group ten years earlier, the Doors. David's version of the song, recorded at Mountain Studios in Montreux, was musically unnerving and deliberately so, with the musicians changing key with every verse and David never singing in the same key with them. It was an interesting experiment, but hard to listen to and even in loyal Britain, as a single it went only to No. 23 (backed with still another version of 'Space Oddity'). It was also a modest hit in Japan, where it was released with the music David composed for a television commercial for Crystal Jun Rock, a saki drink. In America, RCA refused to release it at all.

In April, David was back in Berlin, where he went to hear Jimmy Osterberg at the Metropol, and in May he was back in London to put the finishing touches on *Scary Monsters* with Tony Visconti.

It was during this period that he also plunged back deeply into video, working again with David Mallet, but this time taking more control. The three videos that had been created for *Lodger* (including the by now infamous Bowie-in-drag video for 'Boys Keep Swinging') had been co-directed with Mallet, David said, 'inasmuch as I gave him complete control over what I wanted put in there'. Now, in preparing his video for *Scary Monsters*, David created the storyboards for the films without assistance, actually preparing them in much the same way that Alfred Hitchcock planned his features, sketching them frame by frame by frame. As little as possible was left to chance, a typical Bowie trait.

'Ashes to Ashes' was a surrealist collage of David playing many roles: a deep sea diver, a spaceman, a forlorn Pierrot clown (in the costume used on the album cover) wandering along an inky sea and chatting with a classic British mum.

In June, David met again with Jack Hofsiss, the director of *The Elephant Man*.

'He was staying at the Carlyle Hotel and we talked about the demands of playing a role every night,' the director says. 'I felt the clue to playing the role successfully was to avoid pathos. David felt Merrick's street savvy would have kept him from buying into the hospital sympathy. Up to that time, replacement actors had done variations on the original actor's interpretations, which was mind over matter, that sort of thing, and David came up with an original view.'

Hofsiss told David he wanted him to replace Anglim on the road, to play in Denver for a week, then Chicago for two, then after that, they'd talk about New York.

'How much time do I have to make up my mind?' David asked.

'Twenty-four hours.'

David took a long pull on his cigarette and gave Hofsiss one of his trademark vulpine grins.

David knew he was going to say yes. 'I always look for

parts with an emotional or physical limp,' he said later, 'and I always seem to get them. I kind of like characters with some kind of impediment. It's just an interesting thing to play around with, and I've never gone overboard with the idea of myself as any kind of romantic lead.'

Playing the Elephant Man gave David one more mask to wear, another 'prop', or gimmick, to lean upon, to help him carry the weight. None the less, to say yes was an out-and-out act of faith – of faith in his talent and confidence to take the challenge and run with it.

David flew to London to visit the London Hospital where the skeleton and body casts of the Elephant Man still were on display, along with several other exhibits: the man's hooded hat and clothing, the paper model of a church he constructed as part of his therapy, and drawings of the man, showing his horrifying physical abnormality.

Merrick was a victim of neurofibromatosis, a still incurable condition which distorts the skeletal structure and skin. His head, 36 inches in diameter, looked like a huge and misshapen pumpkin, his face was terribly distended and dominated by a gaping, salivating maw of a mouth, with a thick, protruding, trunk-like upper jaw. Great loose folds of skin, with cauliflower-like fungoid growths covered his chest, back and buttocks. His right hand and arm were monstrously large and useless. Only his left arm, its delicate hand and his sexual organs were left unscathed.

David and Corinne and a few other close friends spent two or three hours in the small hospital museum, looking at the pictures and exhibits and asking questions of the assistant curator, P. G. Nunn.

'David asked pertinent questions,' Nunn says today. 'He wanted to know how Merrick walked, how he spoke. I told him he could not have run, because he had no hips. And there was a great distortion of the mouth, because the tongue was thick and pushed to one side.'

David returned to New York, where Hofsiss introduced him to the cast and crew of the Broadway company, many of whom weren't so sure about him. If David performed adequately in Denver and Chicago and then the decision was made by Hofsiss and David for David to take the lead on Broadway, they didn't want to be embarrassed by

David's lack of 'legitimate' theatrical experience. Moreover, they didn't want to be members of his backup band. This was Broadway, after all, not rock and roll.

David was insecure, too. Because it was impractical, if not impossible, for an actor to hobble around the stage for two hours in some sort of grotesque second skin, the playwright decided that the man playing Merrick would appear in a loincloth and give the illusion of the deformity by twisting and contorting his body and voice. Thus, David knew that to satisfy the demands of a professional cast and crew he would have to adopt the Elephant Man's crippled gait, be obliged to deliver his lines in a fluted, shrilling voice (without facial expression except for that which could be projected by eye and head movements), and on top of all that, *act*, and to do all of this in one of the most critical arenas in world theatre: Broadway. That David had some useful mime experience and that he would open in Denver, where possible disaster might go relatively unnoticed, offered him only slight relief.

(In fact the national press was discouraged from attending the Denver performances. There were no interviews given, no free tickets, no junkets. 'I don't think it's fair to put any scrutiny on David without giving him a chance to work his way into the role,' said Josh Ellis, the play's Broadway press agent. 'If he's marvellous in Denver, he'll be marvellous in Chicago. And if he's not, well, why should we risk exposing him?')

'You better be good,' said Jack Hofsiss on the first day of rehearsal. 'Otherwise, we're both in trouble.'

David and Hofsiss laughed nervously.

David rehearsed for two weeks with the New York company and then flew to San Francisco, where he watched Philip Anglim's final performance and rehearsed for a week with the road company, rehearsing another five days in Denver. Slowly, he and the other professionals gained confidence as a team. Hofsiss says David was never late to a rehearsal, always disciplined, and 'never made any demands. I know that Coco was helping David run his lines at night, so I asked her to attend rehearsals. After that, she began running David's life from his dressing room.'

David opened at the Auditorium Theatre of Denver's

Centre for Performing Arts on 29 July. The first character to appear on the stage was the Elephant Man's doctor, Sir Frederick Treves, who showed a series of slides, made from the original drawings and photographs which were provided by the London hospital. Grotesqueness on a giant screen.

Slowly, a curtain was drawn to reveal David in a nappy-like garment, spotlighted with his legs apart and arms outstretched. As the doctor continued his matter-of-fact lecture about Merrick's rare disease, David adopted the bent-over posture he would hold for most of the rest of the performance.

'In order to play the role, you have to master the physical life and the vocal life of the character very quickly,' says Jack Hofsiss. 'It has to become second nature to you. One approaches it the way one approaches dance or mime: you have to learn the steps before you can really interpret the ballet, for example. We had a series of warm-ups and warm-downs which we taught everybody who played the role. We also found times in the performance when the character was either in the bathtub or in a chair, where you could relax one part of the body, so that it looked like you would still be in the deformed position, but you were being very selective as to which limbs you were twisting, so that the other limbs could rest. There also was somebody like a chiropractor with whom the actor met regularly, so the actor could learn a series of exercises to assist in getting into and out of the part. You could not think about that part, otherwise your mind would not allow you to play the role correctly. . . .'

David himself said later that it was a full week before he stopped thinking about his body and began to act. None the less, the reaction in Denver was positive. Jackie Campbell, the syndicated critic for the Denver *News*, saw nothing unusual about David's appearing in the play, quoting David as once saying, 'I've always played roles with my songs. I wrote the script and played it out on stage and records.' Thus, Campbell wrote, 'it was just a quicksilver side-step for David to submerge himself into the character of Pomerance's freak-show attraction, John Merrick.' David's theatrical debut was 'calmly auspicious,' she said. 'The play is a conjuring feat, rooted in reality and soaring recklessly close to the angels. It is to Bowie's credit that his wings are not singed in the process and he has settled into a difficult role as lightly and effortlessly as a feather.'

A writer for *Trouser Press*, Neil Feineman, said David was 'galvanizing' in the role in Denver and 'when he pounded his hands on the bathtub and repeated phrases over and over, he brought magic and music to the play's language. And, after a powerful final scene, when he came out for bows nattily attired in cravat and formal suit and shirt, graciously holding hands with the rest of the cast, he seemed the perfect incarnation of a stage matinee idol. The Denver audience may not have known it, but they were applauding one of the most courageous and broadening moves yet taken by a rock star.'

David took full advantage of it. Once past the terror of Denver, David rolled into Chicago for two weeks at the Blackstone Theatre with a publicity campaign planned and aggressively put into action by his publicist, Barbara De-Witt, and the people at RCA. 'David did interviews for good reason only,' says RCA's Tony McGrogan. '"Ashes to Ashes" was released the week he opened in Denver, so when he got to Chicago, we started taking writers from all over Europe to see him and do interviews.'

One of those flown to Chicago, at RCA's expense, was Angus MacKinnon, representing the pop weekly *New Musical Express*.

Barbara DeWitt told him, 'You have a one-hour situation with David. I'm afraid that's all he can give you.'

'A one-hour *situation*?' Angus said. 'What's that mean?'

'One hour. You can see him for one hour.'

Angus said, 'I want three.'

'Well, look Angus,' Barbara said, 'we'll have to play it by ear. If he likes you, he can overrule everyone else.'

Angus got his three hours – in two sessions, one in a restaurant and the other sitting on chairs in the middle of the late-night Blackstone Theatre stage. David talked candidly about current and recent events. Yes, he knew some of those in his theatre audience were coming merely to see Ziggy Stardust in his latest incarnation; however, he said, 'I also knew that if I hadn't been successful within the first 15 or 20 minutes, then they'd have got up and started leaving, because it's not the kind of part you can fuck about with, frankly.'

He said he and David Hemmings were still friends, but *Just a Gigolo* was a painful memory. (It had not yet been released in America.) 'The first year or so after I'd made the thing, I was furious, mainly with myself. I mean, oh, God, I really should have known better. Every real, legitimate actor that I've ever met has told me never to even approach a film unless you know the script is good.'

He discussed in great detail the making of the 'Ashes to Ashes' video and revealed, again, his desire to become a film director. He talked about the mythology common in King Arthur's Round Table and Hitler's Nazi Germany . . . about the 'psychological terror' of working with Nicolas Roeg in *The Man Who Fell to Earth* (no anecdotes, however) . . . about the image he felt he had in America: 'I'm still referred to over here as the orange-haired bisexual. Now that is what I am here. Period. Zilch. There's nothing else.'

Well, how did David see himself?

David said he was in his 'old re-examination programme', an ongoing analytical process of self-evaluation.

Angus recited three lines from 'Ashes to Ashes': 'I've never done good things/I've never done bad things/I've never done anything out of the blue.' He wanted to know if that was the way David really felt.

David inhaled his Marlboro cigarette (having abandoned his Gitanes for a while) and nodded. 'Those three particular lines represent a continuing, returning feeling of inadequacy over what I've done.'

David paused and ran a finger around his mouth, as if contemplating what to say next.

'I have an awful lot of reservations about what I've done in-as-much as I don't feel much of it has any importance at all,' he finally said. 'And then I have days when of course it all feels very important to me, that I've contributed an awful lot. But I'm not awfully happy with what I've done in the past, actually.'

'So,' said Angus, 'what would you include amongst your positive achievements?'

'The idea that one doesn't have to exist purely on one defined set of ethics and values, that you can investigate other areas and other avenues of perception and try and apply them to everyday life. I think I've tried to do that. I think I've done that fairly successfully. At times, even if only on a theoretical level, I've managed that. As far as everyday life goes, I don't think so. I have this long chain with a ball of middle-classness at the end of it which keeps holding me back and that I keep sort of trying to fight through. I keep trying to find the Duchamp in me, which is harder and harder to find.'

David laughed nervously.

Angus asked why 'middle-classness' was a problem, wasn't 'that kind of exaggerated class consciousness a peculiarly English affliction?'

'Yes, of course,' David said, 'and class consciousness is a very great wall of contention with me, always getting in my way.'

'What is it that you feel, then,' Angus asked, '– you should have "suffered" more for your art or something?'

'Oh, no, not at all. Not on that level. I just keep finding my vision gets blinkered and becomes narrowed all the time. I'm continually trying to open it up and break it down and do shattering things to it. . . .'

One by one the interviewers were given access, each hour ending with Barbara DeWitt or Corinne entering the interview environment, making cutting motions at their necks, the theatrical sign for stop. Some, like Angus MacKinnon, were given additional time, others were not.

Angus's paper gave the story seven pages a few weeks later and the cover. 'David Bowie is an intelligent, articulate and fascinating man who is still writing messages to himself and sealing them in bottles,' Angus said. 'It's an obsessively private process that for obvious reasons he offers up for public scrutiny. Whatever he may think or feel, Bowie has done both good things and bad things. He has also done a lot more out of the blue than he may ever surmise.'

The Elephant Man opened in Chicago on 3 August and closed on the 31st. Again, the reviews and box office were excellent and New York was assured.

At that time in England, where the rich tradition of cabaret remains, a crossover from rock to theatre was not unusual; Tommy Steele and Cliff Richard, among many more, had successfully performed in both arenas comfortably and profitably. In America, it was rare. It was true that when David was playing *The Elephant Man* in Denver, another popular music personality, Linda Ronstadt, went into a Broadway revival of Gilbert & Sullivan's *Pirates of Penzance*. But that was about it.

'There was,' says Jack Hofsiss of the Broadway announcement, 'an intense curiosity about whether David could pull it off.'

There was one critic, John Simon, writing in *New York* magazine, who hated David's performance saying his 'reedy voice, when distorted as the part demands, becomes a falsetto sawing that slices intelligibility in half, and his androgynously pretty face and street-wise punk-rock sexiness finish off what pathos his acting left intact.'

Everyone else sounded thrilled. *Back Stage* magazine said he 'acquitted himself magnificently' and *Theater* magazine said he had 'the exquisite stillness that the best actors have ... the physical precision of his acting is really something to see.' The New York *Daily News* spoke of his 'restrained, tortured eloquence' and said he knew 'the difference between having an act and acting.' The *Village Voice* said David 'succeeds, breathing new life into *The Elephant Man* ... commands the stage ... is overall not so vulnerable as Philip Anglim and less ironic (he lacks Anglim's boyish beauty), but his portrait is more precise, more colourful, and much funnier.'

'Bowie Blazing on Broadway!' headlined the *New York Post*.

John Corry wrote in the *New York Times*, 'When it was announced that David Bowie would play the title role in *The Elephant Man*, it was not unnatural to think he had been cast simply for the use of his name. Dismiss that thought now. Yes, more young people in designer jeans and leather now show up at the Booth Theatre than before, and yes, they probably show up because Mr Bowie is a celebrated rock star. Fortunately, he is a good deal more than that, and as John Merrick, The Elephant Man, he is splendid.'

Back home in London, the headlines echoed the praise. The *Times* called his performance 'one of the events of New York's theatrical season.'

'Wowie!' exclaimed the *Evening Standard*, 'Bowie is a hit on Broadway.'

'I looked at the third row one day,' says Jack Hofsiss, 'and I saw people aged twenty and eighty and they all had the same colour blue hair. We had to tell an usher once to tell one guy in the audience to turn off the lights on his coat. Definitely, David's fans made a difference. We started to sell out the house again.'

By the 1 September, the weekly box office take had dropped to $61,000, about half capacity. David opened on the 29th and on 1 October, *Variety* began its Broadway roundup story saying, 'Business slumped for most Broadway shows last week, but David Bowie, as the replacement star of *The Elephant Man*, carried the play to its top b.o. [box office] figure and attendance in its 17-month run.'

Gross for the week was now $116,680 and the next week it went to $118,000 and after that to $119,000. These figures were small compared to concert and movie grosses, but for Broadway at the time, they were astonishing. Compared to what he could earn elsewhere, David's income from this venture was also rather minimal: a guaranteed salary with a 10 per cent interest in anything that took the box office past the breakeven point. This meant he was earning under $30,000 for eight performances a week, a figure that wouldn't have covered his hotel bill when he and his band were on the road. It didn't matter. The bottom line was: David was a hit! An actor!

At the same time, he was a hit again on the record charts. In England 'Ashes to Ashes' went straight to No. 2 and if his success in America seemed slight by comparison ('Ashes to Ashes' went only to the 101 position) at least he was on the charts again; previously, David hadn't had one of his new records appear on an American chart in three years. The album sold exceedingly well in *both* markets, going to the top position in England and to a respectable No. 12 in America.

David's financial concerns were, by now, very well organized. Pat Gibbons was still handling his business affairs, through Bewlay Brothers Music and all the other businesses that David had had set up. Tony DeFries was still collecting his 50 per cent directly from RCA for every record sold, but with the success of *The Elephant Man*, this seemed to bother him less, resulting in a burst of new energy.

David talked expansively with friends about touring the following spring. Something new on television, called MTV, was happening, and he was happy that his *Lodger* videos and the more abstract 'Ashes to Ashes' film were included in the opening weeks' playlist. He was still painting, and still threatening to show his art publicly. He met with people about doing another film, and in October, began collaborating with Herman Weigel, a German writer and director who wanted him to appear in a film called *Christine F. Wir Kinder Vom Bahnhof Zoo* (*The Children of Bahnhof Zoo*), the story of teenage drug addiction. David agreed to appear briefly in an in-performance sequence – the plot line had Christine F., the main character, first trying heroin at one of David's concerts – during which he played several songs from his *Heroes* and *Low* albums and the eccentric 'TVC 1–5'. A set recreating the nightclub in Berlin was constructed in Manhattan and David filmed the sequence in a single day. The next day, David and David Mallet moved on to the set, using it for part of their next video production, 'Fashion'.

David enjoyed working on Broadway and enjoyed living again in New York (in rooms at the Carlyle Hotel). By now, he had a favourite Japanese restaurant near the theatre, where he conducted most of his interviews and took many friends (speaking earnest but hesitant Japanese to the waitresses), and his life had fallen into a relaxed, predictable pattern. He liked New York, he told one writer, because he wasn't bothered in public.

'The most you get is "Hi, Dave, how's it going?" It's a very neighbourly characteristic. They don't get as excited at meeting you as in London, which is still a bit star-conscious. Here you see Al Pacino walking around or Joel Grey jogging. It's quite easy to do that. It's great.'

That quote appeared in a story published in the *Times* on 25 November. Two weeks later, something awful happened in New York that made David change his mind, almost permanently.

THE ACTOR, CRACKS REMOVED

On 5 December, David was interviewed by Andy Peebles for the BBC. During the interview, he talked of his work with John Lennon.

The next day, Andy Peebles interviewed John Lennon and Lennon, in turn, talked about David Bowie.

'I must say I admire him for the vast repertoire of talent the guy has, you know. I was never around when the Ziggy Stardust thing came, because I'd already left England while all that was going on, so I never really knew what he was. And meeting him doesn't give you much more of a clue, you know. Because you don't know which one you're talking to.'

Two days later, on 8 December, John Lennon was shot dead walking from a cab to the door of his apartment building.

David panicked, absolutely panicked when John's secretary, May Pang, called. He didn't even want to leave his hotel room and if he hadn't had the play to do, he probably wouldn't have – although he never even mentioned his concern to the people at the theatre.

'There were security problems from the start,' says Jack Hofsiss. 'David had to isolate himself to come down from the performance and avoid the crowds outside the stage door. A lot of theatres on 45th and 46th Streets had connecting passageways, so David could exit the theatre several ways. The day after John was shot, I offered to re-stage the show so that David could leave the stage periodically when he wasn't needed, to keep his time on stage at a minimum. He absolutely refused. We increased the security at the theatre, but *he* made no demands.'

John Lennon's death made David think and one of the things he felt was a desperate longing for family. He had planned to fly Zowie in from Switzerland to spend the

Christmas holidays, anyway. After Lennon was shot, David decided to fly his mum in, too.

It was their first Christmas together in seven years and according to those who were there, it was an awkward reunion, but uneventful. 'There were,' says one, 'no fights.'

By New Year's Eve, with the newspapers still full of stories about John Lennon and his strange, groupie-like murderer, David made two more decisions: not to tour in the spring as he had planned, and not to record for at least a year.

The decision to cancel plans for a tour was understandable. David never liked touring, telling everyone that the only reason he did it was for the money – the large box office grosses and the royalties from increased record sales. Now, with the fear of assassination on every rock star's mind, David wasn't the only one to withdraw and tighten security. Mick Jagger, Rod Stewart, Paul McCartney (who retreated to his remote Scottish farm) and half a hundred more added bodyguards to the payroll.

The decision not to record was unrelated to John Lennon's death. This decision was prompted by his continuing dissatisfaction with RCA and resentment of Tony DeFries. The way David's attorneys explained it to him, 50 per cent of everything released by RCA – past, present and *future* – would go into Tony's pocket automatically and there was, the lawyers said, little that David could do about it. David's response was to leave them with what they already had, and give them nothing new.

Consequently, RCA started doing with David Bowie what it had been doing with Elvis Presley: issuing slightly re-arranged old material in new packaging. Many of these ideas, or concepts, were presented by DeFries. One such plan involved K-Tel, a New York-based company that had marketed more than 100 million album anthologies during the past few years, almost all of them through mail order and telephone sales created by late-night television advertising. The deal Tony made with K-Tel, through RCA, was to repackage 16 of David's bestselling singles, call it *The Best of Bowie*, and begin saturation TV marketing. The only difference between this deal and most made with K-Tel was that K-Tel didn't want the North American rights.

'We didn't feel we'd recoup our money in America,' George Lukan of K-Tel says today. 'We're talking about $500,000 in advertising, which is what we needed to run a successful campaign in 1981. We would have had to sell 700,000 units to break even and we didn't feel we'd be able to do that in the US with Bowie. So we released the album all over Europe and in Australia and Asia. There we did very nicely.'

Indeed. K-Tel's carefully assembled package of hits – presented, more or less, in chronological order, along with presentable annotation and a collection of photographs showing many of David's past characters – was a hit in nearly every country in Western Europe, as well as in New Zealand, Australia and Japan. In England, it went to No. 2 on the album charts, kept away from No. 1 by John Lennon's last album, *Double Fantasy*.

At the same time, his most recent new material continued to sell – 'Fashion' went to No. 1 in England and to No. 70 in the US – as critics began heaping superlatives on his video work.

'What is remarkable about these spots,' said John Rockwell in the *New York Times* of 'Ashes to Ashes' and 'Fashion', 'is not so much the images as the brilliant way they are edited and how they expand on the music itself, rather than merely accompanying it or even contradicting it. These little shorts are genuine music theatre in a new and modern guise, and they deserve to be seen by anyone interested in either rock or opera.'

Rockwell summarized: 'The real hero of the rock-video revolution so far is that perennial pioneer David Bowie.'

It was astonishing. The rock video medium hadn't even been defined yet and the *New York Times* was saying that David had conquered it.

The praise was piling up. Shortly after the *New York Times* review appeared, David gave his final performance as the Elephant Man on 3 January. That same week, his latest single, 'Scary Monsters'/'Because You're Young', started climbing the English record charts and David was named in a *Record Mirror* readers' poll as the No. 1 male singer and co-director of the No. 1 video of the year ('Ashes to Ashes' and 'Fashion'). And a month after that, he received identical recognition as the year's top male vocalist at the 1981 Rock and Pop Awards Ceremony at the New London Theatre. This time, the award came in an annual competition sponsored jointly by the *Daily Mirror* and BBC Radio.

Still cautious after Lennon's death, David went into retreat during the late winter and early spring months of 1981, spending most of his time in his home overlooking Lake Geneva. Friends came to visit. David skied. He wrote songs. On 28 May, he held a small party for Zowie's tenth birthday. He sent Coco out for piles of books. He painted.

Elsewhere in the world it was a time of nostalgically looking backwards. One of the biggest albums of the season was a greatest hits compilation by the Doors, a band that really hadn't existed since its singer died ten years before. Summer 1981 in the US opened with Kim Carnes at the top of the singles list, singing 'Bette Davis Eyes'. This was followed by a string of 'Stars on . . .' disco medleys, which set Beatles songs and hits from the 1960s to a relentless, metronomic disco beat. Even Simon and Garfunkel were getting back together after years apart.

The quiet of David's summer was disrupted occasionally. The first intrusion came in June when Angela published her book, *Free Spirit*. David grimaced as he read the slender book. Clearly Angela had done it for the money. Perhaps to get even, too. But hadn't she thought of Zowie? He was old enough to read. Did she think he'd never see the book? What would Zowie think of his parents? What would he think of his mother for hanging up so much of the dirty linen?

Two pleasanter intrusions into David's Swiss tranquillity came in the form of a band called Queen and an American film director named Paul Schrader. Queen, one of Britain's most successful heavy metal art rock bands, had a track record of hits that included 'We Will Rock You' and the six-minute 'Bohemian Rhapsody'. With its smoke bombs and costumes and a soundtrack for the science fiction spoof *Flash Gordon* behind it, the band was ripe for David, who found them recording in Montreux. They decided to do a song together.

The result was 'Under Pressure', Queen's next hit.

Conversations with Paul Schrader came about because

of David's continuing attempts to get something else happening in film. Schrader started his career in films as a critic, switched to screenwriting (*Taxi Driver*) and then to directing as well, turning out *Blue Collar*, *Hardcore* and *American Gigolo* before deciding to do a remake of the 1942 horror classic *Cat People*. He wanted David to provide the lyrics for a title song to fit the music of Giorgio Moroder who had won an Oscar for his score for *Midnight Express*.

'David enjoyed movie people,' says a friend, 'and he liked Paul Schrader. They had a lot in common. For one thing, Schrader had written an unproduced screenplay about Hank Williams, the country singer, and he was determined to make a film about the life of one of David's favourite authors, the Japanese novelist Yukio Mishima. So they talked and talked and talked. David said he'd like to get involved in the Mishima film if possible.'

In July, BBC Television announced a series of plays soon to go into production for broadcast in 1982. At the top of the list was *Baal*, the difficult play by Bertolt Brecht which depicted scenes in the life of an anarchic, amoral balladeer whose single-minded dedication to his talent was matched by a cold indifference to ordinary human feelings with devastating results for those he encountered in his short, explosive career.

First, Baal seduces his patron's wife. After that, when a student asks his advice about love, Baal takes the student's girlfriend back to his room; she later drowns herself. Then Baal picks up a streetwalker, whom he uses in his cabaret act to illustrate his lewd songs. When she becomes pregnant, he abandons her. Afterwards, Baal's physical condition deteriorates and in the end he stabs his only friend – dying himself, finally, alone in a small hut in the forest.

David was intrigued, in part because the character was so unlikeable: another costume, another mask. He asked to see some of the director's previous work and when approving that, he requested a meeting in Switzerland.

As was the case when he met with Nicolas Roeg for *The Man Who Fell to Earth* and with David Hemmings for *Just a Gigolo*, one meeting was all it took. David talked with director Alan Clarke in the living room of his home, as Corinne chatted with producer Louis Marks on the balcony.

He said he would be available, so long as certain provisions were made. The provisions were standard for a star of David's stature and, given the paranoia still lingering from the death of his friend John Lennon, totally sympathetic.

'He wanted a car and a bodyguard,' Marks says today. 'He wanted to be assured of his privacy and security. Of course, we provided him with what he needed. Otherwise, I might add, he was given no more than any other actor. He worked for the standard BBC fee.'

A full month was set aside for rehearsals. 'He was an actor in the company of actors,' Marks says. 'He was there on time. He worked the full period required. There were no problems. He was utterly exhausted when we finished. The studio was typically overheated and Alan was a perfectionist, so there were at least five or six takes for every scene. The last of the five shooting days we recorded the songs and halfway through the morning, someone in the basement of the BBC started up a pneumatic drill. We lost the entire morning. We started over in the afternoon. David was wearing these tight-fitting boots and he was drenched in sweat at the end of the day, but never a word of complaint. It was always, "You 'appy w'at, Alan? Want me ta do it again?"'

The songs were not exciting. At the time of their creation, Brecht hadn't met Kurt Weill, his later collaborator, so the music was provided largely by someone hired by the BBC. David performed the material adequately, but used a very stagey voice, showing little emotion.

David's physical appearance in the play was more interesting. David Hemmings' attempts to convert David into an ill-kept gardener may have failed, but the BBC's did not. Given a scruffy beard, bags under his eyes, a rag-and-bone-man's wardrobe and blacked-out, rotten teeth, David was, at last, repulsive, even more grotesque than the Elephant Man, and totally lacking in sympathy.

David's commitment to the BBC was completed by 1 September, and the rest of the year was, essentially, a holiday. Flying to New York, he was backstage at Madison Square Garden for a show by the Rolling Stones, followed by a night on the town with his old friend Mick Jagger. And then it was back to Switzerland to be with Zowie. A winter of skiing was upon them. His thirty-fifth birthday was approaching. Rarely did he return anyone's telephone calls. When the 'Under Pressure' single he had made with Queen was released, in November, and the German movie, *Christine F.*, went into distribution in England, in December, David hardly noticed.

*

It had been fifteen months since the release of *Scary Monsters* and RCA was not pleased, especially in America, where record sales had again declined. Consequently, RCA once more did what it had done in the past: worked with Tony DeFries, who was only too willing to help. Tony and the others had suggested another 'greatest hits' anthology, a sequel to *ChangesOneBowie* which was packaged with great success in 1976. In five years, it was argued, surely there was enough new material for *ChangesTwoBowie*.

The record, released in November under that title, was a disappointment. This wasn't a 'greatest hits' collection at all, but was, instead, a hotchpotch of songs that stretched all the way back to *Hunky Dory* (1971) and up to *Scary Monsters*, and only a few of them had been, in America, even minor hits. Most of the tunes were B-side songs, or strictly British hits, or hits for other performers. It was a tribute to David's charisma – and testimony to the loyalty of his following – that the album sold well anyway, going to No. 24 in England and to No. 68 in the US.

The worst was yet to come.

RCA also released a single from the anthology, pairing 'Wild Is the Wind' (a hit for Lou Reed) and 'Golden Years' (a hit for David in 1976), and, because there was no hint that David would deliver any new material soon, plans were made to package the eleven minutes of music in *Baal* on an album.

In response, David decided to extend his moratorium on recording for another year and signed to do another film, reporting for work in London's Mayfair on 1 March.

The Hunger was the story of a vampire named Miriam (Catherine Deneuve), born 4000 years before Christ and endowed with apparent eternal life. Her latest lover, John Blaylock (David Bowie), was born in eighteenth-century

230

England and together in modern-day New York they haunt Manhattan's punk discos for potential blood donors. They live in a sumptuous town house, teach classical music to teenagers, and keep a crematorium in the basement to dispose of their casual guests. Suddenly John (David) begins to age and following a spectacular scene in a doctor's waiting room, where he ages from thirty-five to 135 in about twenty minutes (the critics later amused themselves by saying that was typical for New York), David goes home and climbs into a waiting coffin, while Miriam starts another affair, this time with a doctor (Susan Sarandon).

It was the sort of strangeness that David loved. After all, how do you top being the Elephant Man and Baal? *The Hunger* seemed to answer that question. The director, Tony Scott, had never made a feature film before, yet he was known as one of London's most creative and stylistic directors of television commercials. David was shown a reel of Tony Scott's commercials. He liked them. He also knew that Tony's brother was Ridley Scott, director of *Alien*.

The day after David reported to the Mayfair set, *Baal* was broadcast by the BBC but in competition against an ITV play starring Laurence Olivier. Many of London's critics unfairly used this fact in reviewing David's role.

'Thames Television's production of John Mortimer's *A Voyage Round My Father* had a 25-minute start over BBC's *Baal* last night and possibly only those observing strict, medieval, Lenten penitential rites would have denied themselves the pleasure of watching Laurence Olivier as Mortimer senior to boggle at this baleful piece of Brecht,' said the critic for the *Times*. David 'did as good a job as possible of playing this amoral, anti-social poet,' the *Times* said, but the play wasn't very good and Olivier's play was wonderful. While Hilary Kingsley in the *Daily Mirror* said, 'It seems daft to say we had a contest between Lord Olivier, our greatest living actor, and David Bowie, professional weirdo, rock idol and actor on TV last night.' Kingsley went on to praise the Olivier play and said *Baal* 'was a total flop. I cannot believe even the most besotted of David Bowie's fans could have tolerated more than a few moments of it. The hero, a tramp-poet haunting German high society in 1912, was rotten in every sense – a drunk, a slob, a know-all, a seducer, a murderer, who apparently decomposed before our eyes. That the BBC could spend a small fortune on this repulsive and rightly ignored tableau is a cause for top level concern.'

Others echoed this sentiment. It was 'perverse' to cast David in the role, said the *Daily Telegraph*, 'then subdue him in an emotionless production . . .' Capsuled the *Sunday Times*: '*David Bowie in Baal* the BBC calls it, as if the actor were more interesting than the play, and for once Aunty's right.' While the *Daily Express* said, succinctly, 'The grim Bertolt Brecht play with music is hardly the best vehicle to project the spectacular Bowie style and Mr Bowie's acting talents are swamped in the general *angst*. The BBC revival does nobody any favours. Not least Mr Bowie. There has been a lot of pretentious rot written in advance about the play needing a charismatic star to project the character of Baal. Mr Bowie's own creations – Ziggy Stardust to name but one – are infinitely more interesting.' Even the slight praise was left-handed as when the *Sun* said, 'The BBC's David Bowie in *Baal* was described as a "star vehicle for a big star" as if they were of equal merit. They weren't. Bowie, always more than a pretty face, confirmed that he is a creditable actor. But what an unspeakable play in which to prove it!'

David read the reviews, but was unable to give them much attention. His focus was on *The Hunger* now.

David was brought to the Mayfair house each day by six-thirty in the morning in a limousine, Coco at his side, Tony Mascia at the wheel. Five hours in make-up often followed, as fleshlike material was affixed to each facial muscle, to create the illusion of great age; when David smiled or grimaced, the material attached to muscles used for those expressions moved in an eerie, 'natural' way.

Both Tony Scott, the director, and Michael Thomas, one of the screenwriters, say David was co-operative, easy to work with, totally dedicated and disciplined. Scott was nervous on his first feature, he says, and David 'tried to put me at ease right away and was very friendly'.

'I think the reason he was so pleasant was he was so bloody confident,' Thomas says today, 'as if he was the biggest star in the history of mankind. He feels he can't lose.

He hasn't got any fears or doubts about himself. There was a scene in which he had to play the cello. Most actors would have faked it, appearing only in indirect or long shots, using a professional musician for the closeups. Not David. He fuckin' *learnt* how to play the cello! He worked like a bah-stahd until he could play a decent Bach cantata!'

In the evenings David went out. Those around him remark that he still showed signs of paranoia connected with John Lennon's death, but apparently these fears were dissipating. There was then in London a rash of trendy clubs, and David visited most of them, accompanied always by Tony Mascia and a changing list of friends.

David was enjoying London until, in July when *The Hunger* finished shooting, life came falling in on him when his aunt, Pat Antoniou, convinced him that he should visit his half-brother in Cane Hill Hospital, where Terry had been living for most of the past sixteen years. David did not want to go, and approached the hospital grim-faced, refusing to talk throughout the hour-long drive.

David hadn't seen Terry in nearly a decade and didn't want to see him now, according to Pat (David's mother's sister).

'Terry was in hospital getting £6.99 a month from social security,' Pat says today. 'I took him clothes and money and cigarettes and David gave him nothing, David wouldn't lift a finger. Terry was walking about in rags. His pants were in tatters at the bottoms. And that awful place he's in! Drug addicts and old people shuffling about. Even Angela helped. She came to London once and I visited her at the Hilton. She had lesbians and gay boys all around, she was a debauched person, but she had a heart, a good heart. She asked about Terry. He was out of the hospital then, and married to an alcoholic. I told Angela that he couldn't hold a job. She gave me £200 and told me to give it to Terry.

'Later, Terry went back in the hospital and in 1981 he threw himself from a window in despair and broke both his arms and legs. He had two operations on one arm. It was gangrenous. I forced David to visit him. I wanted him to put Terry in a private nursing home and set up a trust fund. He promised Terry the world. And then he left. I never heard from him again. And neither did Terry.'

David's aunt was unhappy about the meeting and called John Blake of the *Sun*. A few days later, a livid two-page spread was published under the headline: 'I'M TERRIFIED OF GOING MAD, SAYS BOWIE'. The story began, 'In a sad, old Victorian hospital in South London two men met a few days ago with tears in their eyes . . .'

David was appalled and made plans to leave London immediately. At that moment, he got a telephone call from the controversial Japanese director Nagisa Oshima. David had met Oshima backstage at the Booth Theatre a full two years before when he was starring in *The Elephant Man*. Oshima asked him then if he would take the lead role in his next film, a story about a British soldier in a Japanese prisoner-of-war camp in the South Pacific.

'He asked me if I had read the book [that the film, *Merry Christmas, Mr Lawrence*, was based upon] and I hadn't,' Bowie said. 'But I had certainly seen a few of his movies and I immediately agreed to do it without seeing the script, mainly because it was such an opportunity, a once-in-a-lifetime experience to work with someone like Oshima. It didn't really matter if the script was dreadful.'

David had said for years that what he wanted more than anything else was to be a director of films, and he looked upon his acting as a sort of apprenticeship. Consequently, he wanted to work with what he – and most film critics, especially the intellectual ones – regarded as the very best. Nic Roeg was on that list. So was Nagisa Oshima.

Oshima was generally regarded as the first completely modern Japanese film director. An iconoclastic film-maker and an angry and outspoken critic of traditional Japanese values, he also was regarded as a radical spokesman for Japan's younger generation. (As a student, he led a protest against the Emperor, shocking his elders.) David had seen three of his films.

The first of these was *Boy*, an account of a wandering family that fakes road accidents for insurance settlements – a portrait of the moral confrontations forced upon the new Japan. The second, *The Ceremony*, was a bleak but luminous picture of how domestic ritual destroys or perverts the life force in a family. The third was Oshima's most widely known, because it was involved in the most sensational obscenity trial in Japan's history and was pulled out of the 1976 New York Film Festival by nervous censors. *In the Realm of the Senses*, produced with French money because Japanese backers were too conservative, was a psychological study of a man and a woman who compete for sexual ecstasy, and Oshima left nothing to the imagination. By the time David met Oshima in 1980, the film had won major awards in Britain and America and had become known as one of the world's greatest erotic masterpieces.

The script for *Merry Christmas, Mr Lawrence* arrived soon afterwards and when he read it, David was ready to clear his calendar and go. And that was the last he heard from Oshima for two years. Although the budget was only $5 million – a moderate figure for the time – Oshima still was regarded as controversial and one of the script's themes was homosexuality. Thus, Oshima again was forced to go outside Japan for financing, finally finding support in England and New Zealand. It was then that Oshima called David and said, in effect, 'We start in three weeks in Rarotonga. Can you be there?'

David said, 'Yes, of course.'

Later David said, 'I'd just finished *The Hunger* and the last thing I wanted to do was make a movie! I just wanted to have a holiday. So I took advantage of the situation and took my holiday in the South Pacific. I got to know the islands pretty well before Oshima got there with the crew, so by the time everyone arrived I felt pretty much as if I'd been on the island for some time, which, in fact, I was supposed to have been in my role.'

David took several 'friends' with him on that holiday – some of his favourite tapes.

'I wanted something to listen to and I found that my natural inclination was to choose mainly rhythm and blues from the fifties and sixties,' David said. 'I wanted to find stuff that I could play over and over again, because in the South Pacific it can get very boring.

'I really was doing my Desert Island Discs in a way, and I found it was interesting to see what in fact I did choose – everything from James Brown to the Alan Freed Rock and Roll Orchestra, Elmore James, Albert King, Red Prysock, Johnny Otis, Buddy Guy, Stan Kenton. I surprised myself when I eventually got there – there was just about nothing representing the last fifteen or twenty years.

'I asked myself, why have I chosen this music? What is it about it that makes me play it over and over again? The fact was it had such a human emotional quality to it without pinpointing a tight situation, it was very non-uptight music and it comes from a sense of pleasure and happiness. There is enthusiasm and optimism on those recordings.'

David was going back to his original source and driving force, the music that propelled him through his teens: rhythm and blues. The sound of his next album, which he had decided by now would go to his next record company and not to RCA, was being formed.

The movie company filmed for five weeks in the Cook Islands, and two weeks in New Zealand. The pace was quick, unlike anything David had witnessed before.

'Working with him was my first experience of movie-making that wasn't incredibly boring,' David said. 'I've spent more time making movies just sitting on my ass, waiting for my call, then doing ten takes of something and going away for two or three hours while they change the lighting setup. Oshima cancelled that out for me. Two takes and it was done, and then he'd take the film out of the camera and send it, literally in brown paper, back to Japan, where his editor put it all together. It was shot in sequence, the majority of it, and edited in the camera. And for the first time, I was caught up in the momentum of making a film.'

David's co-stars were an intriguing lot. Tom Conti played the put-upon man-in-the-middle in the film, who takes it upon himself to serve as intermediary between the prisoners and the camp commander because he speaks Japanese and had been a diplomat in Tokyo before the war. The tough, samurai-styled commandant was played by another pop star, Ryuichi Sakamoto, and it was his relationship with 'Straffer' Jack Celliers, the Bowie role, that made the film what it was. Homosexuality becomes a metaphor for all the taboos against contact between prisoners and guards, and the film's dramatic triumphs occur when these taboos are broken. Until finally, David kisses Ryuichi on the lips and is killed for it.

David explained his role: 'In the film I embrace the idea

of war because of my guilt about my dealings with my family, specifically my younger brother, who was a hunchback from birth, which reflects badly, as far as I'm concerned, upon my own being, and so I disown him. I disown all responsibility for looking after him to an extent that leads him into terrible social situations, but I just stand there in the wings and watch him undergo terrible humiliations, without ever running to his defence. All this starts to work on me over the years, and comes to a point where my life becomes meaningless because of the dishonourable way I've treated my brother, so when the war comes, I throw myself into it, looking for salvation, but really it's that now I can die, can die honourably doing something. This is what produces this so-called iron will I've got: it's just this enforced feeling that I've got to throw myself into the most dangerous situations so that I can redeem myself.'

David might well have been talking about himself. Although Oshima says they never discussed such things, David certainly must have been reminded throughout the shooting of his own bisexual past and his own half-brother Terry, and as a result must have wondered if, perhaps, he, too, didn't 'throw [him]self into the most dangerous situations so that [he could] redeem [him]self'.

Oshima says he picked Bowie and Sakamoto for two reasons: he knew they might attract a larger, younger audience and help make the film a hit, but, more importantly, he was attracted to the 'honesty' that non-actors project. 'I like working with non-professionals,' Oshima says. 'It has an interesting effect on the professional actors in the cast. When they are confronted by the non-professionals, they become more honest and truthful in their performances.'

Says David on the same subject: 'You'd go through a scene, you'd be done, and then you'd be moving on to the next scene immediately, so you were always your character, with no chance to see the overall thing. You were continually redefining what your character was undergoing, what stresses were involved in his relationships with his own men and with the enemy.

'It was like real life. You only get one shot at it. He [Oshima] doesn't believe in a thousand takes. He'll do two takes, sometimes three, and he's got it. He'd get all geared up and we'd go for it. I asked him if we could do a particular scene again and he said, "If you like. But my editor very old man. So tired these days. No point in taking more. He only look at first one anyway." It was a bit like making old rock and roll records, when James Brown and his band would do it just once.'

Even at this pell-mell pace, there was time for relaxation and play. David and Oshima talked about Japanese film and literature. David and Ryuichi played each other the tapes they'd brought. (Ryuichi later did the soundtrack for the film.) And at the end of the shooting schedule, David staged a deliberately rude but hilarious musical for the members of the cast and crew. Everyone parted friends.

A good thing. What lay immediately ahead was not pleasant at all. It was David's final showdown with RCA.

DAVID BOWIE STRAIGHT

When David returned to New York from the South Seas in November, he discovered that, in the absence of new material, the record company was repackaging the old stuff again. For the holiday season, a 'new' single had been prepared from the five-year-old Bing Crosby television tapes ('Peace on Earth'/'Little Drummer Boy'), along with a limited edition collector's set of ten 45 rpm picture discs including songs that went all the way back to 'Space Oddity' and came forward to 'Ashes to Ashes'. David admitted that the collection showed some taste and imagination, but thought his fans were being milked; the music, after all, was available elsewhere, and all they were getting was glitzy packaging.

David also noticed how much advertising RCA had purchased to promote these records, saying aloud to friends that it would have been nice if he had had advertising budgets like that for *Heroes* and *Low*. It was, he concluded, an obvious attempt to make him feel better. After all, however unhappy RCA may have been about recent sales, the company was offering him millions of dollars to re-sign.

RCA was not alone in the bidding. Four of the six largest American record companies were in the race and all were connected to major entertainment industry conglomerates, so the figures were significant.

David asked his offices in New York to provide business profiles of each of the bidding companies, so that he could look at them, one by one, to see what they had to offer besides money.

First, of course, was RCA. Following an approximate 25 per cent cutback in staff and a 15 per cent reduction in artist roster, RCA was showing signs of recovery from a recent slump. Five years after his death, Elvis was still a big seller – and was being repackaged in a manner that made David's recycling seem tasteful – but RCA had also signed in the past few months two of America's top recording stars, Kenny Rogers and Diana Ross, showing an interest in expansion. RCA was backed by a conglomerate whose interests ranged from television sets to missile guidance systems, and controlled 15 per cent of the record market.

Columbia was the next in line, a part of the CBS Records Group that included Epic Records, the label that had made the CBS family rich with its two greatest stars, Willie Nelson and Michael Jackson. CBS also had the largest overall market share, nearly 25 per cent, as well as 15 per cent of the overseas distribution business. Besides the aforementioned superstars, it had, on the Columbia label, Bob Dylan, Neil Diamond, Paul McCartney, Journey, Billy Joel, Julio Iglesias, Elvis Costello, Miles Davis, Deniece Williams, Men at Work and Pink Floyd, to name but a few.

Geffen Records, the personal creation of David Geffen, was the smallest label in the race by far, but was owned by Warner Communications Inc, the company with the second largest share of the market – 18 per cent. This was a conglomerate whose interests ranged from fast food chains to motion picture production to computer games to books to parking lots. Geffen was known as a tasteful patron of newer acts and counted among his label's artists Berlin, Asia, Irene Cara and Quarterflash, as well as Elton John and Neil Young. Most important, Geffen Records was John Lennon's last record company, the company that put out *Double Fantasy*, and it was Geffen who was on the scene, comforting Yoko and son Sean in the days after John was shot.

The fourth bidder was EMI America. Largely due to the sales of records on the Capitol label, Capitol-EMI America was the fourth-largest company, controlling nearly ten per cent of the marketplace. Capitol was the label of the Beach Boys and the Beatles and, more recently, Anne Murray, Bob Seger, Juice Newton, the Motels and Duran Duran. By comparison, EMI's roster of hitmakers was insignificant, including Kajagoogoo, Naked Eyes, Sheena Easton and only a few others.

David conducted some of his negotiations in a manner befitting the late Howard Hughes. Capitol's chairman and chief executive officer, Bhaskar Menon, told friends that he had to wait for David to call him and he couldn't call David back, because David never said where he was. Berlin? Tokyo? Or right around the corner in New York? Menon never knew. Someone representing David called, usually Coco, to say that David would call the following day at a specified time.

As negotiations continued, David reserved four weeks at New York's Power Plant to record his first album in over two years.

Earlier in the year, he had told his old friend Tony Visconti to put aside three months for the project and Tony kept that period free of commitments. He never heard from David again.

What happened?

David had met the next major influence in his musical life.

This was Nile Rodgers, a black American guitarist whose group, Chic, gave disco music a refreshing shot of wit and sophistication with hits like 'Le Freak' (1978) and 'Good Times' (1979). Nile also worked as a producer for Sister Sledge's 'We Are Family' and Diana Ross's *Diana* LP, which yielded the hits 'I'm Comin' Out' and 'Upside Down'. When David met Nile in a New York club, they began talking and discovered they had many of the same early rhythm and blues heroes. They decided to work together and Nile began writing arrangements for the songs that David had decided to use.

David made it clear that he wanted this album to be unlike any he had done before – not unlike *Young Americans* in *sound*, but warmer, funkier, more positive.

'I felt I was becoming a little static with the kind of synthesizer-techno stuff I'd been doing,' David explained later. 'I wanted to break away from that. Every few years I have to redefine what I'm writing. I had to do it when I moved to Berlin and I had to do it again just recently. I had to think if indeed I want to make another album, do I just want to make another cold album? Is there not another way you can go?'

David said the band had to be able to capture that. Nile recommended Tony Thompson of Chic to take Dennis

Davis's place on drums (Dennis having gone off to join Stevie Wonder since David last recorded). Then David brought in a young, white guitar player from Texas whom he'd heard a year before at the jazz festival in Montreux, Stevie Ray Vaughn. Together David and Nile made up a list of top studio saxophone players – to duplicate the feel of the music David had listened to while filming with Nagisa Oshima.

Working daily from 10.30 a.m. to 6.00 p.m., they completed the record in twenty days. For the first time, David did not pick up a single instrument. 'This was,' he said, 'a singer's album.'

It was also a dancer's album and a lover's album and an album aimed at satisfying the diehard Bowie fatalists, as the title track alone ensured. 'Let's Dance' was a seven-minute evocation to romance, which appeared on the musical surface to be a dance song. Yet, in the pared-down lyric there was what David himself called 'a slightly evasive quality of desperation': 'Let's dance, for fear your grace should fall/ Let's dance, for fear tonight is all.'

'Modern Love' was another up-tempo dance song, created in something of a Motown mode, with a little bit of everything else thrown in: an opening rhythm guitar motif familiar to heavy metal fans, the cry of female harmonies behind David's raw and slicing lead that brought together R&B and pop, and choruses of horns that reeked of tavern funk, with a lyric that made poignant, scary, yet truthful comment: 'Modern love gets me to the church on time/Church on time, terrifies me!'

David also reprieved one of the songs he wrote with Jimmy Osterberg for his album, *The Idiot*. 'China Girl', with its peculiar verse about entering London with swastikas on the brain, was more successful this time around, largely because it was, well, funnier and sexier, complete with whispered lyrics and a hokey guitar riff that smacked of Oriental cliché.

Others included a complete reworking of the title song for the film *Cat People*; an unadorned love song called 'Without You' ('You're exactly who I want to be with/What would I do without you?'), and the album's closer, David's get-down-and-boogie tune, 'Shake It'.

A polished and practised sense of style and grace pervaded all these songs, and the production was big – 'modern big band rock' was what Nile called it, and more than one reviewer later compared the sound to Phil Spector's 'wall of sound' – all of which made it easy to ignore David's often despairing lyrics, lyrics that simultaneously supplied the music with added power for those who chose to listen.

The sessions were fun. Rarely had David enjoyed recording so much, as his entirely American band tried, half-successfully, to turn him into a football fan by making him watch the New York Jets in the televised playoffs. Making the period of the recording even sweeter was the decision he made regarding his future recording career.

'We actually thought he'd stay with us,' says Tony McGrogan at RCA London. 'We knew he'd leave RCA America, but we'd been good to him, even if America wasn't. Keep in mind we also never made any money off of Bowie. He was signed to RCA America and every pound we made in record sales in England went straight to New York. We hoped he would give us our due, so to speak.'

Of course, business is rarely run that way. Usually the record company that gets the artist in a bidding situation is the one offering the most money for the least work, and if the talent roster is compatible and the executive in charge is a likeable bloke, so much the better.

At David Bowie's level, in the winter of 1982–3, such sums and promises were significant. Yes, it was true that his track record was shaky in America, where he had only two Top 10 singles in nearly a decade. None the less, there was an impressive mystique, an aura, a smell of hugeness rarely associated with recording stars. Besides that, he was a consistent record seller internationally and there were rumours of his new album's hit potential that made everyone in on the bidding salivate.

For some time, it was rumoured that David Geffen had the inside track, largely because of the John Lennon connection. But, then, money seemed more important.

'It *was* about money,' says Geffen today, 'and he wanted more than we were able to spend. And that's all I'll say about it.'

The others bidding agree, and the figure finally offered

by EMI was widely reported at first to be in the neighbourhood of $10 million, and then was said to be closer to $17 million, in exchange for five years, with a maximum of an album a year. Neither EMI nor David's offices will confirm or deny the sum. However, RCA's Herb Helman believes that the final figure was even greater.

'Bob Summer, the president of RCA, and Jack Craigo, the head of US and Canada, made every effort to keep David on the label,' Helman says. 'The final EMI figure was more than we could match based on his track record. My business affairs people say he got over twenty million dollars – twenty-one or twenty-two.'

Soon after, David was lying on a beach in Acapulco when he was discovered by Eric Idle, of Monty Python fame. Idle said he and a bunch of loons were making a film up the beach.

'How about it, mate? Want to be a pirate in a B-movie?'

David said, 'Why certainly.'

The film was *Yellowbeard*, a swashbuckling comedy with a cast that included Cheech and Chong, Marty Feldman (in his final film role; he died the last day of shooting), Madeline Kahn, Spike Milligan, Peter Cook, and Monty Python. (As well as a cast of supporting actors that included James Mason, Peter Boyle and Susannah York.) David's role was minuscule and generally went unnoticed. He did it as a lark.

Afterwards, he returned to New York and on 27 January formally signed his contract with EMI America, turned over the master tapes for *Let's Dance*, and then left for Australia, where he planned to make promotional videos for 'Let's Dance' and 'China Girl' with David Mallet. With him were Jee Ling, an exquisite Chinese model David had been dating and whom he planned to use in 'China Girl', and his son, now a long-legged twelve-year-old who looked very much like dad.

David was followed to Australia by Kurt Loder, a writer for *Rolling Stone*. *Rolling Stone* had been interviewing David for more than ten years, since his first visit to America in 1972, when he paraded down Sunset Boulevard in a silk dress. During that period the magazine had chronicled the life and hard times of his vast cast of characters and Loder, an associate editor, was curious who he'd meet this time.

The new 'character' David presented was in the story published in May, when David was on the cover and the cover line read, 'DAVID BOWIE STRAIGHT'. David, Loder said, 'was a man without masks. Open, jokey, very . . . warm is the only word.'

It was no longer hip to be cool, David said, and the biggest mistake he ever made (he added one night after a couple of cans of Foster's lager) 'was telling that *Melody Maker* writer that I was bisexual. Christ, I was so *young* then! I was *experimenting* . . .'

In everything David said, he projected the same down-to-earth, mature, somewhat self-realized image. John Lennon was dead more than two years, but David still felt the pain. 'A whole piece of my life seemed to have been taken away,' he said. 'A whole reason for being a singer and songwriter seemed to be removed from me. It was almost like a warning. It was saying: we've got to do something about our situation on earth.

'Having a child to care for points up one's purpose, it really does. To see him grow, and be excited about the future – and then you think, "Oh, shit, the future, yes, I'd forgotten about that, old son. Um, I'll see what I can do. . . ."'

If David was being a family man, settling into responsibility and oncoming middle age – he was, after all, now thirty-six – he was being no less consummate a professional. David used his presence in Australia to shop for and buy a ranch, and he enjoyed his long days alone with Joey (agreeing to the boy being photographed, though only from behind). But he also created two superb videos during this time, one of which would put him back into the headlines again and, simultaneously, set another new standard in the medium.

By early 1983, there were three general types of video – narratives that told a specific story, usually promoted by the lyric; in-concert footage or films of bands lip-synching; and those which tried to be more artistic and merely matched music with images. David was in the latter group. He had, in fact, been stringing together images without story-line for years. He did the same again in 'Let's Dance' and in 'China Girl' he broke new ground again, making the first great erotic video.

'China Girl' was, in part, an updated version of the classic Burt Lancaster and Deborah Kerr love scene in the film *From Here to Eternity*. In that film, Lancaster and Kerr, in modest bathing suits, steamed up the 1950s cameras in the rolling surf; at the time, it was considered quite daring. In David's update, he and Jee Ling were in exactly the same pose, writhing in the sand and surf, but in 1983 without bathing suits.

David returned to London in March to launch what would be the most intensive publicity campaign for one of his albums since RCA flew a bunch of puzzled journalists from New York to England to see Ziggy Stardust in 1972. He arrived at Heathrow Airport on 16 March and was taken by limousine to Claridge's Hotel, where on the following day he invited seventy-five writers and broadcasters in for champagne and brandy cocktails. David hadn't had a new album in four years, hadn't toured in five. Consequently, the reportage was somewhat breathless.

'Some ten minutes behind schedule, Bowie stepped jauntily into the room – blond, sun-tanned and obscenely well-preserved – perched himself on a table in order to reach the microphones, rumpled his elegant wide-lapelled, beige suit, flashed us a sneak of ankle-sock . . . coolly declared he'd be playing dates in Germany, France, Belgium, Holland, Scandinavia, Britain, America, Australia and Japan . . . and then invited us to fire away.' (Reported *Melody Maker*.)

The press conference that followed was typical. The questions were, largely, inane ('Why aren't you playing Spain?' 'What's your favourite aspect of your career?' 'What time do you go to bed?') and David's answers were as polite as possible. He had learned to play the celebrity game. He could not be ruffled. Even the dumbest question in the world deserved a kind answer.

The press attention was staggering. Even before the formal press conference, his name and picture were spread all over the media. Some, like that which appeared in the *Times*, were positive: 'A cracked actor makes repairs. The rock singer David Bowie, who moulded the style of a generation, returns to the concert stage this year after fruitful ventures into films and theatre.' Other stories were not, for example, 'My Nightmare Fight Against Heroin', a paste-pot collection of old quotes (some from the previous day's *Times* story) which was emblazoned across two pages of the *Sun*. It didn't really matter. The attention was valued none the less because it sold records and tapes and tickets to movies and shows.

Everything was precisely planned, through his own office in New York (Isolar), EMI in New York and London, and Rogers and Cowan (the General Motors of publicity, with offices in London, New York and Beverly Hills). The day after the press conference, EMI released the first single, 'Let's Dance/'Cat People', worldwide. David simultaneously began doing interviews with London's top magazines and radio networks, to each and every one, projecting the new image of normalcy. The days of drink and drugs and kinky sex were past, he said; now it was early to bed with a good book, daily workouts on the punching bag, proper meals, and the joys of single parenting.

Then on 22 March, David and Coco flew to Geneva, where they were met by a limousine and taken to David's home. There, he relaxed with his son and held meetings with various people involved in the forthcoming tour.

There was a problem with the set. David had asked Derek Bozier, who had designed the *Let's Dance* album cover – showing David in boxing gloves and trunks – to develop some ideas for the stage and lighting. What he produced was too elaborate, too expensive; there wasn't time in the schedule or money in the budget to finish it. David put in a call to Jules Fisher, who had done the Diamond Dogs set and he recommended Mark Ravitz, who had assisted him on the Dogs show.

'I got a call Wednesday to see if I was available,' Ravitz says today. 'Thursday I got a confirming call. Friday I was on a Swiss Air jet to Lausanne. He picked me up Saturday and we met all day at his house. I left Geneva at noon Sunday, was home Sunday night, and finished the model by the following Friday.'

It was at this pace that the tour was assembled. In New York, David's business management on 57th Street met with a tour management company in the same neighbourhood, who then rushed to Europe to hold six days of meetings with promoters, as another booking agent (also on 57th Street) completed negotiations back in New York for shows in fifty-nine cities. By the end of April, the set was under construction in San Francisco – construction by the same firm that built the stage for the 1976 Democratic convention and would do the Olympics stage in 1984 – and David was checking final proofs of a stylish 48-page concert programme that would be published in English, French, German and Japanese. Pilots were interviewed and the engines of charter planes actually were disassembled in a search for the safest. Tickets and backstage passes were ordered with a minute flaw so that ticket takers and security guards could immediately detect a counterfeit. More than 9400 hotel rooms were booked. Transportation was arranged for 64,000lb of tour equipment. On and on and on.

And then it was off to Dallas, where David met with his all-American backup band for a week and a half of rehearsals.

There was a serious problem when he arrived. Stevie Ray Vaughn, the guitarist who had given several of the *Let's Dance* tracks so much of its bluesy muscularity, was pulling out of the tour. According to Chesley Millikan, Vaughn's manager, the guitarist was quitting the tour because David's management company had asked him to sign a contract that he regarded as unacceptable. Among other things, Millikan said, David went back on a verbal agreement that Vaughn's trio, Double Trouble, would open some of the concerts in Europe and America. Millikan also charged that David's management originally said Vaughn, while on the tour, could fulfil all publicity commitments for his upcoming solo album, due for release the next month, but then said all interviews and television appearances would have to have their approval. Finally, Millikan said, they were offended by the money being offered, $300 a concert – which Millikan called 'the sort of money that would have been offered to any sideman in need of six months of work.'

David's managers and publicists refused to comment, except to say that they feared Vaughn would be used by various media people to get to Bowie and that's why they wanted publicity approval.

The musicians were not so reluctant to talk. 'We're doing a lot better than that,' said Carlos Alomar. 'David has never made any money before and on this tour there are a lot of people making sure that he's going to make some money. As far as our money situation, come on, that's just fine. Everybody's making over four figures, [$1000 plus a week] plus we have a real good per diem and everything's fine. Plus, once David makes some money, he bonuses everybody out. We're purring like crazy.'

Vaughn was replaced with another guitarist, a heavy metal specialist, Earl Slick, and David returned to his tour preparation, starting each day with two hours of aerobics, followed by another two hours of sparring with a professional boxer, then after lunch, working with the musicians and backup singers until midnight or later.

'This is a long tour and I want to be in shape,' David said at the time. 'I don't want it to be like the old days, when I felt it was almost my duty to end up a wreck. I thought that was what you had to do to be a substantial artist.

'I used to think of a concert as a battle, but I think of it now as more of a date – a courtship, if you will. I'm looking forward to the audience. At one time, I didn't even think of them as human beings. I was the artist and *that* was the audience.'

Finally, it was time to start.

THE $10 MILLION-A-MONTH
MACHINE

David's representatives were calling it the biggest rock spectacle in history and the statistics quoted left little room for argument.

Ninety dates in fifteen countries in over seven months, with a projected audience of two and a half million and a possible gross of $20 million in ticket sales alone.

Add merchandizing (T-shirts, posters, etc) and revenue from television (a one-hour special for America's Home Box Office, followed by a 90-minute videocassette) and increased album sales, and David was being called 'a $10-million-a-month machine'.

The night of the opening concert, in Brussels on 18 May, David had the hottest single and hottest album in America, England and across most of the European continent. The song 'Let's Dance' was No. 1 almost everywhere and the album was headed for the same spot in Britain, No. 4 in America and, according to EMI, was 'the fastest-selling album for the company since the Beatles released *Sgt Pepper* (in 1967).'

At the same time, David was on the cover of London's trendy new punk-chic magazine, *The Face*, and in America on the covers of *Record* and *Rolling Stone*, as well as the subject of a two-page spread in the ultra-stylish *Vanity Fair*:

'Although he was probably the most influential British rock star to emerge in the '70s, David Bowie will always seem something of an imposter. In 1972, when he touched down on the rock world as Ziggy Stardust, ghastly and glamorous, glittering in bright orange hair and swishy futuristic raiment, he seemed an android poseur, a synthetic creation of space-age decadence. His music was cool, campy, and shrill, foreshadowing the second-hand ennui and cutting ironies of new wave. Always a revisionist, in the wake of punk and electronic pop, he had cast off the glitter to explore post-cabaret experimentalism in Berlin, evolving into a kind of jaded Aryan prophet who spins art dancing visions of hedonism and doom.

'Bowie's roles as an actor have also reflected his gifts as a shape-changer. With his mismatched eyes, world-weary voice, and angular grace, Bowie is so alluring one suspects something monstrous beneath the beauty. His eerie performance as a stranded alien in *The Man Who Fell to Earth* was so convincing that he was cast as the misshapen hero in the Broadway production of *The Elephant Man*. And in his latest role, as the aristocrat John Blaylock in *The Hunger*, he portrays a vampire's consort who has remained thirty years old for over 300 years. As Blaylock ages, Bowie becomes both Tithonus and Dorian Gray – telling antecedents for a rock star who has been more immune to time than most.'

It was a summation of his career that David both enjoyed and hated. 'It was well-written,' says one friend, 'and David always admired that, you know. And it was very flattering, too. The writer said some nice things about David as an artist and that pleased David no end. But he also said David was some sort of cold, eerie outsider, like. Now he wanted to be Warm Willie, everybody's teddy bear. He was caught in the middle, I think.'

Caught in the middle, perhaps, but certainly caught at the very top, where superstardom is generally confirmed by gossipy word-of-mouth. And as David played his first dates in Europe, no one around was much riper for gossip.

By now, the 'China Girl' video had been released to great outrage and censorship. Banned by BBC TV's *Top of the Pops* show because of its early evening slot, it was seen by viewers on BBC 2's other longstanding pop arbiter, *The Old Grey Whistle Test* which then went out late at night. There followed in the daily press a rash of headlines like 'BOWIE'S BEACH PARTY', 'BOWIE'S VIDEO – THE NAKED TRUTH', and under the title 'Perils of the Teenage Models', 'MAGIC! MY ROMP WITH NAKED BOWIE IN SURF'.

It was a perfect conversation piece for the grownups that David now wished to add to his audience: the great middle-aged middle-class. Lewd conversations broke out in pubs:

'D'ja see that faggot David Bowie on the telly? Starkers on the beach with a Chinese girl! Fuckin' they were!'

So David was heterosexual, after all!

It all seemed a part of the new, well-dressed shield of normalcy – the early bedtimes, exercise, and time at home with his son. David always had the young in his audience. Now he was going after the mums and dads.

Brussels was the first big test. Would the audience – kids, mums, dads, media – accept it?

The look and feel of the show was quite different from all his previous shows, although once again he depended on lighting that constantly swept and changed to create titanic effect. Four circles of powerful, tiny lights which beamed from the fifty-foot ceiling to the massive stage gave the impression of ancient Greek columns, or the pillars of light from *Star Trek* ('Beam me up, Scotty!'). Forty spotlights swept the stage on cue: jerky, stark white for 'Fame', hot reds and yellow for 'Red Sails', creepy green for 'Scary Monsters'.

David stood in front of (or under) this, looking very much like a young Frank Sinatra – lean, chiselled features beneath a mop of carefully curled, popcorn-coloured hair, a pastel blue silk suit with roomy, pleated, cuffed trousers, belt and suspenders underneath, the collar of his shirt unbuttoned, necktie loose around his neck.

Everywhere you looked there was a fifties feel. The drummer, Tony Thompson, wore a sleeveless, crew-neck sweater with knitted ribs. The two backup singers, Frank and George Sims, wore brightly striped suits and fedoras that made them look like a cross between Preppies and gangsters from *Guys and Dolls*.

Others in the band were clothed in a global mix: Carlos Alomar in a Nehru jacket and hat, the horn section in safari garb, his bassist in ballooning pants that had a Middle Eastern feel.

The use of props was minimal. Twice David sat in a director's chair – once, for a dramatic reading of 'Cracked Actor', he wore a cape and dark glasses, while holding the by-now trademark *Hamlet* skull. And through three or four numbers, a huge, inflatable plastic globe was tossed around the audience. (Beginning, of course, during 'Ashes to Ashes' and 'Space Oddity'.) And that was about it. The backup singers acted or mimed little sketches to provide some visual variety – if you were seated in the first dozen rows, you could see it – and David changed suits, from blue to peach, during the intermission, but that was it. Just as *Let's Dance* was, in David's words, 'a singer's album', the Serious Moonlight Tour was a singer's show.

In all, David performed at least twenty songs, going back to before his days in orange hair, coming up to 'Let's Dance', 'Modern Love' and 'China Girl'. During almost all of them there were no effects, only what could be called an arena-sized, one-man show, a singer singing his songs.

London's music press *loathed* the show.

'This new, very visible Bowie says much to us about the rewards of mediocrity that maintain rock's motion,' grumbled the *New Musical Express*. 'Fighting hard against this growing myopic trend, I soak in the juices of the snobberies of art and consider such spectacles as Bowie . . . being nauseatingly protective and take the "good feeling" they apparently impart about as seriously as Matt Monro's moonlight. The rock right and Bowie's use of it is simply about The Place and keeping people in it.'

Sounds was equally acerbic, only pithier, calling David 'the thinking man's Frankie Vaughan . . . musical fish and chips'.

Melody Maker echoed the rest: 'The concerts confirmed what those singles with Queen and Bing Crosby should already have told us. The man who sold the world can now be safely filed away under family entertainment. And all the family is buying.'

Indeed they were, and so were the critics for the 'straight', or Establishment (Fleet Street), press. The report in the *Daily Express* said, 'For the first time in his thirteen-year career, Bowie played Bowie straight', performing a two-hour show with 'utmost style'. Said the *Evening Standard*: 'Exit Ziggy Stardust, Aladdin Sane and the Thin White Duke. They were the ghosts of David Bowie past, buried in Brussels last night. . . .' Even the *Sun* – circulation 4.5 million and usually concerned only with David's alleged sanity and heroin problems – enthused, saying David had 'the mystique of Bob Dylan' and the 'sheer animal excitement of Mick Jagger'.

By the time these reviews appeared, of course, David and his convoy were on their way to Frankfurt.

Here, again, he played to a sold-out arena and, except for some of the music writers who had tagged along, he received entirely rave reviews. And thence to Munich, Lyons and Nice, where there was more of the same acclaim.

It was also in France that a memo was distributed by Corinne to all the members of the cast and crew to 'beware of strange girls in hotels'. This caused much laughter. 'It's crazy,' said one member of the stage crew, 'because strange girls in hotels is one of the things we do this for!'

The juggernaut was rolling now. The kinks had been worked out. All signs indicated there lay nothing but enormous success ahead. In America and in almost every Western European country and in several in Austro-Asia, 'Let's Dance' was still a Top 10 hit and 'China Girl' was just being released as the follow-up.

At the same time, the original Ziggy Stardust album roared to No. 1 on *Billboard* magazine's relatively new 'Midline' chart (comprised of old albums re-released at discounted prices). *The Hunger* was on general, international release (doing great box office the first week of its run and dropping off abruptly soon after, none the less giving David significant and positive press). And news of advance concert ticket sales was staggering. In Los Angeles alone, 32,000 tickets were sold in 90 minutes. While in England, David's promoter Harvey Goldsmith said requests for tickets were exceeding available seats by 800 per cent, putting David ahead of the Rolling Stones tour of the year before.

David also accepted in May the largest flat fee ever paid a solo performer for delivering a single show. This came from Steve Wozniak, the eccentric co-founder of Apple computers. The 'US festival' was his answer to the 'Me Generation'. It was, he said, time for peace and love and he was willing to pay rock bands almost anything they wanted to announce that in a Woodstockian context. Everyone who came was paid well: the Clash, Van Halen, the Pretenders, Flock of Seagulls, Men at Work, Berlin and

Stevie Nicks. David was booked to close the festival on 30 May – the honoured spot on the bill – and was paid $1 million for doing it.

Some argued that Van Halen got the same price, which they did. But Van Halen was a quartet and David was one man. More important – and what was not revealed at the time – was that Van Halen and all the others in the festival signed away television rights to their performances for a festival special that was being filmed. David kept *his* TV rights for his own special, and he was the only one given that concession.

And then it was back to Europe for sold-out shows in London, Paris, Gothenburg, Bad Segeburg, Sochum, Frejus, Berlin and Edinburgh, in the largest arenas available. In Scotland, 47,000 watched. In Sweden, there were two shows, with 60,000 attending each of them. At Milton Keynes, David performed three times, singing to 175,000.

Everywhere he went, he came out in his ice cream pastels and his yellow candy-floss hair, tossed an inflatable globe around and sang a 90-minute medley of his greatest hits.

All David now needed for confirmation of his massive, international celebrity was the cover of *Time* magazine.

David's publicists at Rogers & Cowan started bombarding America's 'A-list' – the top publications and most popular national television shows – when they signed him the previous November. Week after week after week they drove home each promotable angle in his recent life: new record company! new records! new tour! new lifestyle! And with great passion and ferocity. Rogers & Cowan had done the same thing the year before with Julio Iglesias, virtually transforming him into a world figure in a single six-month period, and the publicists were determined to see lightning strike again.

The last week of June, with David in London, photographs of the massive crowds at Milton Keynes were rushed to New York. They were impressive, there was no denying that. Festival-size crowds were flocking to see a single performer. It was almost Messianic, or so the editors chuckled and remarked. Wasn't it David Bowie who once said he wanted to be Hitler? The man who fell to earth, indeed.

And so it was decided to put David Bowie on the cover

of *Time* on 18 July, the week he was to begin a seventeen-city tour of North America.

For two months, David and his caravan criss-crossed North America, from Quebec to Houston to Philadelphia to Anaheim. In most ways, it was like any of David's tours, sameness marked by small incidents. Hartford, Connecticut, was the first American date, so that was where 5,000 mylar balloons were released over the audience during 'Modern Love', and Philadelphia was where everyone spent an afternoon taping the in-performance video of that song. Philadelphia was also where a female fan grabbed David in the middle of the show and had to be peeled off by Tony Mascia. Vancouver, B.C., was where members of the band played in a softball game with local disc jockeys and Chicago was where Michael Butler, the playboy millionaire who had produced *Hair*, invited them to a polo match.

Houston was where they gave birthday cakes and helium balloons to Tony Mascia and one of the backup singers, George Sims, and virtually everyone inhaled some of the helium, laughing at the squeaky voices the gas gave them. Houston was also where David tried to take his son Joey – who was along on about a third of the tour – to the Six Flags Amusement Park, but the fans got out of hand and they had to leave. Buffalo was where David's luggage was searched when a golden retriever decided there was something illegal inside; nothing was found and the tour continued.

Through it all, David stuck to his healthy regimen as much as possible, eating sushi (a staple in his diet by now), going to bed as early as the shows allowed, even cutting back on the cigarettes, and sending Coco out for books. (He currently enjoyed *Megatrends*, he said, and a book called *Immortal Dreamers*. Always the high-tech romantic.)

It all sounded so ordinary. Of course it was not. David travelled from city to city not on a train or bus as he once had done (when he was afraid to fly) or in a chartered plane (when that fear went away). Now he travelled in a *customized* plane, complete with video room and lounge, as well as a private bedroom. And now entire gossip columns full of celebrities attended the backstage parties. In Los Angeles, he drank with Sissy Spacek, Irene Cara, Henry Winkler,

Sally Struthers, Howie Mandel, Donald Sutherland, Tom Conti, Jacqueline Smith and Prince, and in New York the party included Keith Richards, Yoko and Sean Lennon, Susan Sarandon, Tina Turner, Joe Jackson, Ron Wood, Ian Hunter, Nile Rodgers, Richard Gere, Rick Derringer, Grace Jones and Raquel Welch. David had pulled famous names at earlier tour parties, but never in such quantity or variety. (At once backstage party in Europe, he met Princess Caroline of Monaco, at another, a benefit for Brixton charities, he talked with Princess Michael of Kent.)

It was working as it never had worked before. And the money was rolling in.

The concert grosses were at the top of *Billboard*'s weekly 'Boxscore' (which ranked the week's top shows according to the size of the box office take). In Chicago he played three sellout shows and grossed $716,000. In Detroit there were two shows, with a total of $544,000. In Vancouver he established a single show house record of $1.3 million and the next day he did $1.2 million in Edmonton.

And so it went on: Los Angeles (two shows), $506,000 ... Dallas, $235,000 ... Norfolk, $321,000 ... Toronto, $2.3 million (another attendance and gross record). Plus records and programmes and lapel pins and T-shirts and all the rest. In the middle of September, as David and his band and all the others rested before beginning the Asian leg of the tour, *Billboard* magazine turned one of its business writers loose on the story and he reported that David probably would 'eclipse even the Rolling Stones' record-breaking global trek of last year.'

Billboard was talking about record sales as well as concert ticket sales, giving the story a headline that said, 'EMI, RCA Dancing For Joy Over Bowie's "Moonlight" Tour'. Everywhere in Europe, both record companies had launched major sales campaigns to coincide with regional tour dates, and everywhere the payoffs were great. In Sweden, Norway, Finland, Denmark, Holland, Belgium, France, Germany, England, even in Greece, sales of *Let's Dance* broke records and David's existing catalogue of RCA albums took a tremendous jump.

In August RCA released another collection of early songs, this one called *Golden Years* and sold primarily on the basis that all the songs on the album were being performed on the Serious Moonlight Tour. What made this album unusual, was the fact that it was packaged with David's co-operation.

Earlier in the year, another collection of old songs had been released by RCA. This was called *Bowie Rare*, although only two of the songs of the record's eleven could be called that. Did making available to American and English audiences the Italian version of 'Space Oddity' and the German rendition of 'Heroes' really make the album worthwhile? At the time, David said he thought such compilations were 'horrendous . . . atrocious . . . offensive'. And, he said, if RCA wanted to put out anthologies, he'd appreciate it if they came to him for some good ideas.

And so it was he started working with RCA again. 'He provided the repertoire for the tour with the knowledge we'd issue an album of the tunes we already had on record,' says Don Wardell, head of RCA's marketing. 'And that's what we did.'

Along with the co-operation, however, there came a warning. In no way could the album even hint at being an official tour recording. The words 'Serious' and 'Moonlight' were not allowed. And no new photographs. RCA agreed to everything and then took the package to Tony DeFries. Because he was still in there for 50 per cent and his contract gave him the right.

How did David feel about this continuing DeFries connection? According to friends, David was more accepting now, or, rather, less willing to get emotionally involved. Let the lawyers handle it.

Let the lawyers handle Angie, too. She was separated from Drew Blood and raising her daughter alone, shifting back and forth between a flat in West Los Angeles and a horse ranch in Scottsdale, Arizona, where she raised Polish Arabians. In 1983, she said she never talked to David any more. 'I only talk to Corinne,' she says. 'It's not easy.'

David's mum? She was still living in Beckenham, on a monthly stipend from Isolar, turning away all interviews, seeing David infrequently.

David's half-brother, of course, remained in Cane Hill

Hospital in Surrey, and David's Aunt Pat was still looking for some way to put pressure on David to take up the financial slack.*

Childhood friend George Underwood was making a living as a commercial artist in London.

Ken Pitt was retired, appearing at the odd Bowie fan convention (at one he auctioned off a pair of Bowie's boots). He was still talking about doing something with that half-hour film he had from 1967, *Love You Till Tuesday*, and, according to friends, David's love beads were still hanging from the stairway banister in his London flat.

Hermione Farthingale? Some said she was the key to David's personality, the key to *everything*. And no one had a clue. She had vanished.

Lindsay Kemp was living in Italy and the same month that David went to Australia with his Serious Moonlight Tour, the mime artist opened a month-long retrospective at Sadler's Wells Theatre in London's West End. Yes, he remembered David, he told interviewers; he called him 'my dear sweet boy'.

Mary Finnigan was working as a reporter for one of London's radio networks.

Tony Visconti still had his Good Earth Studio in Soho and was recording a variety of London acts.

Mick Ronson was living in America and producing American and Canadian bands.

Lou Reed was still recording, and so was Jimmy Osterberg, who remained close to David, although Lou Reed did not.

Mick Watts, the interviewer who first asked David if he was gay, was working as a writer-producer for BBC Television.

Cherry Vanilla was working as an assistant to the Oscar-winning composer Vangelis (*Chariots of Fire*).

* As this book went to press, in early 1985, Terry died in a train accident, an apparent suicide.

Toni Basil, who choreographed Diamond Dogs, was a star by now herself, with a No. 1 song, 'Mickey'.

Luther Vandross, one of David's backup singers, was a recording star, too.

The 1983 tour was coming to a close and so was 1983. For David Bowie, it was a good year – his best ever.

His first album and first singles for EMI and several 'new' records for RCA were runaway hits. At year's end, he had had three singles ('Let's Dance', 'China Girl' and 'Modern Love') in America's Hot 100.

David also was nominated (with Billy Joel and Lionel Richie) for a Grammy for the Best Male Singer in America and again he was relatively assured of sweeping all the public opinion polls in Britain.

More important than awards, nominations and opinion polls were the critics' assessment of David's musical significance. Once again, they said, he was in the vanguard. Now he was in the romantic lead, and in the group of performers who led American pop culture into a renewed dance movement, helping to re-establish the link between black music and rock. Romance and dance music made comebacks in 1983 and David was at the forefront, where he'd always been.

At the same time, *Merry Christmas, Mr Lawrence* was on general international release and the reviews of the film and David's performance were mixed, but satisfying. *Playboy* called David's screen presence 'electric', the *Guardian* called it 'formidable'. 'Remarkable,' said *Variety*. 'Superb,' said the *Sunday Telegraph*. 'Acquits himself well throughout,' said *Time Out*. 'A movie star's movie star,' said the critic in the *Village Voice*. Many others were not so complimentary, but David's career as an actor had advanced significantly; there were too many good reviews in good publications and too much praise from fellow actors and directors to deny it any longer.

On several other fronts, fame settled itself around him like a cloak. *Playboy* magazine named him one of its 'Sex Stars of 1983' (along with Clint Eastwood, Burt Reynolds and Eddie Murphy). In England, half a dozen small paperback books and illustrated discographies went back into print and in America, a major publisher commissioned an 'authorized' book about the Serious Moonlight Tour. (Chet Fippo, an editor for *People* magazine, was given the task of writing 15,000 words to go with all the photographs – and had to sign an agreement never to use any of the information he obtained while on the tour in any other publication.) The three videos from the *Let's Dance* album were in 'heavy rotation' on America's 24-hour rock cable network, MTV, and available in stores as a videocassette, and the cassette of *The Hunger* went on to *Billboard*'s bestseller and most popular rental lists. And when his figure went on display at Madame Tussaud's, he became the second most popular attraction, just behind Prince Charles and Lady Di.

David wasn't the only megastar of 1983. In some ways, this really was Michael Jackson's year – the year when *Thriller* sold more than twenty million copies worldwide (compared to David's four million sales of *Let's Dance*), the year when the *Thriller* video outdistanced all the rest (including David's). This also was the year when a 6-foot 4-inch male in a dress who called himself Boy George became an international star, releasing hit after hit after hit and attracting enormous media attention with a band called Culture Club. It is no secret that part of Michael Jackson's appeal is his androgynous looks. Was Boy George a boy, or what? Magazines and newspapers around the world ran stories about this phenomenon. They called it 'Gender Bending'.

Long-time David Bowie fans smiled. He'd done it all more than ten years before.

'Hey,' says one of David's friends, 'I don't want to take anything away from Michael Jackson or Boy George, they're both very talented. But could they have gotten away with this without David breaking ground for them? These things don't happen in vacuums, you know. It's all connected. Call it gender bending, I don't care, call it anything you want. It's experimenting, trying new things, new faces, new personalities. Anything you want. Who do you want to be today?'

It was 8 December in Hong Kong, David's final performance. At the end of the show he came forward and waited for the applause and noise to die completely.

'Last time I saw John Lennon was in Hong Kong,' he said. 'We went to the Hong Kong Market and there was a stall that sold old clothes, and there was a Beatle jacket on the stall and I did something that's not usually in my character. I asked him to put it on, so that I could take a photograph. I took a photograph. I've still got the photograph. The jacket doesn't fit properly. It looks like John had outgrown it.'

David paused. The audience applauded his sentimentality, his loyalty.

David resumed, his voice cracking now. 'On this day, December the 8th, in 1980, John Lennon was shot and killed outside his New York apartment.'

The huge audience roared and whistled in tribute and David sang a song he had never sung in performance before: John Lennon's 'Imagine'.

DISCOGRAPHY

Records are listed by title, label number, date of UK release and highest position recorded in *The Guinness Book of British Hit Singles* and *The Guinness Book of British Hit Albums* by Jo & Tim Rice, Paul Gambaccini and Mike Read.

Singles (45 rpm)

'Liza Jane'/'Louie Louie Go Home' (Davy Jones with the King Bees)
Vocalion-Pop V-9221, June 1964

'I Pity the Fool'/'Take My Tip' (The Manish Boys)
Parlophone R-5250, March 1965

'You've Got a Habit of Leaving'/'Baby Loves That Way' (Davy Jones and the Lower Third)
Parlophone R-5315, August 1965

'Can't Help Thinking About Me'/'And I Say to Myself' (David Bowie and the Lower Third)
Pye 7N-17020, January 1966

'Do Anything You Say'/'Good Morning Girl'
Pye 7N-17079, April 1966

'I Dig Everything'/'I'm Not Losing Sleep'
Pye 7N-17157, August 1966

'Rubber Band'/'London Boys'
Deram DM-107, December 1966

'The Laughing Gnome'/'The Gospel According to Tony Day'
Deram DM-123, April 1967

'Love You Till Tuesday'/'Did You Ever Have a Dream'
Deram DM-135, July 1967

'Space Oddity'/'Wild Eyed Boy From Freecloud'
Philips BF-1801, July 1969 (5)

'The Prettiest Star'/'Conversation Piece'
Mercury MF-1135, March 1970

'Memory of a Free Festival, Parts 1 & 2'
Mercury 6052-026, June 1970

'Holy Holy'/'Black Country Rock'
Mercury 6052-049, January 1971

'Changes'/'Andy Warhol'
RCA 2160, January 1972

'Starman'/'Suffragette City'
RCA 2199, April 1972 (10)

'John, I'm Only Dancing'/'Hang On To Yourself'
RCA 2263, September 1972 (12)

'Do Anything You Say'/'I Dig Everything'
Pye 7NX-8002, October 1972

'The Jean Genie'/'Ziggy Stardust'
RCA 2302, November 1972 (2)

'Drive-In Saturday'/'Around and Around'
RCA 2352, April 1973 (3)

'Life On Mars'/'The Man Who Sold the World'
RCA 2316, June 1973 (3)

'Sorrow'/'Port of Amsterdam'
RCA 2424, September 1973 (3)

'The Laughing Gnome'/'The Gospel According to Tony Day'
Deram DM-123, September 1973 (6) (*re-issue*)

'Rebel Rebel'/'Queen Bitch'
RCA LPBO-5009, February 1974 (5)

'Rock 'n' Roll Suicide'/'Quicksand'
RCA LPBO-5201, April 1974 (22)

'Diamond Dogs'/'Holy Holy'
RCA APBO-0293, June 1974 (21)

'Knock On Wood'/'Panic In Detroit'
RCA 2466, September 1974 (10)

'London Boys'/'Love You Till Tuesday'
Decca F-13579, May 1975

'Young Americans'/'Suffragette City'
RCA 2523, February 1975 (18)

'Fame'/'Right'
RCA 2579, August 1975 (17)

'Space Oddity'/'Changes' & 'Velvet Goldmine'
RCA 2593, September 1975 (1) (*re-issue*)

'Golden Years'/'Can You Hear Me'
RCA 2640, November 1975 (8)

'TVC 15'/'We Are the Dead'
RCA 2682, April 1976 (33)

'Suffragette City'/'Stay'
RCA 2726, July 1976

'Sound and Vision'/'A New Career In a New Town'
RCA PB-0905, February 1977 (3)

'Be My Wife'/'Speed of Life'
RCA PB-1017, June 1977

'Heroes'/'V-2 Schneider'
RCA PB-1121, September 1977 (24)

'Beauty and the Beast'/'Sense of Doubt'
RCA PB-1190, January 1978 (39)

'Liza Jane'/'Louie Louie Go Home'
Decca F-13807, September 1978 (*re-issue*)

'Breaking Glass'/'Art Decade' & 'Ziggy Stardust'
RCA BOW-1, November 1978 (54)

'I Pity the Fool' & 'Take My Tip'/'You've Got a Habit of Leaving' &
'Baby Loves That Way'
EMI 2925, March 1979 (*re-issue*)

'Boys Keep Swinging'/'Fantastic Voyage'
RCA BOW-2, April 1979 (7)

'DJ'/'Repetition'
RCA BOW-3, June 1979 (29)

'John, I'm Only Dancing (Again) (1975)'/'John, I'm Only Dancing
(1972)'
RCA BOW-4, December 1979 (12) (*B-side is re-issue*)

'Alabama Song'/'Space Oddity'
RCA BOW-5, February 1980 (23) (*B-side is re-issue*)

'Ashes to Ashes'/'Move On'
RCA BOW-6, August 1980 (1)

'Fashion'/'Scream Like a Baby'
RCA BOW-7, October 1980 (5)

'Scary Monsters (and Super Creeps)'/'Because You're Young'
RCA BOW-8, January 1981 (20)

'Up The Hill Backwards'/'Crystal Japan'
RCA BOW-9, March 1981

'Under Pressure'/'Soul Brother' (David Bowie & Queen)
EMI 5250, November 1981 (1)

'Wild Is The Wind'/'Golden Years'
RCA BOW-10, November 1981

Baal's Hymn (EP)
'Baal's Hymn'/'Remembering Marie A'/'Ballad Of The Adventurers'/
'The Drowned Girl'/'The Dirty Song'
RCA BOW-11, February 1982 (29)

'Cat People (Putting Out Fire)'/'Paul's Theme (Jogging Chase)'
MCA 770, March 1982 (26)

'I Pity The Fool'/'Take My Tip' (The Manish Boys)/'You've Got A
Habit of Leaving'/'Baby Loves That Way' (Davy Jones & the Lower
Third) (10″ EP)
See For Miles CYM 1, October 1982

FASHIONS – Picture disc pack
'Space Oddity'/'Changes'/'Velvet Goldmine'   BOWP-101
'Life On Mars'/'The Man Who Sold The World' BOWP-102
'The Jean Genie'/'Ziggy Stardust'   BOWP-103
'Rebel Rebel'/'Queen Bitch'   BOWP-104
'Sound And Vision'/'A New Career In Town' BOWP-105
'Drive-In Saturday'/'Round And Round'   BOWP-106
'Sorrow'/'Amsterdam'   BOWP-107
'Golden Years'/'Can You Hear Me'   BOWP-108
'Boys Keep Swinging'/'Fantastic Voyage'   BOWP-109
'Ashes to Ashes'/'Move On'   BOWP-110
All released in limited edition of 25,000, November 1982

'Peace On Earth'/'Little Drummer Boy' (Both duets by David Bowie &
Bing Crosby)/'Fantastic Voyage'
RCA BOW-12, October 1982 (3)

Picture Sleeve Reissues
'Drive-In Saturday'/'Round And Round'   RCA BOW-501
'Life On Mars'/'The Man Who Sold The World' RCA BOW-502
'Rock 'n' Roll Suicide'/'Quicksand'   RCA BOW-503
'Diamond Dogs'/'Holy Holy'   RCA BOW-504
'Knock On Wood'/'Panic In Detroit'   RCA BOW-505
'Young Americans'/'Suffragette City'   RCA BOW-506
'Fame'/'Right'   RCA BOW-507
'Golden Years'/'Can You Hear Me'   RCA BOW-508
'TVC 15'/'We Are The Dead'   RCA BOW-509
'Sound And Vision'/'A New Career In A New Town' RCA BOW-510
'Be My Wife'/'Speed Of Life'   RCA BOW-511
'Beauty And The Beast'/'Sense of Doubt'   RCA BOW-512
'Heroes'/'V-2 Schneider'   RCA BOW-513
'Rebel Rebel'/'Queen Bitch'   RCA BOW-514
'The Jean Genie'/'Ziggy Stardust'   RCA BOW-515
'DJ'/'Reputation'   RCA BOW-516
'John, I'm Only Dancing'/'Hang On To Yourself' RCA BOW-517
'Space Oddity'/'Changes'   RCA BOW-518
'Sorrow'/'Amsterdam'   RCA BOW-519
'Breaking Glass'/'Art Decade'/'Ziggy Stardust' RCA BOW-520
All released June 1983

'Let's Dance'/'Cat People (Putting Out Fire)'
EMI America EA 152, March 1983 (1) (also on 12″ – 12EA 152)

'China Girl'/'Shake It'
EMI America EA 157, May 1983 (2) (also on 12" – 12EA 157)

'Modern Love'/'Modern Love (live version)'
EMI America EA 158, September 1983 (2) (also on 12" – 12EA 158, and on picture disc – EAP 157)

'White Light White Heat'/'Cracked Actor'
RCA 372, November 1983

'Blue Jean'/'Dancing With The Big Boys'
EMI America EA 181, September 1984 (6) (also on 12" – 12EA 181)

'Tonight'/'Tumble And Twirl'
EMI America EA 187, November 1984 (53) (also on 12" – 12EA 187)

Albums (33⅓ rpm)

David Bowie
Deram DML-1007, June 1967
'Uncle Arthur', 'Sell Me a Coat', 'Rubber Band', 'Love You Till Tuesday', 'There Is a Happy Land', 'We Are Hungry Men', 'When I Live My Dream', 'Little Bombardier', 'Silly Boy Blue', 'Come and Buy My Toys', 'Join the Gang', 'She's Got Medals', 'Maids of Bond Street', 'Please Mr Gravedigger'

David Bowie
Philips SBL-7912, November 1969
'Space Oddity', 'Unwashed and Somewhat Slightly Dazed', 'Letter to Hermione', 'Cygnet Committee', 'Janine', 'An Occasional Dream', 'The Wild Eyed Boy from Freecloud', 'God Knows I'm Good', 'Memory of a Free Festival'

The World of David Bowie
Decca (S)PA-58, March 1970
'Uncle Arthur', 'Love You Till Tuesday', 'There Is a Happy Land', 'Little Bombardier', 'Sell Me a Coat', 'Silly Boy Blue', 'The London Boys', 'Karma Man', 'Rubber Band', 'Let Me Sleep Beside You', 'Come and Buy My Toys', 'She's Got Medals', 'In the Heat of the Morning', 'When I Live My Dream'

The Man Who Sold the World
Mercury 6338041, April 1971
'The Width of a Circle', 'All the Madmen', 'Black Country Rock', 'After All', 'Running Gun Blues', 'Saviour Machine', 'She Shook Me Cold', 'The Man Who Sold the World', 'The Supermen'

Hunky Dory
RCA SF-8244, December 1971 (3)
'Changes', 'Oh You Pretty Things', 'Eight Line Poem', 'Life on Mars', 'Kooks', 'Quicksand', 'Fill Your Heart', 'Andy Warhol', 'Song for Bob Dylan', 'Queen Bitch', 'The Bewlay Brothers'

The Rise and Fall of Ziggy Stardust and the Spiders from Mars
RCA SF-8287, June 1972 (5)
'Five Years', 'Soul Love', 'Moonage Daydream', 'Starman', 'It Ain't
Easy', 'Lady Stardust', 'Star', 'Hang On to Yourself', 'Ziggy Stardust',
'Suffragette City', 'Rock 'n' Roll Suicide'

Space Oddity
RCA LSP-4813, September 1972 (17)
Same songs as listed on *David Bowie*, Philips SBL-7912

The Man Who Sold the World
RCA LSP-4816, September 1972 (26)
Same songs as listed on album of same name, Mercury 6338041

Aladdin Sane
RCA RS-1001, April 1973 (1)
'Watch That Man', 'Aladdin Sane', 'Drive-In Saturday', 'Panic in De-
troit', 'Cracked Actor', 'Time', 'The Prettiest Star', 'Let's Spend the
Night Together', 'The Jean Genie', 'Lady Grinning Soul'

Pin-Ups
RCA RS-1003, October 1973 (1)
'Rosalyn', 'Here Comes the Night', 'I Wish You Would', 'See Emily
Play', 'Everything's Alright', 'I Can't Explain', 'Friday On My Mind',
'Sorrow', 'Don't Bring Me Down', 'Shapes of Things', 'Anyway, Anyhow,
Anywhere', 'Where Have All the Good Times Gone'

Diamond Dogs
RCA APL-1-0576, April 1974 (1)
'Future Legend', 'Bewitched, Bothered and Bewildered', 'Diamond
Dogs', 'Sweet Thing', 'Candidate', 'Sweet Thing (Reprise)', 'Rebel
Rebel', 'Rock 'n' Roll With Me', 'We Are the Dead', '1984', 'Chant of
the Ever Circling Skeletal Family'

David Live
RCA APL-2-0771, October 1974 (2)
'1984', 'Rebel Rebel', 'Moonage Daydream', 'Sweet Thing', 'Changes',
'Suffragette City', 'Aladdin Sane', 'All the Young Dudes', 'Cracked
Actor', 'When You Rock 'n' Roll With Me', 'Watch That Man', 'Knock
on Wood', 'Diamond Dogs', 'Big Brother', 'Width of a Circle', 'The Jean
Genie', 'Rock 'n' Roll Suicide'

Young Americans
RCA RS-1006, March 1975 (2)
'Young Americans', 'Win', 'Fascination', 'Right', 'Somebody Up There
Likes Me', 'Across the Universe', 'Can You Hear Me', 'Fame'

Images
Deram DPA-3017/3018, May 1975
Re-issue of *David Bowie*, Deram DML-1007 plus all miscellaneous singles
released on that label

Station to Station
RCA APL-1-1327, January 1976 (5)
'Station to Station', 'Golden Years', 'Word On a Wing', 'TVC 15', 'Stay', 'Wild Is the Wind'

ChangesOneBowie
RCA RS-1005, May 1976 (2)
'Space Oddity', 'John, I'm Only Dancing', 'Changes', 'Ziggy Stardust', 'Suffragette City', 'The Jean Genie', 'Diamond Dogs', 'Rebel Rebel', 'Young Americans', 'Fame', 'Golden Years'

Low
RCA PL-12030, January 1977 (2)
'Speed of Life', 'Breaking Glass', 'What in the World', 'Sound and Vision', 'Always Crashing in the Same Car', 'Be My Wife', 'A New Career in a New Town', 'Warszawa', 'Art Decade', 'Weeping Wall', 'Subterraneans'

Heroes
RCA PL-12522, October 1977 (3)
'Beauty and the Beast', 'Joe the Lion', 'Heroes', 'Sons of the Silent Age', 'Blackout', 'V-2 Schneider', 'Sense of Doubt', 'Moss Garden', 'Neuköln', 'The Secret Life of Arabia'

Peter and the Wolf
RCA RL-12743, May 1978 (with Eugene Ormandy & the Philadelphia Orchestra)

Stage
RCA PL-02913, September 1978 (5)
'Hang On To Yourself', 'Ziggy Stardust', 'Five Years', 'Soul Love', 'Star', 'Station to Station', 'Fame', 'TVC 15', 'Warszawa', 'Speed of Life', 'Art Decade', 'Sense of Doubt', 'Breaking Glass', 'Heroes', 'What in the World', 'Blackout', 'Beauty and the Beast'

Lodger
RCA BOW LP-1, May 1979 (4)
'Fantastic Voyage', 'African Night Flight', 'Move On', 'Yassassin', 'Red Sails', 'DJ', 'Look Back in Anger', 'Boys Keep Swinging', 'Repetition', 'Red Money'

Scary Monsters (and Super Creeps)
RCA BOW LP-2, September 1980 (1)
'It's No Game', 'Up the Hill Backwards', 'Scary Monsters (and Super Creeps)', 'Ashes to Ashes', 'Fashion', 'Teenage Wildlife', 'Scream Like a Baby', 'Kingdom Come', 'Because You're Young', 'It's No Game (No. 2)'

The Best of Bowie
K-Tel NE-1111, December 1980 (3)
'Space Oddity', 'Life On Mars', 'Starman', 'Rock 'n' Roll Suicide', 'John, I'm Only Dancing', 'The Jean Genie', 'Breaking Glass', 'Sorrow', 'Diamond Dogs', 'Young Americans', 'Fame', 'Golden Years', 'TVC 15', 'Sound and Vision', 'Heroes', 'Boys Keep Swinging'

Hunky Dory
RCA Ints 5064, January 1981 (68) (*re-issue*)

Ziggy Stardust
RCA Ints 5063, January 1981 (63) (*re-issue*)

Aladdin Sane
RCA Ints 5067, January 1981 (98) (*re-issue*)

Christiane F. Wir Kinder Vom Bahnhof Zoo (film soundtrack)
RCA RCALP 3074, April 1981
'V-2 Schneider', 'TVC 15', 'Helden' (German version of 'Heroes'), 'Boys Keep Swinging', 'Sense of Doubt', 'Station to Station', 'Look Back in Anger', 'Warszawa'

ChangesTwoBowie
RCA BOWLP 3, November 1981 (24)
'Aladdin Sane', 'On Broadway', 'Oh You Pretty Things', 'Starman', '1984', 'Ashes to Ashes', 'Sound and Vision', 'Fashion', 'Wild Is The Wind', 'John, I'm Only Dancing', 'DJ'

Lodger
RCA Ints 5212, March 1982 (*re-issue*)

Bowie Rare
RCA PL 45406, January 1983
'Velvet Goldmine', 'Helden', 'John, I'm Only Dancing (Again)', 'Moon of Alabama', 'Crystal Japan', 'Ragazzo Solo, Ragazza Sola', 'Round And Round', 'Amsterdam', 'Holy Holy', 'Panic In Detroit', 'Young Americans'

Pin-Ups
RCA Ints 5236, February 1983 (*re-issue*)

The Man Who Sold The World
RCA Ints 5237, February 1983 (*re-issue*)

Let's Dance
EMI America AML 3029, April 1983 (1)
'Modern Love', 'China Girl', 'Let's Dance', 'Without You', 'Ricochet', 'Criminal World', 'Cat People (Putting Out Fire)', 'Shake It'

Golden Years
RCA BOWLP 4, August 1983
'Fashion', 'Red Sails', 'Look Back in Anger', 'I Can't Explain', 'Ashes to Ashes', 'Golden Years', 'Joe the Lion', 'Scary Monsters (and Super Creeps)', 'Wild Is The Wind'

Ziggy Stardust – The Motion Picture
RCA PL 84862 (2) (double LP)
'Hang On To Yourself', 'Ziggy Stardust', 'Watch That Man', 'Medley: 'Wild Eyed Boy from Freecloud'; 'All the Young Dudes'; 'Oh You Pretty Things', 'Moonage Daydream', 'Space Oddity', 'My Death', 'Cracked Actor', 'Time', 'Width Of a Circle', 'Changes', 'Let's Spend the Night

Together', 'Suffragette City', 'White Light White Heat', 'Rock 'n' Roll Suicide'

Tonight
EMI America DB 1, September 1984 (1)
'Loving The Alien', 'Don't Look Down', 'God Only Knows', 'Tonight', 'Neighbourhood Threat', 'Blue Jean', 'Tumble And Twirl', 'I Keep Forgettin'', 'Dancing With the Big Boys'

Aladdin Sane (picture disc)
RCA BOPIC 1, March 1984

Hunky Dory (picture disc)
RCA BOPIC 2, March 1984

Ziggy Stardust (picture disc)
RCA BOPIC 3, March 1984

Pin-Ups (picture disc)
RCA BOPIC 4, March 1984

Diamond Dogs (picture disc)
RCA BOPIC 5, March 1984

Fame and Fashion
RCA PL 84919, April 1984
'Golden Years', 'TVC 15', 'Heroes', 'DJ', 'Fashion', 'Ashes to Ashes', 'Space Oddity', 'Changes', 'Starman', '1984', 'Young Americans', 'Fame'

FILMOGRAPHY

Dates given are dates of release; films are listed in order of production.

The Image (1972)
Negus-Fancey Films
Writer-director: Michael Armstrong
Performers: Bowie, Armstrong
Running time: 15 min

Love You Till Tuesday (Unreleased)
Produced & financed by Kenneth Pitt
Director: Malcolm Thompson
Performers: Bowie, Hermione Farthingale, various musicians
Running time: 30 min

The Virgin Soldiers (1970)
Columbia Pictures
Director: John Dexter
Writer: Leslie Thomas
Performers: Lynn Redgrave, Hywel Bennett
Running time: 96 min
Note: Bowie cast as an extra in a fight scene

Ziggy Stardust (1983)
D. A. Pennebaker Productions
Director: Richard Pennebaker
Running time: 1–2 hours (various edits)
Note: documentary of 1973 'retirement' show

The Man Who Fell to Earth (1976)
British Lion Films
Director: Nicolas Roeg
Writer: Paul Mayersberg
Performers: Bowie, Candy Clarke, Rip Torn, Buck Henry
Running time: 120–140 min (various edits)

Just a Gigolo (1978)
Leguan Films
Director: David Hemmings
Writers: Ennio De Conan & Joshua Sinclair
Performers: Bowie, Sydne Rome, Kim Novak, David Hemmings, Maria
            Schell, Kurt Jurgens, Marlene Dietrich
Running time: 147 min

Stage (Unreleased)
Director: David Hemmings
Note: documentary of 1978 shows

Wir Kinder Vom Bahnhof Zoo (Christine F.) (1981)
Solaris Film Productions
Director: Ulrich Edel
Writer: Herman Weigel
Performers: Bowie, Naja Brunckhorst, Thomas Haustein
Running time: 120 min
Note: includes Bowie concert segment

Yellowbeard (1983)
Orion Pictures
Director: Mel Damski
Writers: Graham Chapman, Peter Cook & Bernard McKenna
Performers: Bowie, Monty Python, Cheech & Chong, Peter Cook, Marty
           Feldman, Madeline Kahn, James Mason, Spike Milligan,
           Susannah York
Running time: 101 min
Note: Bowie uncredited in bit part

The Hunger (1983)
MGM
Director: Tony Scott
Writers: Ivan Davis & Michael Thomas
Performers: Bowie, Catherine Deneuve, Susan Sarandon
Running time: 94 min

Merry Christmas, Mr Lawrence (1983)
Universal Pictures
Director: Nagisa Oshima
Writers: Nagisa Oshima with Paul Mayersberg
Performers: Bowie, Tom Conti, Ryuichi Sakamoto, Takeshi, Jack
           Thompson
Running time: 122 min

VIDEOGRAPHY

Documentaries & Specials

1980 Floor Show (1973)
NBC ('The Midnight Special')
Performers: Bowie, Marianne Faithfull, Troggs
Running time: 60 min

Cracked Actor (1975)
BBC
Director: Alan Yentob
Running time: 50 min

Serious Moonlight (1984)
Home Box Office
Director: David Mallet
Running time: 90 min

Drama

Baal (1982)
BBC
Director: Alan Clarke
Writer: Bertolt Brecht
Performers: Bowie, Zoë Wanamaker, Juliet Hammond-Hill, Jonathan
            Kent, Tracey Childs
Running time: 63 min

Music Videos

'Space Oddity' (1972)
'John, I'm Only Dancing' (1972)
'The Jean Genie' (1972)
'Life On Mars' (1973)
'Be My Wife' (1977)
'Heroes' (1977)
'Look Back In Anger' (1979)
'DJ' (1979)
'Boys Keep Swinging' (1979)
'Ashes to Ashes' (1980)
'Fashion' (1980)
'Under Pressure' (with Queen, 1981)

'Wild Is the Wind' (1982)
'The Drowned Girl' (1982)
'Let's Dance' (1983)
'China Girl' (1983)
'Modern Love' (1983)
'Blue Jean' (1984)

THE STONES BY PHILIP NORMAN

'It's a good thing that a writer of Philip Norman's class has finally produced a book on The Stones'
Pete Townshend, *Time Out*

'I have not read a better book on the real world of rock and roll'
Craig Brown, *The Mail on Sunday*

Here, at last, from the bestselling biographer of The Beatles (SHOUT! Also available in Corgi paperback) is the complete and unexpurgated story of The Rolling Stones – from their origins in the seamy nightlife of London to their meteoric rise to fame and the multimillion pound tours. Here are the famous 'Mars bar' drug raid of 1967; the vengeful and ludicrous trial of Mick and Keith; the mysterious death of Brian in a child's dream garden; the terrifying Altamont festival where a spectator was butchered by Hell's Angels in front of The Stones as they played. This is The Stones as they've never been seen before – the music, the magic, the madness.

'Something special. Not only is its subject one which must be of compulsive interest to anyone between the ages of 45 and 15 with an ounce of naughtiness and vitality in them, but it has been written by a stylist, a wit and an aficianado'
Lucy Hughes-Hallett, *Options*

'A narrative of gathering pace and excitement makes *The Stones* virtually unputdownable'
John Walsh, *Books & Bookmen*

0 552 12487 7   £3.50

CATCH A FIRE
The Life of Bob Marley
BY TIMOTHY WHITE

'Superb . . . as fine and moving a biography as Marley could have wanted'
New Musical Express

Bob Marley – undisputed sovereign of reggae music, the pre-eminent political visionary of the Third World, a revolutionary soul-prophet whose music had a massive impact on people of all races throughout the world. His death from cancer at the age of thirty-six in 1981 was mourned by the millions who were inspired by his vision and mesmerised by his haunting power.

  Catch A Fire – a vivid and dramatic chronicle of Bob Marley's life and career, from poverty in Kingston's Trench Town to international superstardom. An insightful exploration of the historical, cultural, religious and folkloric milieu that shaped Marley's spiritual and political beliefs and out of which the uniquely Jamaican version of rock music, later known as reggae, was spawned.

* MANY NEVER-BEFORE-SEEN PHOTOGRAPHS
* THE FIRST COMPLETE DISCOGRAPHY
* EXHAUSTIVE BIBLIOGRAPHY

'Exhaustively researched . . . brilliant . . . spellbinding and authoritative'
Time Out

'So vivid and authoritative is White's work that it's certain to become the yardstick by which others are judged'
Black Music

0 552 99097 3   £3.95

A SELECTED LIST OF AUTOBIOGRAPHIES AND BIOGRAPHIES FROM CORGI

WHILE EVERY EFFORT IS MADE TO KEEP PRICES LOW, IT IS SOME-TIMES NECESSARY TO INCREASE PRICES AT SHORT NOTICE. CORGI BOOKS RESERVE THE RIGHT TO SHOW NEW RETAIL PRICES ON COVERS WHICH MAY DIFFER FROM THOSE PREVIOUSLY ADVERTISED IN THE TEXT OR ELSEWHERE.

THE PRICES SHOWN BELOW WERE CORRECT AT THE TIME OF GOING TO PRESS (APRIL '86).

☐	09332 7	Go Ask Alice	*Anonymous*	£1.95
☐	12708 6	Knockwood	*Candice Bergen*	£2.50
☐	99065 5	The Past is Myself	*Christabel Bielenberg*	£2.95
☐	12548 2	Klaus Barbie: Butcher of Lyon	*Tom Bower*	£1.95
☐	09373 4	Our Kate (Illus.)	*Catherine Cookson*	£1.95
☐	12553 9	Swings and Roundabouts	*Angela Douglas*	£2.50
☐	11772 2	'H' The Autobiography of a Child Prostitute and Heroin Addict	*Christiane F.*	£1.95
☐	12501 6	Beyond the Highland Line	*Richard Frere*	£1.95
☐	12675 6	Mafia Princess	*Antoinette Giancana & Thomas C. Renner*	£2.50
☐	99066 3	Namesake	*Michel Goldberg*	£1.95
☐	99098 1	Autumn of Fury	*Mohamed Heikal*	£3.95
☐	12033 2	Diary of a Medical Nobody	*Dr. Kenneth Lane*	£1.75
☐	12465 6	West Country Doctor	*Dr. Kenneth Lane*	£1.95
☐	12452 4	Out on a Limb	*Shirley MacLaine*	£2.95
☐	11568 1	Evita: The Woman With the Whip	*Mary Main*	95P
☐	12389 7	Indecent Exposure	*David McClintick*	£2.50
☐	12655 1	Bunny: The Real Story of Playboy	*Russell Miller*	£2.95
☐	12378 1	Coroner to the Stars	*Thomas Noguchi*	£1.95
☐	12487 7	The Stones	*Phillip Norman*	£3.50
☐	11961 X	Shout!	*Phillip Norman*	£2.50
☐	12710 8	Bardot	*Glenys Roberts*	£2.95
☐	12577 6	Place of Stones	*Ruth Janette Ruck*	£1.95
☐	08433 6	Every Night, Josephine	*Jacqueline Susann*	£1.50
☐	12589 X	And I Don't Want to Live This Life	*Deborah Spungen*	£2.50
☐	99097 3	Catch a Fire – The Life of Bob Marley (Illus.)	*Timothy White*	£3.95

All these books are available at your bookshop or newsagent, or can be ordered direct from the publisher. Just tick the titles you want and fill in the form below.

CORGI BOOKS, Cash Sales Department, P.O Box 11, Falmouth, Cornwall.

Please send cheque or postal order, no currency.

Please allow cost of book(s) plus the following for postage and packing:

U.K. CUSTOMERS – Allow 55p for the first book, 22p for the second book and 14p for each additional book ordered, to a maximum charge of £1.75.

B.F.P.O. & EIRE – Allow 55p for the first book, 22p for the second book plus 14p per copy for the next seven books, thereafter 8p per book.

OVERSEAS CUSTOMERS – Allow £1.00 for the first book and 25p per copy for each additional book.

NAME (Block Letters) ....

ADDRESS ....

....